This book is about Your rings

To be given to

_____ by _____
BRIDE   GROOM

and to

_____ by _____
GROOM   BRIDE

Who met and fell in Love on

_____
MONTH / DAY / YEAR

Who decided to become engaged to one another on

_____
MONTH / DAY / YEAR

Who celebrate their Wedding on

_____
MONTH / DAY / YEAR

And whose rings will be
for all the world to see...
the sign of their Love and
Commitment to each other.

Engagement
& Wedding
Rings

3rd Edition

THE DEFINITIVE BUYING GUIDE

FOR PEOPLE IN LOVE

Antoinette Matlins, P.G.
Antonio C. Bonanno, F.G.A., A.S.A., M.G.A.

GEMSTONE PRESS
WOODSTOCK, VERMONT

Engagement & Wedding Rings, 3rd Edition:
The Definitive Buying Guide for People in Love

Cover photos courtesy of:

At top: Tiffany-style solitaire, courtesy of the Diamond Information Centre.
Second row, l–r: Diamond solitaire framed by shield-shaped rubies. Designed by Carvin French and Antoinette Matlins. Photo: Tibor Ardai, with permission of David and Agnes Sarns. Emerald ring framed by diamond baguettes, courtesy of Benjamin Zucker, Precious Stones, Company, New York. Gold engraved band by Memoire Paris. Photo: Rudy Hellman Photography. Three-stone ring designed by Brian Sholdt of Sholdt Design. Gabrielle diamond, courtesy of Suberi Brothers Inc.

Third row, l–r: Diamond eternity band from JB International. Photo: Peter Hurst. Natural color sapphire ring, courtesy of a private collection. Photo: Tibor Ardai. Diamond solitaire with channel-set diamonds. Designed by Carvin French and Antoinette Matlins. Photo: Tibor Ardai. Courtesy of a private collection. Art Deco yellow diamond ring, courtesy of Antiquorum.
At bottom: courtesy of Paul Tacorian of Tacori.

Library of Congress Cataloging-in-Publication Data
Matlins, Antoinette Leonard.
Engagement & wedding rings : the definitive buying guide for people in love / Antoinette Matlins.— 3rd ed.
    p. cm.
Includes bibliographical references.
ISBN 0-943763-41-X (Paperback)
1. Diamonds—Purchasing. 2. Gems—Purchasing. 3. Rings—Purchasing. 4. Betrothal. 5. Marriage customs and rites. I. Title: Engagement and wedding rings. II. Bonanno, Antonio C. III. Title.
HD9677.A2 M38 2003
739.27—dc21
2002153846

10 9 8 7 6 5 4 3 2 1
Manufactured in Canada

Text design by Terry Bain
Color insert design by Bridgett Taylor
Illustrations by Kathleen Robinson

GemStone Press
A Division of LongHill Partners, Inc.
Sunset Farm Offices, Route 4, P.O. Box 237
Woodstock, VT 05091
Tel: (802) 457-4000 Fax: (802) 457-4004
www.gemstonepress.com

"Two torches in one ring of burning fire.
Two wills, two hearts, two passions are
bonded in marriage . . ."

Inscription within the Sforza Marriage Ring, 15th century

Dedication

To my daughter, Dawn, and my sons,
Andrew and Seth,
with the hope that you will each find
that special someone
to surround in a love that,
like the rings you will place upon each other's finger,
knows no beginning and no end.
A love for all eternity.

And to my husband, Stuart,
who is that special someone for me.

Contents

Acknowledgments

All of the charts that appear here were especially designed and executed for use in this book; however, in some cases, charts from other publications were used as inspiration and reference. Grateful acknowledgment is given to Gemological Institute of America (GIA) for use of the charts appearing on pages 34, 66, and 67 in their book *The Jewelers' Manual*.

Some of the material appearing in this book is condensed from the author's *Jewelry & Gems: The Buying Guide, 5th Edition* (GemStone Press).

Grateful acknowledgment is also given to the following for use of their reports and valuable assistance:

Accredited Gemologists Association (AGA), San Diego
American Gem Society (AGS), Las Vegas
American Gem Trade Association (AGTA), Dallas
American Gemological Laboratories, Inc. (AGL), New York
American Society of Appraisers (ASA), Washington, DC
Antiquorum Auctioneers, Geneva and New York
Diamond Information Centre, New York and London
The Gold Information Center, New York
The Platinum Guild International, Newport Beach, CA
Benjamin Zucker, Precious Stones Company, New York

I thank the wonderful staff at GemStone Press for their dedication, hard work, and aesthetic input.

Special thanks to the Bonanno family for their loving support, encouragement, and professional expertise: Kathryn Bonanno, F.G.A., P.G.; Kenneth Bonanno, F.G.A., P.G.; Karen Bonanno Ford DeHaas, F.G.A., P.G.; and Ruth Bonanno, Wife and Mother.

Introduction

"With this ring, I thee wed."

These were the words my husband and I said to each other, and the words that you, too, will be saying one day soon. Our rings have been a symbol of our love and commitment to each other and of our hopes and dreams for the future. Your rings will have the same deep meaning.

As we've learned in working with clients over the years to acquire gems and create distinctive rings in which to set them, the purchase of your engagement and wedding rings is one of the most significant purchases you'll ever make, both financially and emotionally. No other single piece of jewelry will ever be as important. No matter how successful you become, no matter how magnificent other jewelry purchases might be, nothing carries with it the same excitement and magic.

But today's couple has many more choices than did couples in earlier generations. To begin with, there are more jewelers than ever before—each anxious for your business—and more Internet vendors and auction sites. There are more stones from which to make a selection, and a wider range of sizes, shapes, qualities, and prices. There are also more treatments being used to alter or conceal the true quality of a stone, and more forms of deception against which to be on guard. And once you've chosen the stone, there's an almost endless variety of ring settings from which to choose. It's easy to feel dazed. But it really doesn't have to be overwhelming, and it won't be if you know how to go about it. More importantly, *knowing how* is the key to experiencing the thrill and excitement that should be part of making this most significant acquisition.

After the publication of our first book, *Jewelry & Gems: The Buying Guide*, readers and clients alike urged us to write a book dedicated exclusively to engagement and wedding rings—a book that combined our knowledge of gems and jewelry design with our own experience helping couples with this meaningful purchase. After searching the literature at that time, we were surprised to find that there was nothing that covered what we thought couples really needed to know. Given the importance of this purchase, and being the romantics that we are, we agreed that this book had to be written, and thus the first edition of *Engagement & Wedding Rings: The Definitive Buying Guide for People in Love* was published.

In the decade following the first edition, new diamond shapes were introduced, several exciting new gemstones were discovered, new designs and styles became popular, and, most important, new treatments were developed to enhance the appearance of gems (such as using glass fillers in diamonds to hide cracks). These developments led to the second edition, where all this critical information—which was not available elsewhere—was added.

In today's market you will continue to find new gemstones, new cutting innovations, and new designs. You'll find antique and heirloom rings alongside fashionable contemporary designs, and you'll find new alloys in gold and platinum. You'll find the treatments we discussed in the second edition, along with new treatments for both diamonds and colored gemstones. But perhaps the most significant change since the second edition is the presence of a new treatment technique that may be the most important in diamond history—a technique that can permanently transform very tinted yellowish or brownish diamonds into colorless "gems" or even rare "fancy" colors. A high-pressure, high-temperature technique (HPHT), as this treatment method is called, is being used increasingly here and abroad (see chapter 7). To be a savvy diamond buyer today, you must know about HPHT-treated diamonds and how to verify whether or not any diamond you are considering has been treated in this way.

Yet once again, we could find nothing up-to-date in terms of what couples really need to know before making this important decision. And thus, we bring you the new, third edition of *Engagement & Wedding Rings: The Definitive Buying Guide for People in Love*.

From our own experience in working with couples, we know how often the excitement and anticipation you should be feeling is replaced by anxiety. If you feel you don't even know where to begin, you're not alone. Most people feel overwhelmed, intimidated, and confused at the prospect of buying an engagement and wedding ring. This is a shame, but it's no surprise.

In this third edition of *Engagement & Wedding Rings* we share our own and our clients' experiences with you, and provide a practical guide through a process we developed as a result of working with so many couples over the years. It is important for you to understand, however, that there is no right or wrong choice in terms of the type or quality of stone you select; selecting the right stone and the right ring is a personal choice that should reflect your *own needs*— emotional, symbolic, and monetary. What is most important is not *what* you choose, but that whatever you choose is, in fact, what you have been *told* it is. Only by knowing how to ensure proper representation of the facts can you be sure you are making a wise choice and paying a fair price for what you have selected.

With this new edition of *Engagement & Wedding Rings: The Definitive Buying Guide for People in Love* you'll find all the information you need to feel more confident about making the right choice, including:

- Romantic traditions behind engagement and wedding rings
- What factors affect quality differences in diamonds and colored gemstones
- How to spot differences in stones that may appear to be the same quality
- How to compare prices
- How to select the right style and design
- How to get what you want on a budget
- How to select your jeweler, appraiser, and insurer
- Types of misrepresentation to guard against, and how to protect yourself
- Questions you need to ask when buying particular stones
- What to get in writing
  ...and much more.

We hope you enjoy *Engagement & Wedding Rings* and find it to be an indispensable guide. Most of all, we hope it will remove your fear and enable you to enjoy this special time to the fullest, to truly experience the wonder, surprise, and romance that should all be part of creating that perfect moment...and that perfect ring with which to begin your marriage and life together.

Antoinette Matlins

PART ONE

Engagement and Wedding Rings through the Ages

A proud Maximilian of Austria gave a sparkling diamond to Mary of Burgundy in 1477, in celebration of their decision to marry.

CHAPTER 1

The Romance of the Ring

Just as the blushing dawn gives promise of the glory of the sunrise, so the betrothal ring, as the token of a pledge, serves to herald, as it were, an emblem that denotes the fulfillment of the vow.
—From a Victorian ladies' magazine

The romantic traditions associated with rings, especially those containing diamonds and precious gems, resound throughout history. In fact, evidence of the engagement tradition dates back as far as the caveman. The Pharaohs of Egypt, however, are credited with being the first to use a ring in the form of a circular band as a symbol of eternity. The Egyptians regarded the circle, a shape that has no beginning and no end, as a heavenly reminder that life, happiness, and love have no beginning and no end.

By Roman times, it was an established tradition to give a ring, a symbol of the cycle of life and eternity, as a public pledge that the marriage contract between a man and woman would be honored. These early rings were made of iron, according to the accounts of Roman historian C. Plinius Secundus. Gold was introduced some time in the second century A.D. Soon, the Christians adopted the custom, and the ring became an integral part of the marriage service.

It wasn't long before the symbolism of the circular ring was further enhanced by the addition of gems. By medieval days, wealthy citizens were married with gem-set rings—diamonds, colored gems, and diamonds combined with colored gems became the fashion. Colored gems were often used because of the symbolism of particular colors. For rings of love, ruby was a particular favorite because

---

Some of the material in chapter 1 and chapter 2 has been condensed from *The Power of Love,* copyright © 1988, The Diamond Information Centre, London, England. Reprinted by permission.

13th-century
bezel-set
sapphire in
gold ring

it was the color of the heart. Sapphire was also popular since it was the color of the heavens. Other colored gems believed to hold certain magical properties (see chapter 14) also became popular choices for betrothal rings.

Diamond held a particularly regal position at this time. It was one of the rarest and costliest of gems. And it was prized above other gems for marriage because of the unique properties described below, and the many special powers attributed to it. While reserved for only the most privileged, it became the choice for those fortunate enough—or powerful enough—to acquire one.

❖ The Allure of Diamond

Diamond, nature's hardest substance—uniquely able to resist both fire and steel, and therefore all of man's early efforts to alter it—epitomized unyielding power and invincible strength. It seemed truly indestructible. What more natural symbol for the marriage covenant, and for the edict "What God Has Joined Together, Let No Man Put Asunder." If the many properties of diamond and its indestructibility were in fact transferred to the wearer, a marriage sealed with the diamond would certainly last forever.

Elaborate
14th-century
ring set with an
uncut diamond
crystal

Indeed, throughout history, the diamond has been one of the most coveted gems. Uncut diamonds adorned the suits of armor of the great knights; cut diamonds have appeared in the crowns of kings and queens all through the ages. Legends of the diamond's mythical properties have been passed along for centuries.

In India, where diamonds were first discovered hundreds of years before Christ, the diamond was valued even more for its strength and magic than for its great beauty. The diamond was thought to protect its wearer from snakes, fire, poison, illness, thieves, and all the combined forces of evil. It was a favorite choice for rings given in love, some of which date back to earliest Indian history.

As the gemstone of the zodiac House of Aries, symbolized by the Ram, the diamond was believed by ancient astrologers to be powerful for people born under the planet Mars. They thought the diamond could provide fortitude, strength of mind, and continuous love in marriage, as well as ward off witchcraft, poisons, and nightmares.

Each culture has prized the diamond for its unique properties. The Romans believed a diamond worn against the skin of their left arm would help them remain brave and daring in battle and give them strength over their enemies. An ancient passage reads: "He who carries a diamond on the left side shall be hardy and manly; it will guard him from accidents to the limbs; but nevertheless a good diamond will lose its power and virtue if worn by one who is incontinent, or drunken." Another Roman practice was to set diamonds in fine steel that would then serve as a charm against insanity.

The word diamond derives from the Greek *adamas*, meaning "the unconquerable"; its Latin equivalent is *diamas*. The diamond has a long and extensive history in books of importance to mankind, with the earliest references occurring in the Bible, Book of Exodus, chapter 28. Here, in describing the details of the tabernacle and its furnishings, a description is given of the High Priest's breastplate: "And the second row shall be an emerald, a sapphire, and a diamond." It was believed that the diamond worn by the Jewish High Priest had special powers to prove innocence or guilt—if the accused was guilty, the stone grew dim; if innocent, it shone more brilliantly than ever! Thus diamonds came to be associated with innocence, justice, faith, and strength. Early Christians also endowed the diamond with special powers, believing it to be an antidote against both moral and physical evil.

The Hindus classed diamonds according to the four castes of their social strata: The Brahmin diamond (colorless) gave power, friends, riches, and good luck; the Kshatriya (brown/champagne) prevented old age; Vaisya (the color of a "kodali flower") brought success; and the Sudra (a diamond with the sheen of a polished blade, probably gray or black) brought all types of good fortune. Red and yellow diamonds were exclusively royal gems, for kings alone. The Chinese treasured the diamond as an engraving tool, while the Italians trusted it to protect against poison.

Through the ages, diamonds have been associated with almost

everything from sleepwalking to producing invincibility and spiritual ecstasy. In the 1500s it was believed that diamond would enhance the love of a husband for his wife. To dream of diamonds was considered symbolic of success, wealth, happiness, and victory. Even sexual power has been strongly attributed to the diamond. There is a catch, however, to the powers associated with it—some believe that one must find the diamond "naturally" to experience its magic, that it loses its powers if acquired by purchase. However, when offered as a pledge of love or friendship, its powers return!

CHAPTER 2

Engagement and Wedding Ring Traditions

❖ The Middle Ages Set the Stage for Betrothal Traditions

As early as the fifteenth century, the diamond, although only available to a very few, was prized above all others as the gem for betrothal. It was acknowledged as the ultimate symbol because of its unique properties, especially its ability to resist destructive forces.

In 1477, we find one of the first recorded accounts of the use of diamond in a betrothal ring. Desiring to please his prospective father-in-law, Archduke Maximilian of Austria proposed to Mary of Burgundy, heeding the words of a trusted advisor who wrote:

At the betrothal your grace must have a ring
set with a diamond and also a gold ring.

Maximilian wed his beloved Mary within twenty-four hours of the betrothal ceremony. Thus began a tradition that has spanned centuries. At the time of Mary and Maximilian, goldsmiths often used thin, flat pieces of diamond called "hogback" diamonds that had "cleaved" (split) from a natural diamond crystal. The imaginative jeweler could create intricate and interesting details using hogbacks, such as the beautiful letter "M" you see in Mary's ring above. Diamonds in their natural *crystal* form were also used. Certainly this was in part because it was the hardest natural substance known and man lacked the knowledge and skill to cut it. But perhaps there was more to it than that. Diamond crystals look like two pyramids joined together base-to-base. From the time of the Pharaohs, the shape of the pyramid was identified with power, strength, and

---

Natural diamond crystal

Beautifully enamelled ring with uncut diamond crystals (15th century)

A 17th-century posy ring, engraved on the inside "I doe rejoyce in thee my choyce."

A 15th-century table-cut diamond ring

mystery, so the "pyramidal" shape of the diamond crystal itself may have added to diamond's allure, to the mystery and power identified with it. The very shape of the natural diamond crystal may have made it all the more attractive as the choice to symbolize the power of love and marriage.

One might think that using an uncut diamond would have detracted from the beauty of these early rings. However, this was not the case. Medieval goldsmiths used imagination and ingenuity to create beautiful mountings to hold the diamond crystal. Ornate and complex settings distinguished by elaborate enamel detail made up for the somewhat crude condition of the rough diamonds they held.

At the same time, the inside of the ring took on added significance as the "posy" ring gained popularity. These rings were known for the little poems and romantic messages inscribed inside the hoop of the ring, a tradition that has continued until today, although with inscriptions somewhat more concise than the poems of old!

The first significant breakthrough in diamond cutting techniques occurred by the end of the fifteenth century, enabling a cutter to apply the first "facet" to the natural diamond crystal. These early cut diamonds were called table-cut because the big, flat facet resembled the top of a table. This was the initial step toward diamond cutting and polishing, and the first step in unlocking the diamond's hidden fire, brilliance, and dazzling beauty.

❖ Sixteenth-Century Craftsmen Reach New Heights

The table-cut diamond became a great challenge to the goldsmiths of the sixteenth century as they strove to create designs that could exhibit the rare stone to its fullest potential. As they refined their art—with the full support of the royal court—their efforts reached a peak of perfection. The results are masterpieces of delicate design and fine enameling, combined with pointed or table-cut stones. An impressive example is the wedding ring of Duke Albrecht V of Bavaria, a rosette set with sixteen small diamonds.

Renaissance Jewish Wedding Rings

Some of the most beautiful and intricate rings ever created were those associated with the Jewish wedding ceremony during the Renaissance period. These Jewish wedding rings, however, were used only during the wedding ceremony, as they were far too unwieldy for daily wear. In many of these elaborately ornamented rings, the bezel took the form of a gabled building, a synagogue, or Solomon's Temple. They were further enhanced with extensive detailing in enamel, as well as Hebrew inscriptions.

Intricately worked Jewish wedding ring (German, 16th century)

The Gimmel Ring

The increasing technical know-how of Renaissance goldsmiths also created a new style of marriage ring called the gimmel, from the Latin *gemelli,* meaning twins. The gimmel, or twin ring, has two hoops (sometimes three) that fan open from a pivot at the base. When open, they often contained intricately sculptured forms symbolizing eternity by using figures that represented both life and death. When shut, the hoops slid together so perfectly that only a single ring could be seen. The gimmel ring thus symbolized the coming together of two lives truly as one. When three hoops were used, the third symbolized the presence of God in the marriage. This symbolic allusion to marriage was further emphasized by an inscription on the hoop taken from the marriage service: "Whom God Has Joined Together Let No Man Put Asunder." Martin Luther and Catherine Bora were married in 1525 with an inscribed gimmel ring.

Renaissance Jewish wedding rings representing some of the most beautiful and intricate rings ever made

Around 1600, the gimmel began to incorporate another romantic symbol—two clasped hands. In the ring known as the *fede* (Italian for faith), the gimmel hoops ended in hands which, when the ring was closed, joined together. Another symbol was also added in this period—a heart—and in some

An open gimmel-type ring showing two figures, symbolizing the life cycle and the couple's role in it

German gimmel ring

A typical fede betrothal ring showing two clasped hands symbolizing faithfulness. The red ruby symbolized the heart.

of the more elaborate fede rings we find delicately enameled hands embracing a sumptuous diamond heart.

In addition to its prevalence in the fede ring, the symbol of the heart was very popular in seventeenth-century rings. This natural symbol of love and romance was often depicted "aflame with desire," incorporating rose- and table-cut diamonds, or colored gems.

At this time we also see a reaction against the increasing use of rings, especially the more elaborate examples. In contrast to an atmosphere in which expensive symbols of romance were fashionable, the Puritans, rebelling against Church ritual, attempted, unsuccessfully, to abolish the wedding ring. This test of tradition ultimately proved that the symbolism surrounding the custom of the wedding ring was too powerful to be destroyed!

An early 17th-century gimmel-type fede ring in which the hands clasp a heart, shown here in both the open and closed positions. The heart contains a diamond and ruby, combining the associations of love (identified with ruby) and eternity (symbolized by diamond).

The Tradition of the "Fourth Finger"

Wedding rings of the seventeenth century were frequently worn on the thumb. During the marriage ceremony, however, the fourth finger was most commonly used. There are differing theories as to the origin for the tradition of placing the ring on the fourth finger. According to one source, the custom stems from the Christian wedding service in which the priest arrives at the fourth finger after touching three fingers of the left hand: "In the Name of the Father . . . Son . . . and Holy Ghost." A more romantic legend that harkens back to Egyptian times holds that the fourth finger of the left hand follows the *vena amoris* (vein of love), a vein that was believed to run from that finger directly to the heart. The more practical explanation is that the fourth finger is the most protected finger, so by placing the ring there, one could best avoid damage to it.

❖ In the Eighteenth Century Diamonds Abound

The eighteenth century produced a sparkling variety of betrothal and wedding rings. The discovery of diamonds in Brazil dramatically increased the supply so that diamond jewelry became more widely available. Simultaneously, improved candle-lighting increased the number of social events held in the evening, when sparkling diamonds could be admired to the fullest. A woman appearing with her fingers glittering with diamonds reflected the height of fashion. Providing *enough* diamond jewelry became the major preoccupation of the eighteenth-century jeweler.

Rings that glittered with diamonds became the vogue in the 18th and 19th centuries.

An 18th-century ring making use of two diamond hearts

Polishing techniques underwent improvement to meet the demand for glittering stones, and the rose cut was replaced by an early version of the round, brilliant cut. Settings were pared down to show more of the diamond, and silver settings were created to enhance the diamond's white sparkle. Stones also were often backed with metallic foil to add greater brilliance and sparkle, or to emphasize or enhance color—*red* foil to enhance the red of ruby, *green* foil for emerald, and so on.

Mid-Eighteenth Century Introduces Diamond "Keeper Ring"

By the mid-eighteenth century, jewelry design began to show the effects of the fanciful rococo spirit. Colored gems (including colored diamonds) became increasingly popular and the stones themselves increasingly became the centerpiece of the design, especially when used in combination with white diamonds. In keeping with its romantic tradition, the heart motif was especially popular, often set with both white and colored diamonds, and colored gems such as ruby. Delicate, feminine jewelry of this kind expressed the elegant and refined taste of the time.

Rings that symbolized love and romance were cherished, particularly the betrothal ring. In 1761, King George III of England started what was to become a popular tradition

A replica of Queen Charlotte's **keeper ring**— to **keep** her engagement ring safe (1761). Today a similar style, a single row of diamonds encircling the finger, is popular as a wedding or anniversary band.

when he presented Queen Charlotte a diamond *keeper ring* on their wedding day. This was a simple diamond band worn on the finger next to the engagement ring to *protect* it and, perhaps, the marriage itself. The symbolism of the diamond combined with that of the circle was clear—diamond was indestructible and would protect; the unending circle represented eternity. We find a contemporary version of Queen Charlotte's keeper ring in today's diamond wedding or anniversary band, a band that usually contains a single row of diamonds encircling the finger.

❖ The Nineteenth Century: Forerunners of Modern Traditions

At the start of the nineteenth century, the idealized status of women was reflected in the style of their jewelry—pretty, feminine, and sentimental. Symbols of love—hearts, crowns, flowers—followed them from the previous century. But as the century progressed, jewelry began to play a more important role and increasingly became a status symbol in nineteenth-century society. The Industrial Revolution provided greater wealth for more people than ever before. Men could now afford extravagant gifts for the women they loved. Gem-studded jewelry became the favored choice. Diamonds were increasingly in demand but until the last quarter of the century supply remained very limited, so they were still available to only a few. Then, in 1870, supply greatly increased when a major diamond deposit was discovered on the African continent. Diamond, the gem that most could only dream about, suddenly became available to a far wider public.

And so, with the rich new supply of diamonds, the nineteenth century would see the diamond's full beauty revealed. The supply of rough diamonds from Africa not only influenced availability and jewelry design, but also resulted in greater experimentation with cutting and polishing. Soon diamonds showed a truly unique beauty; they began to exhibit a brilliance and fire unknown in any other gem. Thus, set alone, the glorious diamond became the height of fashion.

During the nineteenth century, Queen Victoria was the most avid collector and visible promoter of the jewelry of the period. She not only maintained an immense collection, but spent many thousands of pounds with her Court jeweler, Garrard. In 1850, she excitedly accepted the magnificent 105.602 carat Koh-i-Noor (the largest in the world at that time), a gift from the East India Company.

❖ The Twentieth Century and the Tiffany Setting

Dramatic changes in jewelry design took place in the late nineteenth century. As the role of women changed from docile and demure to increasingly strong and independent, jewelry correspondingly became larger, bolder, and more assertive. Then, in reaction to the boldness, a romantic, freethinking spirit emerged in the form of what came to be called Art Nouveau. This movement brought a fluid delicacy back to design that continued into the early twentieth century. And, as diamonds continued to be the central element in rings of love, it was the perfect environment to introduce the revolutionary new "Tiffany mount" at the close of the nineteenth century. This exciting setting began a tradition for the diamond solitaire (a ring with a single large stone at the center) that carried into the twentieth century and continues to be the most popular choice for the engagement ring.

Tiffany, the famous New York jeweler, invented a dramatic "open" mount. In this innovative setting, the stone was held up prominently by six tiny prongs (like little fingers). This setting allowed the fullest amount of light to enter the stone, so that it could exhibit maximum brilliance and sparkle. Unlike old style settings, which concealed most of the stone (and many of its flaws), the new Tiffany style revealed the diamond fully, along with its overall quality; the cut, color, and clarity of the diamond was now clearly visible and could be fully appreciated.

Today, modern cutting and polishing techniques have been refined and enable the full beauty of a diamond to be revealed as light radiates from each of its facets. Modern materials such as platinum and new alloys have also provided greater freedom in design and setting, opening up fresh new vistas for twentieth-century craftsmen. Design now concentrates more on finding the

The famous
Tiffany six-
prong setting

right balance between personal style and emphasis on the stone.

The skills of present-day designers continue to delight lovers with exquisite new ways of presenting the stone of their choice and incorporating the symbolism and traditions of centuries. When today's bride receives her engagement and wedding rings, she will become connected to men and women in love in both past and future generations. She will become part of a tradition of love that has spanned centuries.

PART TWO

Getting to Know Gems

CHAPTER 3

Becoming Intimate with Gems

The major cost of the engagement ring is often the sparkling diamond or shimmering colored gemstone that you select to adorn it. To avoid costly mistakes, it is very important to learn as much as possible about the stone you are considering. The best way to take the risk out of buying a particular gem is to familiarize yourself with the gem. While the average consumer can't hope to make the same precise judgments as a qualified gemologist whose scientific training and wealth of practical experience provide a far greater data base from which to operate, the consumer can learn to judge a stone as a "total personality" and learn what the critical factors are—color, clarity (sometimes referred to in the trade as "perfection"), sparkle and brilliance, and weight—and how to balance them in judging the gem's value. Learning about these factors and spending time in the marketplace looking, listening, and asking questions before making the purchase will prepare you to be a wise buyer more likely to get what you really want, at a fair price.

Try to learn as much as you can about the gem you want to buy. Examine stones owned by your family and friends, and compare stones at several different jewelry stores, noting differences in shades of color, brilliance, and cut. Go to a good, established jewelry store and ask to see fine stones. If the prices vary, ask why. Let the jeweler point out differences in color, cut, or brilliance, and if he can't, go to another jeweler with greater expertise. Begin to develop an eye for what constitutes a fine stone by looking, listening, and asking good questions.

After gaining an initial impression of a stone, you may want to examine it more carefully. Once you start to look at stones seriously, even a beginner can start to see differences between stones that they might not otherwise have noticed.

As you examine stones more closely, we recommend that you follow these key steps:

❖ The Six Key Steps in Examining a Stone

1. *Whenever possible, examine stones unmounted.* They can be examined more thoroughly out of their settings, and defects cannot be hidden by the mounting or side stones.

2. *Make sure the gem is clean.* If buying a stone from a retail jeweler, ask that it be cleaned for you. If you are not someplace where it can be cleaned professionally, breathe on the stone in a huffing manner in order to "steam" it with your breath and then wipe it with a clean cloth or handkerchief. This will at least remove any superficial oily film that might affect the appearance of the stone (when a stone is handled by several people who hold the stone with their fingers to examine it, an oily residue from the oil in skin quickly builds up on the stone's surface).

3. *Hold the unmounted stone so that your fingers touch only the edge.* As mentioned above, putting your fingers on the top and/or bottom of a stone will leave traces of oil, which will affect color and brilliance.

    The *careful* use of tweezers instead of fingers is recommended only if you feel comfortable using them. Make sure you know how to use them and get the permission of the owner before picking up the stone. It is easy for the stone to pop out of the tweezers and to become damaged or lost, and you could be held responsible.

4. *View the gem under proper lighting.* Many jewelers use numerous incandescent spotlights, usually recessed in dropped ceilings. Some use special spotlights that can make any gemstone —even glass imitations—look fantastic.

    Fluorescent lights may also *adversely* affect the appearance of some gems. Diamonds will not show as much sparkle under fluorescent lighting, and many colored gems, such as rubies, look much better in true daylight or incandescent light ("warm" light, such as that produced by standard lightbulbs).

To get a sense of how the stone will look when mounted in the ring, examine it with the light coming from above or behind you, shining down and through the stone, so that the light traveling through the stone is reflected back up to your eye.

5. *Rotate the stone in order to view it from different angles.*
6. *If using a loupe, focus it both on the surface and into the interior.* To focus into the interior, shift the stone slowly, raising or lowering it, until you focus clearly on all depths within it. This is important because if you focus on the top only, you won't see what is in the interior of the stone.

❖ How to Use a Loupe

A loupe (pronounced "loop") is a special type of magnifying glass. The use of the loupe can be very helpful in many situations, even for the beginner. With a loupe you can check a stone for chips and scratches or examine certain types of noticeable inclusions more closely. Remember, however, that even with a loupe, you will not have the knowledge or skill to see or understand the many telltale indicators that an experienced jeweler or gemologist can spot. No book can provide you with that knowledge or skill. Do not allow yourself to be deluded or let a little knowledge give you a false confidence. Nothing will more quickly alienate a reputable jeweler or mark you faster as easy prey for the disreputable dealer.

The loupe is a very practical tool to use once you master it, and with practice it will become more and more valuable. The correct type is a 10x (ten-power) "triplet," which can be obtained from any optical supply house. The triplet-type is recommended because it corrects two problems other kinds of magnifiers have: the presence of traces of color normally found at the outer edge of the lens; and visual distortion, also usually at the outer edge of the lens. In addition, the loupe must have a black housing around the lens, not chrome or gold, either of which might affect the color you see in the stone.

The loupe *must be* 10x because the Federal Trade Commission in the United States requires grading to be done under 10-power magnification. Any flaw that does not show up under 10x magnification is considered nonexistent for grading purposes.

A 10X triplet
loupe

With a few minutes' practice you can easily learn to use the loupe. Here's how:

1. Hold the loupe between the thumb and forefinger of either hand.
2. Hold the stone or ring similarly in the other hand.
3. Bring both hands together so that the fleshy parts just below the thumbs are pushed together and braced by the lower portion of each hand just above the wrists (the wrist portion is actually a pivot point).
4. Now move the hands up to your nose or cheek, with the loupe as close to the eye as possible. If you wear eyeglasses, you do not have to remove them.
5. Get a steady hand. With gems it's very important to have steady hands for careful examination. With your hands still together and braced against your face, put your elbows on a table or countertop. (If a table isn't available, brace your arms against your chest or rib cage.) If you do this properly you will have a steady hand.

Practice with the loupe, keeping it approximately one inch (more or less) from the eye, and about an inch from the object being examined. A 10x loupe is difficult to focus initially, but with a little practice it will become easy and you will soon be able to see through it clearly. You can practice on any object that is difficult to see—the pores in your skin, a strand of hair, a pinhead, or your own jewelry.

Play with the item being examined. Rotate it slowly, tilt it back and forth while rotating it, look at it from different angles and different directions. It won't take long before you are able to focus easily on anything you wish to examine. If you aren't sure about your technique, a knowledgeable jeweler will be happy to help you learn to use the loupe correctly.

How to hold
a loupe when
examining a
stone

❖ What the Loupe Can Tell You

With practice and experience (and further education, if you're really serious), a loupe can tell even the amateur a great deal. For a gemologist it can help determine whether the stone is natural, synthetic, glass, or a doublet (a composite stone, to be discussed later) and reveal characteristic flaws, blemishes, or cracks. In other words, the loupe can provide the necessary information to help you know whether the stone is in fact what it is supposed to be.

For the beginner, the loupe is useful in seeing:

1. *The workmanship that went into the cutting.* As you will see in chapter 6, there are many factors in how a stone is cut that affect value. Some are easy to check with the loupe. For example, you can see whether or not the edge of the stone has been cut dangerously thin, whether or not the symmetry of the stone is balanced, or whether or not it has the proper number of facets. Few cutters put the same time and care into cutting imitations as they do into cutting a diamond.

2. *Chips, cracks, or scratches.* Some gemstones are softer or more brittle than others and will scratch or chip easily. Zircon, for example, looks very much like diamond because of its pronounced brilliance and relative hardness, but it chips easily Therefore, careful examination of a zircon will often show chipping, especially around the top or edge of the stone. Glass, which is very soft, will often show scratches, and even normal wear can cause it to chip or become scratched. Also, if you check around the prongs, the setter may even have scratched it while bending the prongs to hold the stone.

   In such stones as emeralds, the loupe can also help you determine whether or not any natural cracks are really serious, how close they are to the surface, how deep they run, or how many are readily visible.

3. *The sharpness of the facet edges.* Harder stones will have a sharp edge, or sharper boundaries between adjoining planes or facets, whereas many imitations are softer and under the loupe the edges between the facets are less sharp and have a more rounded appearance.

4. *Inclusions and blemishes.* Many inclusions (often called flaws) that cannot be seen with the naked eye are easily seen with the loupe. The word "inclusion" simply refers to something that formed inside the stone as it was forming in nature; "blemish" refers to something on the *outside* of the stone such as a small nick on the edge. After you decide on a particular stone, the loupe can often enable you to find something inside that stone—a particular inclusion—that can become an "identifying mark." This can be very reassuring, helping you recognize your stone, for example, after it has been set, or at some future time should your ring need to be resized or repaired. But remember, many are not easily seen unless you are very experienced. (All gemstones contain inclusions, and many have some type of blemish. It is important to understand what they are and how they affect value. This is discussed in detail in chapter 8.)

The presence of inclusions is not as serious in colored stones as in diamonds, and they don't usually significantly reduce the value of the stone. However, the *kind* of inclusions seen in colored stones can be important. They often provide the necessary key to positive identification, or to determining whether a stone is natural or synthetic, and possibly, its country of origin (which may significantly affect the value of a colored gemstone). With minimal experience, the amateur can also learn to spot the characteristic bubbles and swirl lines associated with glass and cheap synthetics.

With a little practice the loupe can tell you a great deal about the workmanship that went into cutting a gem and help you see how well made the ring is. It can also help you locate internal characteristics that are part of the unique makeup of your stone. It can help a professional decide whether a gem is natural, synthetic, or an imitation, or whether or not the stone has been artificially enhanced. It can provide the clues about the gem's authenticity, its durability, and its place of origin. But spotting these clues takes lots of practice and experience.

When you use a loupe, remember that you won't see what the experienced professional will see, but with a little practice, it can still be a valuable tool that might save you from a costly mistake.

CHAPTER 4

Looking for a Gem That's a "Cut Above"

One of the most important things to learn is how to look at a gem, but before beginning you should become familiar with the terms you will be hearing to describe what you will be seeing, and what you want, especially terms pertaining to the stone's "cut" and the names for the parts of a cut stone.

It's important to be familiar with a few general terms that are commonly used when referring to faceted stones. The parts of a stone can vary in proportion to one another, and these variations result in differences in a stone's appearance. This will be discussed later in greater detail.

Girdle. The girdle is the edge or border of the stone that forms its perimeter; it is the edge formed where the top portion of the stone meets the bottom portion—its "dividing line." This is the part usually grasped by the prongs of a setting.

Crown. The crown is also called the *top* of the stone. This is simply the upper portion of the stone, the part above the girdle.

Pavilion. The pavilion is the bottom portion of the stone, the part from the girdle to the point at the bottom.

Culet. The culet refers to the "point" at the bottom, which is really not a point but another tiny facet. The smaller the culet the better. Today, many diamonds are cut without a culet, and colored gemstones are often cut in styles that lack the culet.

Table. The table is the large, flat plane (facet) at the very top of the

Parts of a Faceted Stone

Table facet

Girdle

Culet

Crown
(top portion)

Pavilion
(bottom portion)

stone. It is the largest facet on a stone, often called the *face*. The term *table spread* is used to describe the width of the table facet, often expressed as a percentage of the total width of the stone.

❖ The Cut of the Stone

The most important—and least understood—factor that must be evaluated when considering any gem is the *cutting*. When we talk about how a stone is cut, we are not referring to the shape, but to the care and precision used in creating a finished gem from the rough. There are many popular shapes for gemstones. Each shape affects the overall look of the stone, but whatever the shape, it must be well cut in order to see its full beauty; the better the cutting, the greater the sparkle and brilliance, and the higher the value.

For most people, choosing a shape is simply a matter of personal taste. Some of the most popular traditional shapes are pictured here. New shapes are discussed in chapter 6.

Traditional Shapes

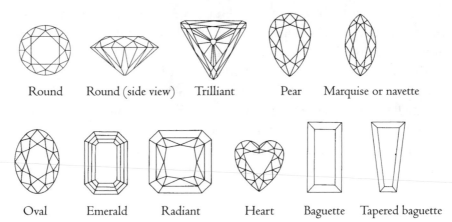

Round   Round (side view)   Trilliant   Pear   Marquise or navette

Oval   Emerald   Radiant   Heart   Baguette   Tapered baguette

❖ *Make* Makes a Big Difference

The shape of the stone may affect its look and overall "personality," but it is the precision of the cutting that releases its full beauty. A term used by professionals to describe the overall quality of the cutting is *make*. Having a "good make" is especially important in diamonds. A diamond with an "excellent make" will sell for much more than one with a "fair make." The difference in price between a well-cut and poorly cut diamond can be as much as 50 percent or more. Even more important, careless cutting, or cutting to get the largest possible stone from the rough, can sometimes result in faults that may make a stone more fragile and vulnerable to breakage. Such stones should sell for much less, although the fault may not be visible without careful examination by an expert. Here we will discuss cutting in a general way. It will be discussed in greater detail later.

❖ How to Know If a Stone Is Well Cut

The precision of the cutting dramatically affects the beauty and value of any stone. This is especially true in faceted stones, those on which a series of tiny flat planes (called facets or faces) have been cut and polished. (Nonfaceted stones are called cabochons; these are discussed in the section on colored gemstones). By following some general guidelines and tips for looking at faceted gemstones, you can better determine both the quality of the stone and the quality of the cut.

The first thing to keep in mind is that in any stone, if the material is of good quality, the way it is cut will make the difference between a dull, lifeless stone and a beautiful, brilliant one. In diamonds, the cutting and proportioning of the stone have the greatest influence on the stone's brilliance and fire. In colored gems, the perfection of the cut is not as important as it is with diamonds, but proportioning remains critical because it can significantly affect the depth of color as well as the stone's brilliance and liveliness.

As you view the stone, first look at it "face up," that is, through the top (table). This is the most critical area to view, since this is the one most often noticed. If looking at a diamond, does it seem to sparkle and dance across the whole stone, or are there dead spots? In a colored gem, does the color look good from this direction? Is the table centered and symmetrical?

A quick way to check the symmetry of a round diamond is to look at the table edges, as shown on the next page. The lines should be straight, regular, and parallel to one another. The table edges should form a regular octagon, with the edges meeting in sharp points. If the lines of the table are wavy, the overall symmetry is not good, and the symmetry of the adjoining facets will also be affected.

Table centered
but lines of octagon
are not symmetrical

Table centered and
symmetrical,
forming perfect
octagon—the ideal

Table off-
center and lines of
octagon asymmetrical

Next, look at the stone from the side. Note the proportioning of the top (crown) and bottom (pavilion) portions of the stone; how thin or thick is the portion above the girdle? Below the girdle?

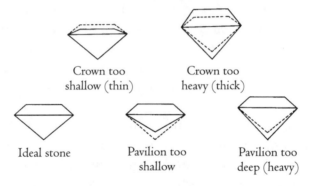

Crown too
shallow (thin)

Crown too
heavy (thick)

Ideal stone

Pavilion too
shallow

Pavilion too
deep (heavy)

A diamond's proportioning—whether the crown or pavilion are too thin or too thick—will have a marked affect on its overall beauty. With colored stones, the thickness or thinness will vary greatly depending upon the inherent optical properties of different gems, as well as where and how the color is dispersed throughout the stone. This will be discussed later in greater detail.

When considering colored stones, as a general guide keep in mind these three points:

1. If the stone appears lively and exhibits an appealing color when viewed through the table, no matter how the proportioning appears (thick or thin), it is usually correct and acceptable proportioning for that particular stone.
2. The depth of color (tone) will become darker as the stone is cut thicker, particularly if the bottom portion (pavilion) is deep and broad.

3. A stone's depth of color will become lighter as the stone is cut thinner. This is especially important when considering a pastel colored stone. A pastel stone should always have fairly deep proportioning.

The effects of the cutting and proportioning for diamonds will be discussed fully in chapter 6, and for colored gemstones in chapter 16 since the effects are somewhat different for diamonds and colored gems. As a first step, however, it is important simply to begin to look at stones and familiarize yourself with what they should look like, and to begin to have a feeling about what looks "right." You'll be surprised at how quickly you begin to notice differences between stones and begin to zero in on what appeals most to you.

❖ As You Begin

As you shop for your ring, keep in mind the importance of visiting fine jewelry stores to look at stones and compare them. Many of the factors discussed in the following chapters will become clearer when you have actual stones before you to examine, and you will gain a deeper understanding and appreciation for the gem you are considering. Knowledgeable jewelers will also be happy to take time to help you understand quality and cost differences.

Also keep in mind the importance of buying only from a knowledgeable, well-trained jeweler with a good reputation. Remember, you are not an expert. The information provided here should help you begin your search more confidently and gain insights that will make the experience more fun, more challenging, and more fulfilling. But perhaps just as important, we hope it will help you make a wiser decision about the jeweler with whom you decide to do business, and about his or her knowledge, professionalism, and integrity. If so, this book will have provided a valuable service and, perhaps, saved you from a costly mistake.

PART THREE

Diamond Engagement
and Wedding Rings

CHAPTER 5

Selecting the Diamond

The diamond engagement ring has emerged as the universal symbol of love and commitment between two people. Not only is it the formal beginning—the visible "announcement" of your engagement—but the centuries-old symbolism surrounding diamond reflects both the preciousness of the moment and the commitment made by two people in love to cherish each other forever.

While some women prefer other gems to diamond, or opt for the special significance of a family heirloom, a diamond is the overwhelming choice of today's bride. Some brides-to-be have no doubt been taken by surprise with the unexpected presentation of an engagement ring, but it is probably safest to go about the task of selecting the ring *together*. While the element of surprise is very romantic, keep in mind that the engagement ring is meant to be worn for a lifetime. So it is especially important that the bride-to-be really loves it; that it reflects her personal taste and style. If you are a die-hard romantic who wants to surprise her, we suggest placing a *photo* of a ring you like inside the "tiny black ring box" and presenting her with this instead; it combines romance with practicality, and you are sending another important message: not only do you love her, but you understand the importance of working *together* on such an important decision!

The following chapters will give you everything you need to know to purchase a diamond with greater confidence—whether you're shopping for an engagement ring, wedding or anniversary band, or simply a beautiful piece of diamond jewelry to commemorate an important moment. The greater your awareness of the elements that determine diamond quality, the better your chances of knowing what you want, getting exactly what you're after, and deriving lasting pleasure from it.

Some modern diamond engagement rings

❖ What Is Diamond?

Chemically speaking, a diamond is the simplest of all gemstones. It is plain, crystallized carbon—the same substance, chemically, as the soot left on the inside of a glass globe after the burning of a candle; it is the same substance used in lead pencils.

The diamond differs from these in its crystal form, which gives it the desirable properties that have made it so highly prized—its hardness, which gives it unsurpassed wearability; its brilliance; and its fire. (But note that while diamond is the hardest natural substance known, it can be chipped or broken if hit hard from certain angles, and if the "girdle" has been cut too thin it can be chipped with even a modest blow.)

The transparent white (or, more correctly, *colorless*) diamond is the most popular variety, but diamond also occurs in colors. When the color is prominent it is called a *fancy* diamond. Diamond is frequently found in nice yellow and brown shades. Colors such as pink, light blue, light green, and lavender occur much more rarely. In diamonds, the colors seen are usually pastel. Deep colors in hues of red, green, and dark blue are extremely rare. Historically, most colored diamonds have sold for more than their colorless counterparts, except for light yellow or brown varieties. Yellow or brown in *very* pale shades may not be fancy diamonds but *off-color* stones that are very common and sell for much less than colorless diamonds or those with a true "fancy" color.

In addition to natural-color diamonds, "fancies" that have obtained their color artificially, through exposure to certain types of radiation and heating techniques, are readily available. The bill of sale (and any accompanying certification, appraisal, etc.) should specify whether the color is natural or induced. If induced, the price should be much less, although the gem will often be just as beautiful as one with a natural color.

❖ The Four Factors That Determine Diamond Value

Diamond quality and value are determined by four factors. These factors are called the "Four C's." If we were to rank them based on their importance in determining the value of a diamond, we would list them as follows:

1. Color (body color)
2. Clarity (degree of flawlessness)
3. Cutting and proportioning (often referred to as the *make*)
4. Carat weight (which affects the size)

In terms of determining beauty, however, we would rank them in a different order:

1. Cutting and proportioning
2. Color
3 Clarity
4. Carat weight

Because each factor is a lesson in itself, we have devoted a chapter to each. We will begin with a discussion of diamond cutting and proportioning because it is the least understood and because we think it's the most important factor in terms of the stone's beauty. Equally important, as we mentioned earlier, the cutting of a diamond has a significant effect on cost and can even affect the stone's durability.

CHAPTER 6

The Importance of Cutting and Proportioning in Diamond

It is important to distinguish exactly what "cut" means in reference to diamonds and other stones. *Cut* does not mean *shape*. Shape pertains to the outline of the diamond's perimeter. The selection of shape is a matter of individual preference. No matter which shape is selected, its *cutting* must be evaluated.

There are several different cutting styles: *brilliant* cut, *step* cut, or *mixed* cut. A brilliant cut uses many facets, usually triangular and kite-shaped, arranged in a particular way to create maximum brilliance. A step cut uses fewer facets, usually trapezoid or rectangular in shape, arranged in a more linear pattern (as you see in the emerald cut). Although usually less brilliant than those cut in a brilliant style, step-cut diamonds can produce a lively, fiery stone with a very elegant and understated personality. You often see step-cut triangle, square, and trapezoid shapes in Art Deco period jewelry (1920s). A mixed-cut style incorporates elements from both the step-cut and brilliant-cut styles.

The term "cut"—also referred to as the stone's "*make*"—is especially important because of its effect on the beauty and personality of the diamond. When we evaluate the cut, we are really judging the stone's proportioning and finish, the two factors that are most directly related to producing the *fire* (the lovely rainbow colors that flash from within) and *brilliance* (the liveliness, the sparkle) that sets diamond apart from all other gems. Regardless of the shape or cutting style, a stone with an excellent make will be exciting, while a stone with a poor make will look lifeless; it will lack the sparkle and personality we identify with diamond. In addition, diamonds are often cut to make them *appear* larger. But a stone that looks much larger than another of the same weight will not be as beautiful as a smaller stone that is properly cut.

Differences in cutting can also affect the *durability* of a diamond. Some cutting faults weaken the stone and make it more susceptible to breaking or chipping.

Fine cutting requires skill and experience, takes more time, and results in greater loss of the "rough" from which the stone is being cut, resulting in a stone that yields less weight when finished. For all these reasons, a well-cut diamond commands a premium and will cost much more than one that is cut poorly.

There are many popular shapes for diamonds. Each shape affects the overall look of the stone, but if the stone is cut well, beauty and value endure no matter which shape you choose. We will begin the discussion of diamond cutting with the round brilliant cut, since this is the most popular shape.

A modern round brilliant-cut diamond has fifty-eight facets. There are thirty-three on the top, twenty-four on the bottom, plus the culet—the "point" at the bottom, which normally is another tiny facet (although many diamonds today are cut without a culet). Round brilliant-cut stones that are small in size are referred to as "full-cut" to distinguish them from "single-cut" stones that have only seventeen facets, or "Swiss-cut" with only thirty-three facets. Older pieces of jewelry such as heirloom diamond bands, or inexpensive pieces containing numerous stones, often contain these cuts instead of full-cut stones. They have less brilliance and liveliness than full-cuts, but with fewer facets they are easier and less expensive to cut. Rings containing single- or Swiss-cut stones should sell for less than rings with full-cut stones.

When a round brilliant-cut diamond is cut well, its shape displays the most liveliness because it enables the most light to be reflected back up through the top. This means that round brilliant-cut diamonds will have greater brilliance, overall, than other shapes, but other shapes can also be very lively. New shapes are also appearing, some of which compare very favorably to round stones for overall brilliance and liveliness.

As a rule of thumb, if the top portion of the stone (the crown) appears to be roughly one-third of the pavilion depth (distance from girdle to culet), the proportioning is probably acceptable.

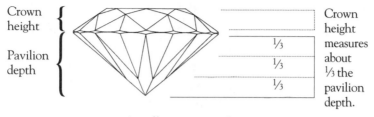

Crown height {

Pavilion depth {

Crown height measures about ⅓ the pavilion depth.

⅓
⅓
⅓

A well-proportioned stone

❖ Types of Diamond Proportioning

The proportioning—especially the height of the crown in relation to the depth of the pavilion, and the width of the table facet in
relation to the width of the stone—is what determines how much
brilliance and fire the stone will have. Several formulas for correct
proportioning have been developed for round diamonds. Stones
that adhere to these very precise formulas are considered to have an
"ideal" make and will cost more than other diamonds because of the
extra time and skill required to cut them, and because more diamond "rough" is lost in the cutting.

How Cutting Affects Brilliance

Light Reflection in an Ideally Proportioned Diamond
Ideal proportions ensure the maximum brilliance. When
light enters a properly cut diamond, it is reflected from facet
to facet, and then back up through the top, exhibiting
maximum fire and sparkle.

Light Reflection in a Diamond Cut Too Deep
In a diamond that is cut too deep, much of the light is reflected
to opposite facets at the wrong angle and is lost through the
sides. The diamond appears dark in the center.

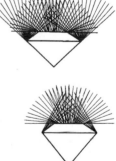

Light Reflection in a Diamond Cut Too Shallow
A diamond cut too shallow (to make it look larger) loses
brilliance. The eye sees a ring of dull reflection instead
of the great brilliance of a well-cut diamond.

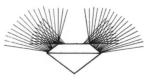

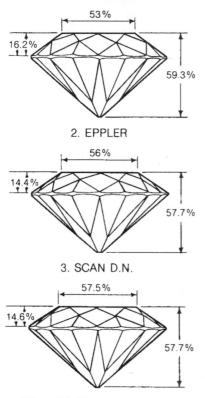

1. TOLKOWSKY

53%

16.2%

59.3%

2. EPPLER

56%

14.4%

57.7%

3. SCAN D.N.

57.5%

14.6%

57.7%

Three "ideal" standards for diamond proportioning. Note the differences in table widths and crown heights.

❖ What Is Ideal?

Today great emphasis is placed on "ideal makes" to help people better understand the effect of precision cutting on the beauty and cost of a diamond, and to provide guidelines to help in selecting a diamond that exhibits brilliance, fire, and overall scintillation (the "sparkle" that results from the fire and brilliance working together). There are exceptions to all rules, however, and there are many diamonds that do not adhere to "ideal" parameters, yet are as brilliant and fiery as those that do.

Diamond cutting is an art form that is still evolving, and technological advances continue to shed new insights on how cutting affects the way light travels through diamond to create a scintillating diamond. Today there are several slightly differing formulas for cutting an "ideal" stone, and there is no consensus as to what is "best," but each results in an exceptionally beautiful stone. Generally speaking, diamonds that are cut with smaller tables exhibit more fire; those with larger tables exhibit more brilliance. Larger tables seem to be more in fashion today. But, as common sense may tell you here, both can't excel in the same stone. A larger table can create greater brilliance but may cause some reduction in fire; a smaller table area can increase fire but may reduce brilliance. The ideal would be a compromise that would allow the greatest brilliance and fire simultaneously. No one has come to agreement, however, on what the percentages should be, since some people prefer fire to brilliance, and vice versa. This is one reason why there are several different types of proportioning found in diamonds, and "best" is usually a matter of personal preference.

In 1919, Marcel Tolkowsky developed what he thought would be the best combination of angles to allow light to enter the stone and be reflected back in such a way as to create the most vivid fire combined with intense brilliance. The Tolkowsky cut provided the basis for the modern American ideal make, but today there are several variations of Tolkowsky's formula, some with "brand" names such as the *Lazare Kaplan Ideal®*, the *EightStar®*, and the *Hearts on Fire®*. These ideal cuts often create perfectly aligned arrows or a hearts-and-arrows pattern that can be seen with a special viewer. Whatever "ideal" you choose, each results in a very beautiful diamond, but you must compare them for yourself to discover which "ideal" you prefer.

EightStar® Diamond

When purchasing a round diamond, ask how the make would be graded: ideal, excellent, very good, good, fair, or poor. A diamond with a "fair" or "poor" make should sell for less than a diamond with a "good" make. A diamond with a "very good," "excellent," or "ideal" make will sell for more. (See chapter 11 for more information on grading the make.)

Keep in mind that despite the effect of cutting on a diamond's beauty, durability, and cost, most laboratories do not yet "grade" the cut or indicate "ideal." The American Gem Society Laboratory (AGS), American Gemological Laboratories (AGL), and Professional Gem Sciences (PGS) do so. Diamond reports from the Gemological Institute of America (GIA) and other laboratories provide information about cutting that relates to the diamond's make, but you must understand how to interpret this information. (See chapter 11.)

Diamonds exhibit somewhat different "personalities" depending on the make. An "ideal" make will exhibit one personality, while another diamond with different proportioning will exhibit a different personality. Not everyone will prefer stones cut to a particular "ideal" formula, and diamonds don't have to be cut to "ideal" proportions to show strong fire and brilliance, to be beautiful or desirable.

We've seen diamonds with "ideal" proportions that were not as brilliant and fiery as diamonds cut to "non-ideal" proportions, and vice versa. Many people prefer diamonds with wider tables than are found in an "ideal," and we have seen diamonds with tables exceeding 64 percent that were surprisingly beautiful and very desirable.

Your eye will be responsible for making the final determination. In general, when you look at a diamond that has a lot of brilliance and fire, the cutting and proportioning probably are acceptable. A stone that appears lifeless and seems to be "dead" or dark at the center probably suffers from poor cutting and proportioning. The more time you take to look at and compare diamonds of different qualities and prices, the better trained your eye will become to detect differences in brilliance and fire, lifelessness and dullness.

No matter what the proportions are, before making a final decision on a particular stone, ask yourself whether or not you think it is beautiful. If you like it, don't allow yourself to be overly influenced by formulas.

❖ New Technology Provides *Ideal* Solution

Rather than relying rigidly on formulas or subjective perceptions, new technology may provide the "ideal" solution to the dilemma of judging the overall make of a diamond. Increasingly we are finding new tools on the jewelry store counter—including the *FireScope®*, introduced by EightStar® Diamond Company, the *BrillianceScope™ Analyzer,* and the *BrillianceScope™ Viewer,* developed by GemEx, and the *Gilbertson Scope*—to make it easier for you to know whether or not a diamond is cut to exceptional standards.

One of the first to be developed was the FireScope®. With it, you can compare the cutting of several diamonds side by side very quickly. When a precisely cut diamond—one in which each of the fifty-eight facets has been properly shaped, angled, and aligned—is viewed through the scope, the diamond will produce a pattern showing eight black arrows against a red background. When you see this, you know the diamond exhibits high brilliance, fire, and scintillation.

The BrillianceScope™ Analyzer and the BrillianceScope™ Viewer also enable you to compare several diamonds, but rather than relying on patterns they actually *measure* how much brilliance, fire, and scintillation is seen in the diamond. The latest, the Gilbertson Scope, is similar to the FireScope® but produces a pattern in three colors for a more precise impression of the fire and scintillation.

What is most exciting about these new technologies is that they are providing information about what is really important; that is, what the diamond is *doing* with the light that enters it. With viewers such as those mentioned here, even the most inexperienced consumers will be able to see how light is performing in a specific stone, compare the brilliance and the fire—the overall personality—of different stones, and pick what they really like best. As more jewelers acquire such diamond viewers, it will become much easier for consumers to judge not only the cutting of a diamond, but the final result: its beauty.

Six diamonds, as seen with the FireScope®, showing the progression of cutting perfection. The diamond on the far right is not very well cut, while the diamond on the far left, one of the "super ideal" cuts known as an EightStar® diamond, shows eight perfect arrows, telling you the diamond is precision-cut; that is, each of the fifty-eight facets is perfectly shaped, angled, and aligned.

❖ Faulty Cutting

Many errors that affect the appearance and value of a diamond can occur in the cutting. Remember that some cutting faults will make a stone more vulnerable to breakage. We recommend avoiding such stones unless they can be protected by the setting.

There are several cutting faults to watch for in round diamonds. First, look carefully for a *sloping table* or a table that is not almost perfectly perpendicular to the point of the culet.

Second, the culet can frequently be the source of a problem. It can be chipped or broken, open or large (almost all modern cut stones have culets that come nearly to a point), off-center, or it can be missing altogether.

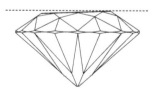

A brilliant-cut stone
with a sloping table

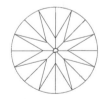

Chipped and "open" culet
(viewed from the bottom)

Off-center culet

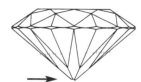

Broken or chipped culet

Poor symmetry

Stone with extra facets

Third, repairs to chipped areas can result in *misaligned facets,* which destroy the stone's symmetry.

Sometimes, too, as a result of repair, an *extra facet* will be formed, often in the crown facets, but also on or just below the girdle. These extra facets may slightly affect the stone's brilliance.

❖ Girdle Faults

The girdle is often the source of faults. *Bearded* or *fringed girdles* are common. A fringed girdle exhibits small radial cracks penetrating into the stone; these can result from a careless or inexperienced cutter. A bearded girdle is similar but not as pronounced a fault and can be easily repaired by repolishing, with minor loss in diamond weight.

The relative thickness of the girdle is very important because it can affect the durability as well as the beauty of the stone. Any girdle can be nicked or chipped in the course of wear, or by careless handling, but if the girdle is too thin it will chip more easily. Some chips can be easily removed by repolishing, with minimal diamond weight loss. If there are numerous chips, the entire girdle can be repolished. Chips or nicks in the girdle are often hidden under the prongs or concealed by the setting.

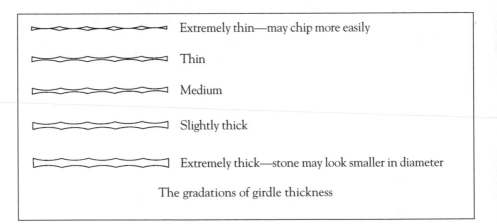

The gradations of girdle thickness

If the girdle is too thick, the stone may look smaller because a disproportionate amount of its weight will be in the girdle itself; such stones, for their weight, will be smaller in diameter than other stones of comparable weight. The girdle can also be *wavy, rough,* or *entirely out-of-round.*

Wavy girdle

Out-of-round girdle

A *natural* at the girdle

A *natural* may not be a fault. It's actually a piece of the natural surface of the diamond crystal. In cutting, a cutter may decide to leave part of the "natural" rough surface in order to get as large a diamond as possible from the rough stone. If this natural is no thicker than the thickness of the girdle and does not distort the circumference of the stone, most dealers consider it a minor defect at worst; if it extends into the crown or pavilion of the stone, it is a more serious fault.

Sometimes if the natural is somewhat large but slightly below the girdle, it will be polished off. This produces an extra facet.

❖ Other Popular Shapes

Unlike round diamonds, "fancy" shapes—all shapes other than round—have no set formulas, so evaluating the make of a fancy is more subjective. Table and depth percentage can vary widely among individual stones of the same shape, each producing a beautiful stone. Personal taste also varies with regard to what constitutes the "ideal" for shapes other than round. Nonetheless, there are certain visual indicators of good or poor proportioning—such as the bow tie effect—which even the amateur can learn to spot. There are recommended ratios for overall shape and symmetry, but a preferred shape is largely a personal matter. Ranges for what is acceptable or unacceptable have been developed (see chapter 11). As you gain experience looking at specific shapes, you will be able to spot faults, and begin to determine what is within an acceptable range. Moderate deviations will not significantly affect the beauty or value of a stone; however, extreme deviations can seriously reduce a stone's beauty and value.

❖ Cutting Faults in Popular Fancy Shapes

One of the most obvious indicators of poor proportioning in fancy shapes is the *bow tie* or *butterfly* effect: a darkened area across the center or widest part of the stone, depending on the cut. The bow tie is most commonly seen in the pear shape or marquise, but it may exist in any fancy shape. Virtually all fancy shapes cut today will exhibit some

Marquise
with a
pronounced
bow tie,
or butterfly

minimal bow tie effect. Nonetheless, the presence or absence of a bow tie is an indicator of proper proportioning. In poorly proportioned stones there is a pronounced bow tie; the more pronounced, the poorer the proportioning. The less pronounced the bow tie, the better the proportioning. The degree to which the bow tie is evident is the first indicator of a good or a poor make. A diamond with a pronounced bow tie should sell for much less than one without.

As with the brilliant-cut diamond, fancy shapes can also be cut too *broad* or too *narrow,* and the pavilion can be too *deep* or too *shallow.*

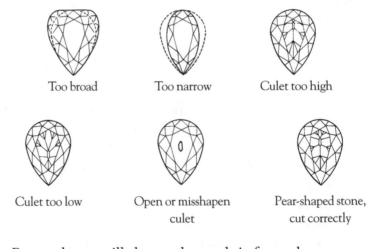

Too broad   Too narrow   Culet too high

Culet too low   Open or misshapen   Pear-shaped stone,
                        culet   cut correctly

Personal taste will always play a role in fancy shapes—some prefer a narrow pear shape, for example, while others might prefer a fatter pear. Whatever the shape you are considering, you must ask yourself whether or not you find the stone exciting. Does it have a pleasing personality? Does it exhibit good brilliance and fire? Is the entire stone brilliant, or are there "dead" spots? Are there any cutting faults that might make it more susceptible to chipping? Then you must make the choice.

❖ New Shapes Create Excitement

Today we can choose from many shapes and cuts, ranging from the classics—round, oval, pear, marquise, emerald cut, and heart shape—to new shapes that appear as cutters continue to experiment with novel looks. Here are some of the most popular:

The *radiant cut* is perfect for the person who likes the shape of an emerald cut but wants more sparkle. It has the shape of the classic emerald cut—square or rectangular— but much greater brilliance, giving it a personality very similar to a round diamond. The *Crisscut®* is a wonderful blend between the two, more understated than the radiant but livelier than an emerald cut.

Radiant Crisscut®

The *princess cut,* a square brilliant cut, is ideal for bezel and channel settings (see chapter 22) or any setting in which you want the stone to be flush with the mounting. The *Quadrillion™* was the first trademarked "princess," cut to unique specifications for maximum brillance and fire.

Standard Quadrillion™
princess

The *trilliant cut,* a popular shape for use as a center stone or as side stones, is also a thin cut, giving a large appearance for its weight. Extra facets and precision cutting produce high brilliance. When flanking either side of another diamond, trilliants produce a much larger diamond appearance overall. The *Noble Cut™*, a newly branded elongated "kite" shape with 29 facets, is ideally suited for classic, linear designs.

Trilliant Noble Cut™

The *Gabrielle®* cut has 105 facets arranged in a unique alignment that creates more scintillation, more sparkle, than is seen in traditional cuts. The Gabrielle® comes in all the classic shapes. The *Spirit Sun®* is a revolutionary new cut with only 16 facets and a pointed crown. It represents an entirely new approach to diamond cutting, and its almost pinwheel-like facet alignment achieves intense brilliance and reflectivity.

Gabrielle® Spirit Sun®

Tiffany has patented its own new cut, the *Lucida™*, a square brilliant cut that blends the modern brilliant cut and old-mine cut (cushion) with its high crown and small table. This cut is available only from Tiffany, although similar cuts are entering the market. Another of the new "square" cuts, the *Context®*, creates a wholly new look. The epitome of simplicity, it can be fashioned only from rare, perfectly formed diamond crystals—one in one

Lucida™ Context®

hundred thousand—and it achieves an amazing luminosity without altering the inherent shape of the natural crystal.

Royal Asscher®   Modern cushion

The *Royal Asscher®* is a contemporary 74-facet version of the original Asscher, an older cut that is enjoying renewed popularity (see page 48). A square cut characterized by exaggerated corners, the Royal Asscher® reveals intense fire. The overall look is elegant, classic, and important. The distinctive *modern cushion cut,* a blend between a rectangular and oval shape, is a contemporary version of a cut that dates back prior to the turn of the nineteenth century (see page 48). The modern version is more brilliant and not as "heavy" in its make, so it looks somewhat larger than earlier cushion cuts of the same weight.

As we learn more and more about diamond cutting and how various facet arrangements and angles affect the way light performs in a diamond, new cuts continue to emerge. These include the *New Century®*, a patented 102-facet, round, super brilliant cut; the *Zoë,* a scintillating 100-facet cut; the extra fiery 82-facet *Royal 82;* the 80-facet *Spirit of Flanders™*; the *Lily Cut®,* shaped like a four-leaf-clover; the 66-facet *Leo Diamond™*; and the new 97-facet, 12-sided *Escada®* that was created exclusively for the great fashion house.

In addition to the new cuts above, we are also seeing cutting innovations in baguettes, with new brilliant-cut baguettes, such as the *Princette™* and the *Bagillion™*. They occur in straight and tapered shapes. There are also Crisscut® baguettes and tapered baguettes. These are gaining in popularity because they have greater brilliance than traditional baguettes. They can be used to flank diamonds or other stones in traditional settings, or are used in very contemporary jewelry design with straight, clean lines.

❖ Early Cuts Enjoy Renewed Popularity

Interest in antique and period jewelry is growing rapidly. As it does, the diamonds that adorn them are arousing renewed attention and gaining new respect. If you are considering an antique or estate piece for your engagement and/or wedding ring, or are lucky enough to be receiving a diamond that has been passed down through the family, it is important to know about earlier cuts and how they compare to modern cuts.

The way a diamond is cut is often one of the clues to the age of a piece. Older diamonds can be replaced or recut to modern proportions, but replacing or recutting stones mounted in antique or period pieces could adversely affect the value of the jewelry. To preserve the integrity of the piece, antique and period jewelry connoisseurs want original stones, or, if stones have been replaced, at least stones cut in the manner typical of the period. The market is becoming increasingly strong for diamonds with older cuts, and prices are also strengthening.

As these early-cut diamonds receive more and more attention, a growing number of people are beginning to appreciate them for their distinctive beauty and personality and for the romance that accompanies them. The romantic element—combined with a cost that is more attractive than that of new diamonds—is also making them an increasingly popular choice for engagement rings.

As we mentioned in chapter 2, cutters didn't know how to actually cut diamond until the end of the fifteenth century; the earliest diamond rings contained natural, uncut diamonds, often in their octahedral crystal form (see color insert). The earliest *cut* was the *table cut*, followed by the *rose cut*, the *old-mine cut*, and the *old-European cut*. (Before 1919, when America began to emerge as an important diamond cutting center, most diamonds were cut in Europe. Thus most "old European" diamonds were cut before the first quarter of the twentieth century.)

The *table cut* illustrates history's earliest cutting effort. By placing the point of a diamond crystal against a turning wheel that held another diamond, the point could be worn down, creating a squarish, flat surface that resembled a *tabletop*. Today we still call the flat facet on the very top of the stone the *table* facet.

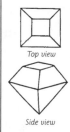

Table Cut

Top view

Side view

A table-cut diamond. Note the table-like flat surface on the top, where the crystal point was polished off. The remainder of the crystal is left unchanged.

The rose cut is a sixteenth-century cut, usually with a flat base and facets radiating from the center in multiples of six, creating the appearance of an opening rosebud. The rose cut appears in round, pear, and oval shapes.

The *old-mine* is a precursor to the modern round. This cut has a squarish or "cushion" shape (a rounded square). Proportions follow the diamond crystal, so the crown is higher and the pavilion is

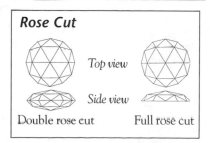

Rose Cut

Top view

Side view

Double rose cut   Full rose cut

low the diamond crystal, so the crown is higher and the pavilion is

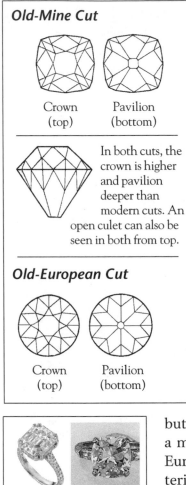

Old-Mine Cut

Crown
(top)

Pavilion
(bottom)

In both cuts, the crown is higher and pavilion deeper than modern cuts. An open culet can also be seen in both from top.

Old-European Cut

Crown
(top)

Pavilion
(bottom)

Old Asscher in a modern setting

Old cushion cut (note shape is *not* round)

Trapezoid

Half-moon

deeper than in modern stones. The table is very small, and the culet is very large and is easily seen from the top (resembling a "hole" in the diamond). These lack the brilliance of modern stones but often exhibit tremendous fire. The old-mine is enjoying a resurgence in popularity today.

Appearing in the mid-1800s, the *old-European* is similar to the old-mine cut but is *round* rather than squarish, with fifty-eight facets. The crown is higher than in modern cuts but not as high as in the old-mine cut; it has a deep pavilion, but not as deep as in old-mines. The culet is still "open" but smaller than in old-mines. This was replaced by the modern "American" round brilliant cut.

In addition to the early cuts described above, there are two other older cuts that are enjoying renewed popularity: the *cushion cut*, with a small table, high crown, and large culet, which resembles the old-mine but is usually more elongated; and the *Asscher cut*, a more or less square emerald cut that, like old-European and old-mine cut diamonds, is characterized by a very high crown, deep pavilion, small table, large culet, and very canted corners (in some cases the angles formed at the corners are so pronounced that the stone resembles an octagon). Although exhibiting less brilliance than modern-cut diamonds, the cushion and Asscher both exhibit very fiery personalities, and offer a distinctive look with a classic character.

Older cutting styles once popular for use as side stones, or to create interesting design elements, are also enjoying renewed popularity. Among the most popular are the trapezoid and half-moon.

Step-cut *trapezoid* and *half-moon* shapes are often seen in Art Deco period jewelry (1910–1920s) and make especially elegant choices to use with colored gemstones and emerald-cut diamonds (which are also step cut). Here the understated character of the trapezoid or half-moon is very complementary; while lively, their brilliance is not overpowering as it often is with modern brilliant cuts.

Old cuts can be very beautiful. The finest examples of these earlier cutting styles are very fiery and have tremendous allure. Although they have more "fire," by today's standards they have less "brilliance," and an overly large culet may also detract from the stone's beauty.

❖ Are Diamonds with Old Cuts Valuable?

Until recently, old-mine cut and old-European cut diamonds have been evaluated by comparison with modern-cut stones. Value has been determined by estimating the color, the clarity, and the weight the stone would *retain* if it were recut to modern proportions. However, this practice is now changing because of the increasing demand for old cuts among collectors and connoisseurs of antique jewelry.

We don't suggest recutting old diamonds if they are in their original mountings. The overall integrity of the piece—and its value—would be adversely affected.

If the setting has no special merit, the decision must be an individual one, based on whether or not the stone appeals to you. As we have said, some older cuts are very lovely, while others may look heavy, dull, or lifeless. An unattractive older cut may benefit from recutting, and although it will lose weight, it may have equal or greater value because of the improved make. In addition, recutting can sometimes improve the clarity grade of an older stone. Finally, before deciding whether or not to recut, you should note that the increasing popularity of older cuts is driving prices higher since they are difficult to find. In addition to their unique personalities, old cuts can have a distinctive character that sets them apart from more modern cuts.

A Word about Recutting Diamonds

There are many fine diamond cutters in the United States—New York City is one of the most important diamond cutting centers in the world for top-quality diamonds—and many diamonds can be greatly improved by recutting.

If you have an old-cut diamond that you don't care for, or a damaged diamond, your jeweler can consult with a diamond cutter—or refer

Retail Price Guide for Old-European Cut Diamonds*
Prices are per carat in U.S. dollars

COLOR†	½ CARAT	1 CARAT	2 CARATS
Color D–F			
VVS–VS	6,750–9,375	10,300–15,280	17,500–28,000
SI	5,175–6,050	8,320–9,380	13,600–14,340
I₁	2,725–3,050	5,750–6,400	6,400–6,920
Color G–H			
VVS–VS	5,100–7,050	8,060–10,560	13,440–17,820
SI	4,025–4,550	7,020–7,780	10,880–12,640
I₁	2,200–2,350	5,125–5,425	6,825–7,525
Color I			
VVS–VS	4,025–4,775	6,900–7,540	11,340–11,740
SI	3,400	7,475	9,380
I₁	2,075	4,650	6,500
Color J–K			
VVS–VS	2,900–3,700	6,725–7,800	7,160–9,100
SI	2,575–3,088	6,075–6,663	6,520–7,410
I₁	1,700–1,850	3,750–4,175	5,100–5,725
Color L–M			
VVS–VS	2,275–2,900	4,650–6,400	6,150–6,520
SI	2,150–2,550	4,200–5,600	5,250–6,875
I₁	1,275–1,425	2,850–3,450	3,600–4,375

*Retail prices are based on *The Guide,* Gemworld International, Inc.
† See pages 54 and 69 for color and clarity grades.

you to one—to determine whether or not your stone can be improved by recutting and, if so, what risks and costs might be involved.

Normally, the cost to recut a diamond ranges from approximately *$150 per carat* to as much as *$350 per carat,* depending on the skill required and the labor involved. In rare instances, the cost might be more. Thus, if the labor estimate to recut a stone is $150 per carat, recutting a two-carat diamond will cost $300.

A knowledgeable jeweler can help you decide whether or not a diamond should be recut, make arrangements for you, and help assure you that you've received the same stone back. For your own comfort and security, as well as the cutter's, we recommend that you obtain a diamond grading report or a thorough appraisal before having a stone recut, so that you have a point of reference when the stone is returned.

CHAPTER 7

Body Color

Color is one of the most important factors to consider when selecting a diamond because one of the first things people notice is whether or not the diamond is white, or, more accurately, *colorless* (there actually are *white* diamonds, usually milky white in color and translucent, but they are very rare and most people do not find them attractive). The color grade of a diamond, a measure of the stone's *colorlessness*, is also one of the most significant factors affecting value.

Color refers to the natural body color of a diamond. The finest and most expensive "white" diamonds are absolutely colorless, as in pure springwater. Most diamonds show some trace of yellowish or brownish tint. Diamonds also occur in every color of the rainbow. Natural-colored diamonds are called *fancy-color* diamonds. For engagement rings, "white" diamonds are the traditional choice, but blue, pink, lavender, and yellow diamonds are also found in engagement rings and offer a colorful alternative to symbolize the rarity and preciousness of your love...for those lucky enough to be able to afford them.

❖ How to Look at a Diamond to Evaluate Color

In colorless diamonds, color differences from one grade to the next can be very subtle, and a difference of several grades is difficult to see when a diamond is mounted. Keep in mind that it is impossible to accurately grade color in a mounted diamond. When looking at an unmounted stone, however, even an amateur can learn to see color differences if the stone is viewed properly.

Because of the diamond's high brilliance and dispersion (fire), the color grade cannot be accurately determined by looking at the stone from the top, or face-up, position. It is best to observe color by examining the stone through the *pavilion*, with the table down. Use a flat white surface such as a folded white business card or a grading trough, which can be purchased from a jewelry supplier.

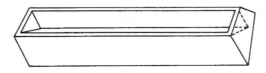

A grading trough, available in plastic or in
handy disposable folding white cardboard
stand-up packs. Be sure to use a *clean* trough.

Position 1. Place table-side down and view the stone
through the pavilion facets.

Position 2. Table-side down, view the stone through the
plane of the girdle.

Position 3. Place the pavilion down with the culet pointing
toward you. View the stone through the girdle
plane.

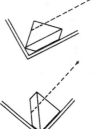

Position 4. Place table-down in a grading trough and view
the stone through the girdle plane.

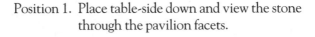

Position 5. Place pavilion-down in a grading trough, with
the culet pointing toward you. View the stone
through the pavilion facets.

❖ What Is Body Color?

When we discuss body color in colorless diamonds, we mean
how much yellow or brown tint can be seen. We are not referring
to rare natural-color diamonds.

Today, most colorless diamonds in the United States and other
countries are graded on an alphabetical scale beginning with the letter D. This letter designation is part of a color grading system introduced by the Gemological Institute of America (GIA) and is used
extensively in the diamond trade worldwide. The GIA classification
progresses from D, the rarest classification on this scale (colorless),

through the alphabet to Z, getting progressively more tinted. The grades D, E, and F are exceptionally rare and are the only grades that should be referred to as colorless. (Technically, E and F are not colorless, since they possess a trace of yellow or brown, but the tint is so slight that referring to them as colorless is acceptable.)

A diamond with the color grade D exhibits the most prized color. It is essentially colorless—like crystal-clear spring water—and is considered the most desirable. Diamonds with D-color are very rare, and a significant premium is paid for them. A diamond with the color grade E also is exceptionally rare and is almost indistinguishable from D except to the very experienced. Nonetheless, diamonds graded E in color cost significantly less per carat than those graded D, despite the difficulty in seeing the difference. The next color grade is F, and it is close to E, but there is more gradation in color than the difference observed between D and E.

❖ What Color Grade Is Most Desirable?

The colors D, E, and F can all be grouped as exceptionally fine, rare colors and may be referred to as *colorless, exceptional white,* or *rare white,* as they are often described by diamond dealers. The colors G and H may be referred to as *fine white* or *rare white*. These grades are also rare and considered very fine. The I and J colors are slightly more tinted than G and H, and sell for less, but diamonds possessing color grades G through J are very fine colors and are classified as *near colorless*. The colors K and L show a stronger tint of yellow or brown, but settings can often mask the tint. Grades M through Z will show progressively more and more tint of yellowish or brownish color. Grades D through J seem to have better resale potential than grades K through Z. This does not mean, however, that diamonds having less rare color grades are less beautiful or desirable. Sometimes a more tinted diamond can exhibit a warmth not shown by other diamonds and create a very beautiful ring with a unique appeal.

❖ To What Extent Does the Color Grade Affect Value?

To an untrained eye, discerning the difference in color from D down to H in a mounted stone, without direct comparison, is almost impossible. Nevertheless, the difference in color greatly affects the value of the diamond. A one-carat, flawless, excellently proportioned, D-color diamond might retail for $30,000, while the same stone with H-color might sell for only \$12,000 and the same stone with K-color might sell for only \$7,500. And, of course, if the stone were not flawless, it could sell for much less (see next chapter). This sounds complicated, but color differences and their effect on price will become clear to you the moment you begin looking at stones. It is important to understand your options and to be watchful when you go to purchase a stone.

In diamonds over one carat, the whiter the stone, the more critical it becomes to know the exact color grade because of its effect on value. On the other hand, as long as you know for sure what color the stone is and are paying the right price, choosing one that is a grade or two lower than another will reduce the cost per carat but there will be little, if any, visible difference when the stone is mounted. Therefore, for the difference in cost, you might be able to get a larger diamond, or one with better cutting or a better clarity grade, depending on what is most important to you.

Diamond Color Grades

COLORLESS	D E F	Loose diamonds appear colorless.
NEAR COLORLESS	G H I J	When mounted in a setting, these diamonds may apppear colorless to the untrained eye.
FAINT YELLOWISH* TINT	K L M	Smaller diamonds look colorless when mounted. Diamonds of 1/2 carat or more show traces of color.
VERY LIGHT YELLOWISH* TINT	N O P Q R	
TINTED LIGHT YELLOWISH*	S T U V W X Y Z	These diamonds show increasingly yellow tints to even the untrained eye, and appear *very "off-white."*

*Usually yellow, but can be brown or gray

Commonly Used Color Grading Systems

The GIA and American Gem Society (AGS) grading systems are the most commonly used in the United States. The GIA system is the most widely used in the world. Scandinavian diamond nomenclature (Scan D.N.) is often used in Scandinavian countries, as well as a system developed by CIBJO (the International Confederation of Jewelry, Silverware, Diamonds, Pearls, and Stones.) Participating member nations include most European nations, Japan, and the United States. Another system, HRD, is applied by the Belgian Diamond High Council.

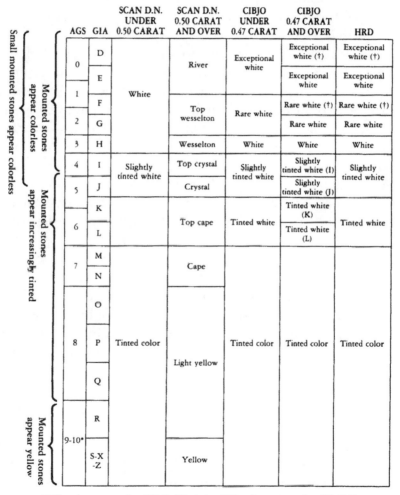

Left-margin brackets (top to bottom): Small mounted stones appear colorless · Mounted stones appear colorless · Mounted stones appear increasingly tinted · Mounted stones appear yellow

AGS	GIA	SCAN D.N. UNDER 0.50 CARAT	SCAN D.N. 0.50 CARAT AND OVER	CIBJO UNDER 0.47 CARAT	CIBJO 0.47 CARAT AND OVER	HRD
0	D	White	River	Exceptional white	Exceptional white (†)	Exceptional white (†)
0	E				Exceptional white	Exceptional white
1	F		Top wesselton	Rare white	Rare white (†)	Rare white (†)
2	G				Rare white	Rare white
3	H		Wesselton	White	White	White
4	I	Slightly tinted white	Top crystal	Slightly tinted white	Slightly tinted white (I)	Slightly tinted white
5	J		Crystal		Slightly tinted white (J)	
6	K	Tinted color	Top cape	Tinted white	Tinted white (K)	Tinted white
6	L				Tinted white (L)	
7	M		Cape			
7	N					
	O					
8	P		Light yellow	Tinted color	Tinted color	Tinted color
	Q					
9-10*	R					
	S-X -Z		Yellow			

*AGS grade 9 corresponds to GIA, R–U inclusive. AGS grade 10 corresponds to GIA, V–Z inclusive. † The use of the term *blue-white* is discouraged today since it is usually misleading.

❖ Natural Color or HPHT Processed

Color differences can be subtle, but the difference in cost can be extreme. It is important to know the precise color grade, but it is even more important to know whether the color is natural or the result of some type of treatment.

A new product entered the market in the 1990s, resulting from years of research. Briefly, the product was created by a new process involving the use of high-pressure/high-temperature annealing (often referred to as the *HPHT* process). With it, very tinted, off-white diamonds can be transformed into colorless and near-colorless stones, ranging from D through H in color. In addition to using this process to create colorless through near-colorless stones, the process can also be used to produce "fancy" colors, including yellow, yellowish green, pink, and blue. The innovators of this process believe that they have created a new diamond category that will provide new alternatives to consumers. The color of these stones, originally referred to as *GE-POL* diamonds, is permanent and irreversible.

It is also important to understand that it is not possible to transform all tinted diamonds into colorless or near-colorless diamonds with this new process. Only very rare diamond types respond to HPHT *whitening* techniques. Of all diamonds mined, reports estimate that less than 2 percent are in these rare categories.

The color-enhanced "colorless" diamonds produced by GE are now sold under the name Bellataire™ through exclusive arrangements with selected retailers. They are usually cut in fancy shapes (approximately 85 percent) and are available in colors ranging from D through H, with clarity grades VS_2 or better (see chapter 8). Each Bellataire diamond is laser inscribed on the girdle with the Bellataire logo and a registered number, but there have been cases where the laser inscription has been polished off.

In terms of cost, it is unclear how they will be priced. At this time, they are selling for 30 to 50 percent less than diamonds with comparable natural color. For many, these newcomers are a beautiful and exciting "high-tech" alternative. Ultimately, it will be consumer acceptance and demand that will determine their pricing.

In addition to Bellataire™ colorless and fancy yellow, blue, and pink diamonds, other companies are using HPHT annealing techniques to whiten diamonds and to produce a range of colors. Lucent Diamonds™ *Luminari* brand offers a wide range of yellow, deep yellow, orange-yellow, and yellow-green diamonds, and Nova™ Diamonds is offering yellowish green to greenish yellow, among other colors. Diamonds are even being transformed into mysterious *black* diamonds through HPHT methods, and who knows what alluring colors await us in the future. In fancy colors, these treated diamonds should sell for significantly less than natural-color fancy diamonds.

Major laboratories will grade HPHT diamonds and indicate the treatment on diamond reports (see chapter 11). However, caution needs to be taken. Once again, the availability of this new product in the marketplace provides yet another reason to obtain laboratory verification prior to the purchase of any important diamond. There have already been incidents of HPHT-treated diamonds having been sold without disclosure. More importantly, before becoming aware of the use of this technology on diamonds, gem-testing laboratories were not checking for it, nor did they have the data to understand how to detect it. Today most diamonds treated in this manner can be identified, but prior to the year 2000, HPHT-treated stones may have slipped through the world's labs undetected.

❖ What Is Fluorescence?

If the diamond you are considering is accompanied by a diamond grading report issued by the GIA or another respected lab, it will indicate whether or not the diamond has some degree of *fluorescence*. Fluorescence refers to whether or not a stone produces a color reaction when exposed to ultraviolet radiation—a color seen *only* when the stone is exposed to ultraviolet radiation. Whether or not a diamond flouresces, and the strength of its fluorescence (faint, weak, moderate, strong, very strong), are determined by viewing the diamond with a special lamp called an ultraviolet lamp, which emits only ultraviolet radiation. When we say a colorless diamond flouresces blue, we mean that its color will appear to be blue when we view it under the pure ultraviolet light produced by the ultraviolet lamp. The stone is really a colorless diamond and will appear colorless in normal light. Some diamonds fluoresce; others do not. A diamond can fluoresce any color, but most diamonds fluoresce blue, white, or yellow. The results of a recent study conducted by the GIA showed that consumers found the presence of blue fluorescence to be a benefit; participants in the study actually preferred diamonds that fluoresced blue to other diamonds because they seemed "whiter," despite the fact that you will not really notice fluorescence with the naked eye.

It is important to note whether or not a diamond fluoresces, and what color it fluoresces, because there are varying wavelengths of ultraviolet radiation all around us. Ultraviolet radiation is present in daylight (that's what causes sunburn) and wherever there are fluorescent light fixtures (those long tube lights you see in the ceilings of many stores and office buildings). This means that, depending upon the strength of a diamond's fluorescence and the intensity of the ultraviolet radiation in the light source, its color may not appear the same in all lights.

A diamond that fluoresces a strong blue, for example, might appear whiter in daylight, or in an office with fluorescent lights, because the ultraviolet radiation present will cause the diamond to emit some degree of blue, masking any faint yellow or brown tint that might be present. The same stone might appear less white when seen at home in incandescent light—any warm light, such as a household lightbulb—where you see the stone's true body color without the benefit of any fluorescence stimulated by ultraviolet radiation. A diamond that fluoresces "strong yellow" can look more yellow in some lights. But remember, whatever color is produced by fluorescence, it occurs *only* in daylight or fluorescent light.

To ensure that the true body color is being graded, a professional always tests a diamond for fluorescence with an ultraviolet lamp before color grading it. Blue fluorescence is more common than white or yellow. Some diamonds that fluoresce blue may actually look blue-white in the right light.

❖ Does Fluorescence Affect Value?

Generally, the absence or presence of fluorescence has little if any effect on value. However, if the stone has a strong yellow fluorescence it should sell for at least 10 to 15 percent less, since this will make the stone appear more yellow in some lights than another stone with the same color grade.

Blue fluorescence may be considered an added benefit—a little bonus—because it may make the stone appear whiter in some lights; and yet there may be no difference in cost or the stone may sell at a slight *discount* (although this may change after the results of the GIA study). You must be careful, however, to look closely at stones with *very strong* fluorescence—some will have an oily or murky appearance. If the stone appears murky or oily in daylight or fluorescent light, it should sell for at least 15 to 20 percent less than comparable stones without the murky cast.

If a diamond fluoresces, its true body color can be misgraded. This can be costly to the buyer, but the error can be easily avoided. Knowledgeable jewelers or appraisers will always test a diamond to see whether or not it fluoresces, and to what degree, in order to color grade it accurately.

❖ What Is a "Premier"?

At this point we should mention a type of flourescent diamond that is not encountered often, but which occurs frequently enough to warrant a brief discussion. It is called a *premier*. This does not mean the diamond is better than others. In fact, it should sell for much less than other white diamonds.

The true color of any premier diamond will be yellowish (referred to in the trade as *cape*), but the yellow color is masked by strong blue fluorescence. As with other diamonds that fluoresce blue, the premier will appear whiter than it really is in certain light. It may actually have a bluish tint, sometimes with a greenish cast. However, a premier will *always* have a murky or oily appearance in daylight or fluorescent light, resulting from the coupling of the yellow with the blue. The murkiness detracts from its beauty and causes a reduction in the value. The price of the premier varies depending on the degree of yellow present and the degree of murkiness.

Do not confuse a premier diamond with one that exhibits some normal blue fluorescence. Many diamonds exhibit some degree of fluorescence. Many have a very fine white body color to begin with. But most important, they differ from the premier because they will not appear oily or murky in daylight-type light.

❖ Some Plain Talk about "Fancy"-Color Diamonds

Let's spend a moment discussing fancy-color diamonds. While white diamonds are preferred by most as the choice for engagement rings, those who love color are increasingly turning to colored diamonds. Diamonds have been found to occur naturally in almost every color and shade—blue, red, green, yellow, lavender, pink, gunmetal gray, cognac brown, and black. The color can be intense or very pale.

Some colored diamonds are very rare and expensive, while others are more common than white diamonds and very affordable. The most common fancy colors are shades of brown, yellow, and orange. Some of these shades, in paler tones, are referred to as "champagne" colors and are more affordable than white diamonds. Except for the very pale yellow and brown shades—which are very common and not considered "fancy" but more properly as "off-white"—colored diamonds often sell for more than fine white diamonds. Among the most rare and costly are the reds and blues, pinks and lavenders, and intense, vivid yellows.

One must be aware, however, that it is possible with the use of sophisticated radiation technology to alter poor-quality brownish and yellowish diamonds to look like beautiful fancy-colored stones. These should sell for much less than their naturally occurring counterparts, so if you are considering a colored diamond, be sure that it is accompanied by a laboratory report confirming whether or not the color is natural, or have it examined by a professional gemologist who can perform the necessary tests. If you are considering a fancy-color diamond, see *Diamonds: The Antoinette Matlins Buying Guide* for in-depth information.

❖ Special Tips on the Subject of Color

Keep It Clean if You Want the Color to Look Its Best

A dirty diamond will not look white, nor will it sparkle. An accumulation of dirt, especially greasy dirt, will give a diamond a yellowish cast, so if you want to see and enjoy its full beauty, keep your diamond clean.

This principle applies especially when you are looking at old jewelry for possible purchase. When you are considering old diamond pieces, pay particular attention to whether or not it is impacted with dirt accumulated by years of use. If it is, there is a possibility that the diamond will have a better color grade than it may appear to have at first glance. This is because the dirt may contain varying amounts of fatty deposits (from dishwashing, cosmetics, etc.), which yellow with age. When this type of dirt builds up and is in contact with the diamond, it will also make the diamond appear more yellow.

White or Yellow Gold Setting?

The color of the metal in the ring setting can affect your perception of the color of the stone—sometimes adversely and sometimes beneficially. A very white diamond should be held in a white metal such as white gold, platinum, or palladium. If you prefer yellow gold, it's possible to have just the portion of the setting that holds the diamond itself fashioned in white metal. For example, a diamond ring can be made with a yellow gold shank to go around the finger and a white metal head to hold the diamond. An all-yellow setting may make a very white diamond appear less white because the yellow color of the setting itself is reflected into the diamond.

On the other hand, if the diamond you choose tends to be more yellow than you'd like, mounting it in yellow gold, with yellow surrounding the stone, may make the stone appear whiter in contrast to the strong yellow of the gold.

The yellow gold environment may mask the degree of yellow in a yellow diamond, or it may give a colorless diamond an undesirable yellow tint. The setting can also affect future color grading should you ever need an updated insurance appraisal.

CHAPTER 8

Clarification on Clarity

How Flaws Affect Diamonds

Flaw classification—also called the *clarity* grade—is one of the criteria used to determine the value of a diamond. As with all things in nature, however, there is really no such thing as "flawless." Even though some very rare diamonds are classified "flawless," the term is somewhat misleading and you must be sure you understand what it really means.

When we talk about this classification, we are referring to the presence of tiny, usually microscopic, imperfections. The word "flaw" suggests something bad, but this is not really the case; rather, the flaw grade simply provides part of the complete description of the stone. It is important to understand that as a diamond forms in nature, *every* diamond develops certain types of internal characteristics. They might be microscopic cracks shaped like feathers—some are quite lovely when viewed with the microscope—or microscopic diamond crystals, or even crystals of some other gemstone!

Every diamond contains distinctive internal characteristics. In the jewelry trade these internal characteristics are called *inclusions*, something *included* within the stone as it was forming in nature. Each diamond's internal picture—its internal character—is unique. No two are alike, so the clarity picture can be an important factor in identifying a specific diamond.

❖ To What Extent Does Clarity Affect the Beauty of a Diamond?

It is very important to understand that clarity may have little or no effect on the *beauty* of a diamond if it falls within the first eight grades discussed later in this chapter (FL–SI). Few people can discern any visible difference between stones until they reach the imperfect grades, and even then it is sometimes difficult to see anything in the stone without magnification.

Many people mistakenly believe that the clarity grade affects a diamond's brilliance and sparkle. This is not true; the clarity grade has little effect on a diamond's visible appearance except in the very lowest grades. Many people think that the better the "clarity," the more brilliant and sparkling the diamond. Perhaps it is the term itself, "clarity," that leads to the confusion (and the reason we don't like the term "*clarity* grade"). Whatever the case, as discussed in chapter 6, it is the precision of the *cutting* that determines how brilliant and sparkling a diamond will be.

To the buyer, the flaw or clarity grade is important because it indicates, on a relative basis, how "clean" the diamond is and this ranking has a significant effect on cost. The cleaner the stone, the rarer; the rarer the stone, the costlier. But diamonds don't have to be "flawless" to be beautiful and sparkling.

As you will see as you shop and compare, you can find very beautiful, sparkling diamonds in a wide range of clarity grades. Juggling the clarity grade can give you tremendous flexibility in getting a whiter or larger diamond for your money. Just keep in mind that you won't *see* differences with the eye alone, so you must take care to know for sure what the specific clarity grade is.

❖ How Is the Clarity Grade Determined?

Diamonds used in jewelry are usually very clean, and little, if anything, can be seen without magnification. This is starting to change as an increasing number of diamonds with visible cracks or other inclusions enter the market—stones in the I_1–I_3 range and below—but for the most part, differences in clarity cannot normally be seen simply by looking at the stone with the naked eye. The clarity grade is based on what can be seen *when the diamond is examined using 10-power (10x) magnification* under a loupe. The "flawless" grade is given to a stone in which no imperfections can be seen internally or externally when it is examined with 10-power, although at higher power inclusions will be visible, even in a flawless diamond. For clarity grading purposes, if an inclusion can't be seen at 10x, it doesn't exist.

Clarity grading requires extensive training and practice, and proper grading can only be done by an experienced jeweler, dealer, or gemologist. The grade is based on the number of inclusions and their color, size, and placement. If you want to examine a diamond with the loupe, remember that only in the *lowest* grades will an inexperienced person be able to see inclusions or blemishes easily, and even with the loupe it will be difficult to see what a professional will see easily; few amateurs will see anything at all in the highest clarity grades.

Today, a jeweler might use a microscope with a video monitor to help you see what is inside a diamond you are considering. Be sure that the jeweler focuses at different depths into the stone and that the microscope is set at 10-power. And remember, don't panic; what you are seeing is magnified ten times!

We recommend that you first examine the stone carefully with your eyes alone, then with a simple loupe, saving the microscope, when offered, for last. Examining a diamond in this way will help you become familiar with the particular characteristics of the stone you purchase, and may give you information that will enable you to always recognize your diamond should it be necessary at some future time (after having it mounted in the ring, for example).

❖ Types of Internal and External Characteristics

Basically, clarity grading systems grade the stone according to the presence or absence of internal and external characteristics, generally referred to as "flaws." They are called *inclusions* when internal, *blemishes* when external. Flaws can be white, black, colorless, or even red or green in rare instances.

We will discuss some of these flaws here, so that you have a working vocabulary of diamond imperfections.

Internal Flaws or Inclusions

Pinpoint. This is a small, usually whitish dot (although it can be dark) that is difficult to see. There can be a number of pinpoints (a cluster) or a "cloud" of pinpoints (often hazy in appearance and difficult to see).

Dark spot. This may be a small crystal inclusion or a thin, flat inclusion that reflects light like a mirror. It may also appear as a silvery, metallic reflector.

Colorless crystal. This is often a small crystal of diamond, although it may be another mineral. Sometimes it appears very small, sometimes large enough to substantially lower the flaw grade to SI, or even I. A small group of colorless crystals lowers the grade from a possible VS to I₃.

Cleavage. A cleavage is a particular type of crack that has a flat plane, which, if struck, could cause the diamond to split, or cleave, as though it had been sliced cleanly with a saw. A large cleavage in the upper part of the diamond can be a serious flaw.

Feather. This is another name for a crack. A small feather is not dangerous if it does not break through the surface of the stone on the top portion where you might accidentally strike it. (In colored gemstones, thermoshock or ultrasonic cleaners can worsen a crack or make it larger.)

Bearded girdle or girdle fringes. These are usually the result of hastiness on the part of the cutter while rounding out the diamond. The girdle portion becomes overheated and develops small radial hair-like cracks that resemble small whiskers going into the diamond from the girdle edge. Sometimes the bearding amounts to minimal "peach fuzz" and can be removed with slight repolishing. Sometimes the bearding must be removed by faceting the girdle. If the bearding is very minimal, a diamond can still be graded IF.

Growth or grain lines. These can be seen only when examining the diamond while slowly rotating it. They appear and disappear, usually instantaneously. They will appear in a group of two, three, or four pale brown lines. If they cannot be seen from the crown side of the diamond and are small, they will not affect the grade adversely.

Knaat or twin lines. These are sometimes classified as external flaws because they appear as very small ridges, often with some type of geometrical outline; or as a small, slightly raised dot with a tail resembling a comet. They're difficult to see.

Laser line. Laser techniques are used today to make black flaws less visible, and thus improve the stone aesthetically. Using laser technology, it is possible to "vaporize" black inclusions so they practically disappear. With the loupe, however, an experienced jeweler or gemologist can see the "path" cut into the diamond by the laser beam. This path looks like a fine, straight, white thread starting at the surface of the stone and penetrating into it. See the section on "Clarity Enhancement" later in this chapter.

External Flaws or Blemishes

A natural. A natural is a remnant of the original skin of the diamond, and is often left on the girdle by the cutter in order to get the largest possible diameter from the rough. They are usually seen on the girdle and appear to be a rough, unpolished area. A natural may look like a scratch line or small triangle (called a trigon). If it is no wider than the normal width of the girdle or does not disrupt the circumference of the stone, it may not be considered a blemish. Often naturals are polished and become an extra facet, especially if they occur below the girdle edge.

Nick. This is a small chip, usually on the girdle, and can be caused by an accidental knock or blow in the course of wearing the diamond (especially if the girdle is on the thin side). Sometimes a nick or chip can be seen on the edge where the facets meet. If small, the bruised corner can be polished, creating an extra facet. This usually occurs on the crown.

Girdle roughness. This blemish appears as crisscrossed lines, brighter and duller finishing, and minute chipping. This can be remedied by faceting or repolishing.

Pits or cavities. Pits or holes on the facet. When on the table facet, especially if they are deep, the presence of pits or cavities will quickly lower the grade of the stone. Removing a pit may involve recutting the whole top of the stone and can also shrink the stone's diameter.

Scratch. A scratch is usually a minor defect that can be removed with simple repolishing. Remember, however, that in order to repolish the stone, you must remove it from its setting, and then reset it after it has been polished.

Polishing lines. Many diamonds exhibit polishing lines. If they appear on the pavilion side and are not too obvious, they do not lower the value. In some small diamonds these scratch lines can be obvious and are usually the result of a badly maintained polishing wheel.

Abraded or rough culet. The culet has been chipped or poorly finished. This is usually a minor flaw.

❖ Commonly Used Clarity Grading Systems

There are several recognized clarity grading systems in use worldwide, but the system used most widely in the United States and an increasing number of other countries was developed by the Gemological Institute of America (GIA). The terms clarity grade and flaw grade may be used interchangeably, but today the term "clarity" is more commonly used.

The most widely recognized clarity grading scales were introduced by:

1. **CIBJO** (International Confederation of Jewelry, Silverware, Diamonds, Pearls, and Stones). Participating member nations who use this system include Austria, Belgium, Canada, Denmark, Finland, France, Great Britain, Italy, Japan, Netherlands, Norway, Spain, Sweden, Switzerland, United States, and West Germany
2. **Scan D.N.** (Scandinavian Diamond Nomenclature)
3. **GIA** (Gemological Institute of America)
4. **AGS** (American Gem Society)
5. **HRD** (Hoge Raad voor Diamant, the Diamond High Council of Belgium)

The chart on the following page shows the relationship between the GIA system and others used internationally.

❖ How Does the Clarity Grade Affect Diamond Value?

We will use the GIA system to explain clarity and its effect on value because it is the most widely used in the United States. As you can see from the comparison chart, other systems now use similar classifications; should you have a diamond with a report from one of these, you can use this chart to find the corresponding GIA grade.

On the GIA scale, FL is the grade given to a stone that has no visible flaws, internal or external, when examined under 10x magnification. Only a highly qualified person will be able to determine this grade. If you are using a loupe as you examine diamonds, remember that it is very difficult for the inexperienced viewer to see flaws that may

Commonly Used Clarity (Flaw) Grading Systems

CIBJO UNDER 0.47 CARAT	CIBJO 0.47 CARAT AND OVER	HRD	SCAN D.N.	GIA	AGS
Loupe clean	Loupe clean	Loupe clean	FL	FL	0
			IF (Internally Flawless)	IF	1
VVS	VVS_1	VVS_1	VVS_1	VVS_1	
	VVS_2	VVS_2	VVS_2	VVS_2	2
VS	VS_1	VS_1	VS_1	VS_1	3
	VS_2	VS_2	VS_2	VS_2	4
SI	SI_1	SI	SI_1	SI_1	5
	SI_2		SI_2	SI_2	6
Piqué I	Piqué I	P_1	1st Piqué	I_1 (Imperfect)	7
					8
Piqué II	Piqué II	P_2	2nd Piqué	I_2	9
Piqué III	Piqué III	P_3	3rd Piqué	I_3	10

VV = Very, Very
V = Very
S = Slight or Small
I = Inclusion or Included or Imperfect (Imperfection)

For example, VVS may be translated to mean: Very, Very Slightly (Included); Very, Very Small (Inclusion); or Very, Very Slightly (Imperfect). Some jewelers prefer to classify the stone as "very, very small inclusion" rather than "very, very slightly imperfect," because the former description may sound more acceptable to the customer. There is, in fact, no difference.

No difference can be seen between these two diamonds with the unaided eye, but accurate grading is important because it can dramatically affect price.

FLAWLESS   SI$_2$

be readily observable to the experienced jeweler, dealer, or gemologist and you will not have the experience to determine whether or not a diamond is flawless. Often the novice is unable to see any flaws, even in SI grades, even with use of the loupe. A flawless, colorless, correctly proportioned stone, particularly in a one-carat size or larger, is *extremely* rare and is priced proportionately much higher than any other grade. Some jewelers insist there is no such thing available today.

IF is the grade given to a stone with no internal flaws and with only minor external blemishes that could be removed with polishing, such as nicks, small pits not on the table, and/or girdle roughness. These stones, in colorless, well-proportioned makes, are also rare and priced proportionately much higher than other grades.

VVS$_1$ and *VVS$_2$* are grades given to stones with internal flaws that are *very, very* difficult for a qualified observer to see. These are also difficult grades to obtain and are priced at a premium.

VS$_1$ and *VS$_2$* are grades given to stones with very small inclusions, difficult for a qualified observer to see. These stones are more readily available in good color and cut, and their flaws will not be visible except under magnification. These are excellent stones to purchase.

SI$_1$ and *SI$_2$* grades are given to stones with flaws that a qualified observer will see fairly easily under 10x magnification. They are not as rare as the higher grades and so they are less costly; in these grades, flaws may sometimes be visible without magnification when examined from the back side or laterally. These grades are still highly desirable and, since they cannot normally be seen with the naked eye when mounted, may enable one to select a stone with a higher color, or in a larger size, when working with a limited budget.

Imperfect grades are given to stones in which the flaws may be seen by a qualified observer without magnification; they are readily available and are much less expensive. They are graded I_1, I_2, and I_3.

(These grades are also called "1st piqué" [pee-kay], "2nd piqué," and "3rd piqué" in some classifications.) Stones graded "I" may still be desirable if they have good color and are well cut, and so should not be eliminated by a prospective purchaser who desires lovely diamond jewelry. As a general rule, however, imperfect grades are less desirable for engagement rings unless they are from heirloom pieces or have other characteristics that give them character and allure. They are also difficult to resell and do not appreciate in value as rapidly as better grades.

❖ How Does the Position of a Flaw Affect Diamond Grading and Value?

As a general rule, the position of any given inclusion will downgrade and devalue a diamond progressively as indicated below.

- *If seen* only from *the pavilion side,* or clearly only from the pavilion side, it has the least adverse effect, since it is the least visible from the top.
- *If positioned near the girdle,* while perhaps more visible than described above, it is still difficult to see, and hardly noticeable from the top. This flaw can be easily covered with the prong of a setting.
- *Under a crown facet* (other than a star facet), except when near the girdle, a flaw is more easily visible.
- *Under a star facet,* a flaw will be much more easily noticed.
- *Under the table* is the least desirable position since it places the flaw where it is most noticeable and may have the greatest effect on visibility (depending on size, color, etc.).

Sometimes a small black or white flaw may be in such a position that it is reflected within the stone. This can occur as a reflection to the opposite side of the stone, or, it may reflect itself as many as eight times around the

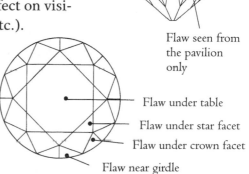

Flaw seen from the pavilion only

Flaw under table

Flaw under star facet

Flaw under crown facet

Flaw near girdle

bottom or near the culet of the stone. A diamond with such a flaw will have a lower flaw grade because of the eight-fold reflection resulting from its unfortunate position.

❖ A Word about Clarity Enhancement

Today technological advances have made it possible to improve diamond clarity. Several clarity enhancement techniques are available, some more or less permanent, and others definitely not permanent. Unfortunately, clarity enhancement frequently is not disclosed, either to jewelers themselves or by jewelers to their customers. It is important to buy diamonds from knowledgeable, reputable jewelers who check for such treatments. In addition, prior to buying any diamond you must *ask* whether or not the stone has been clarity-enhanced. If the stone has been enhanced, ask what method was used, and be sure this is stated on the bill of sale. In addition, be sure to ask about special care requirements that might be necessitated by the process.

The two most widely used methods of clarity enhancement are lasering and fracture filling.

Lasering. As we mentioned earlier, laser treatment is used today to make flaws less visible and thus improve the stone aesthetically. Using laser technology, it is possible to "vaporize" black inclusions so they practically disappear. With the loupe, however, an experienced jeweler or gemologist can see the "path" cut into the diamond by the laser beam. This path looks like a fine, white thread starting at the surface of the stone and traveling into it. The effects of the laser treatment are permanent. If a lasered diamond is accompanied by a GIA diamond grading report, the report will state that the stone is lasered.

A lasered stone should cost less than another with the "same" clarity, so it may be an attractive choice for your ring—as long as you *know* it's lasered and pay a fair price for it. But you must be sure to ask whether or not the stone has been lasered because some countries don't require disclosure, and jewelers in the United States are no longer required to disclose lasering. Jewelry industry organizations are trying to get the Federal Trade Commission to reverse this ruling, but in the meantime, you must ask explicitly. If a diamond is not lasered, a statement indicating "not lasered" should be included on the bill of sale; if it turns out that the stone *is* lasered, the written statement serves as proof of misrepresentation and will provide you with recourse.

Fracture filling. Fractures—cracks or breaks—that would normally be visible to the naked eye and detract from the beauty of a diamond can often be filled with a nearly colorless, glass-like substance. After filling, these breaks virtually disappear and will no longer be seen, except under magnification. Filling is not a permanent treatment, and special precautions are required when cleaning and repairing jewelry containing a filler. With proper care, such stones may remain beautiful for many years. Careless handling, however, can cause the filler to evaporate or change color, resulting in a much less attractive diamond. Some filling materials are much more stable than others, but at present it is usually not possible to know what filler has been used in a particular stone. Should the filler be accidentally removed, your jeweler can have the treatment repeated to restore the stone's original appearance. GIA will *not* issue a grading report on a filled diamond.

Filled diamonds cost much less—about 50 percent less—than other diamonds. They can be a very affordable alternative as long as you know what you are buying, understand the limitations, and pay the right price. Be sure to ask explicitly if the stone has been fracture-filled, and get a statement as to whether or not it has been on the bill of sale.

If you are considering a filled diamond for your engagement ring, however, be sure your fiancée knows; you won't want her to receive an unpleasant surprise should she take the diamond to a jeweler to have it appraised or re-sized!

❖ An Important Closing Word about Flaws

Remember, a diamond does not have to be flawless to be a very fine stone and of high value. Personally, we prefer a stone that is slightly imperfect (SI), but has fine color and brilliance, over a flawless stone with less sparkle and a less fine color. We consider *color* and *brilliance* the most important factors in terms of a stone's beauty and desirability. And remember: Even a diamond graded I_1 is still 97 percent clean!

CHAPTER 9

Carat Weight

❖ What Is a Carat?

Diamonds are sold by the carat (ct), not to be confused with *karat* (kt), which in the United States refers to gold purity. Since 1913, most countries have agreed that a carat weighs 200 milligrams, or 1/5 gram.

Before 1913, the carat weight varied depending on the country of origin—usually weighing *more* than the modern carat. The Indian carat didn't weigh the same as the English carat; the French carat was different from the Indian and the English. This is important if you have, or are thinking of buying, a very old piece that still has the original bill of sale indicating carat weight. Since the old carat usually weighed *more* than the post-1913 *metric carat,* an old three-carat stone will often weigh more than three carats by modern standards. Today the term *carat* means the metric carat, the 200-milligram carat with five carats weighing one gram.

What are points? Jewelers often refer to the carat weight of diamonds in terms of *points.* This is particularly true of stones under one carat. There are 100 points to a carat, so if a jeweler says that a stone weighs 75 points, he means it weighs 75/100 of a carat, or 3/4 carat. A 25-point stone is 1/4 carat. A 10-point stone is 1/10 carat.

The carat is a unit of weight, not size. We wish to stress this point, since most people think that a one-carat stone is a particular size. Most people, therefore, would expect a one-carat diamond and a one-carat emerald, for example, to look the same size or to have the same apparent dimensions. This is not the case.

Comparing a one-carat diamond with a one-carat emerald and a one-carat ruby easily illustrates this point. First, emerald weighs less than diamond, and ruby weighs more than diamond. This means that a one-carat emerald will look larger than a one-carat diamond, while the ruby will look smaller than a diamond of the same weight. Emerald, with a mineral composition that is lighter, will yield greater mass per carat; ruby, with its heavier composition, will yield less mass per carat.

Let's look at the principle another way. If you compare a one-inch cube of pine wood, a one-inch cube of aluminum, and a one-inch cube of iron, you would easily choose the cube of iron as heaviest, even though it has the same *volume* as the other materials. The iron is like the ruby, while the wood is like the emerald and the aluminum like the diamond. Equal *volumes* of different materials can have very different weights, depending on their density, also called mass or specific gravity.

Equal volumes of materials with the same density, however, should have approximately the same weight, so that in diamond, the carat weight has come to represent particular sizes. These sizes, as we've discussed, are based on diamonds cut to ideal proportions. Consequently, if properly cut, diamonds of the weights given in the charts on pages 77 and 78 should be approximately the sizes illustrated. Remember, however, *that these sizes will not apply to other gems.*

❖ How Does Carat Weight Affect Value in Diamonds?

Diamond prices are usually quoted *per carat*. Diamonds of the finest and rarest quality are sold for the highest price per carat, and diamonds of progressively less rare quality are sold for a progressively lower price per carat. For example, a rare-quality diamond might sell for $20,000 per carat. So, a stone in this quality weighing 1.12 carats would cost $22,400. On the other hand, a stone of exactly the same weight, in a less rare quality, might sell for only $10,000 per carat, or $11,200.

Also, as a rule, the price increases per carat as we go from smaller to larger stones, since the larger stones are more rare. For example, stones of the same quality weighing 1/2 carat will sell for more per carat than stones weighing 1/3 carat; stones weighing 3/4 carat will sell for more per carat than stones of the same quality weighing 1/2 carat. For example, the per carat price of a particular quality 1/2 carat stone might be $5,000, while the per-carat price for a 1/3-carat stone of the same quality would be $3,000. The stones would cost $2,500 (1/2 x $5,000) and $1,000 (1/3 x $3,000) respectively.

Sizes and Weights of Various Diamond Cuts

Weight (ct)	Emerald	Marquise	Pear	Brilliant
5				
4				
3				
2½				
2				
1½				
1¼				
1				
¾				
½				

Diameters and Corresponding Weights of Round Brilliant-Cut Diamonds

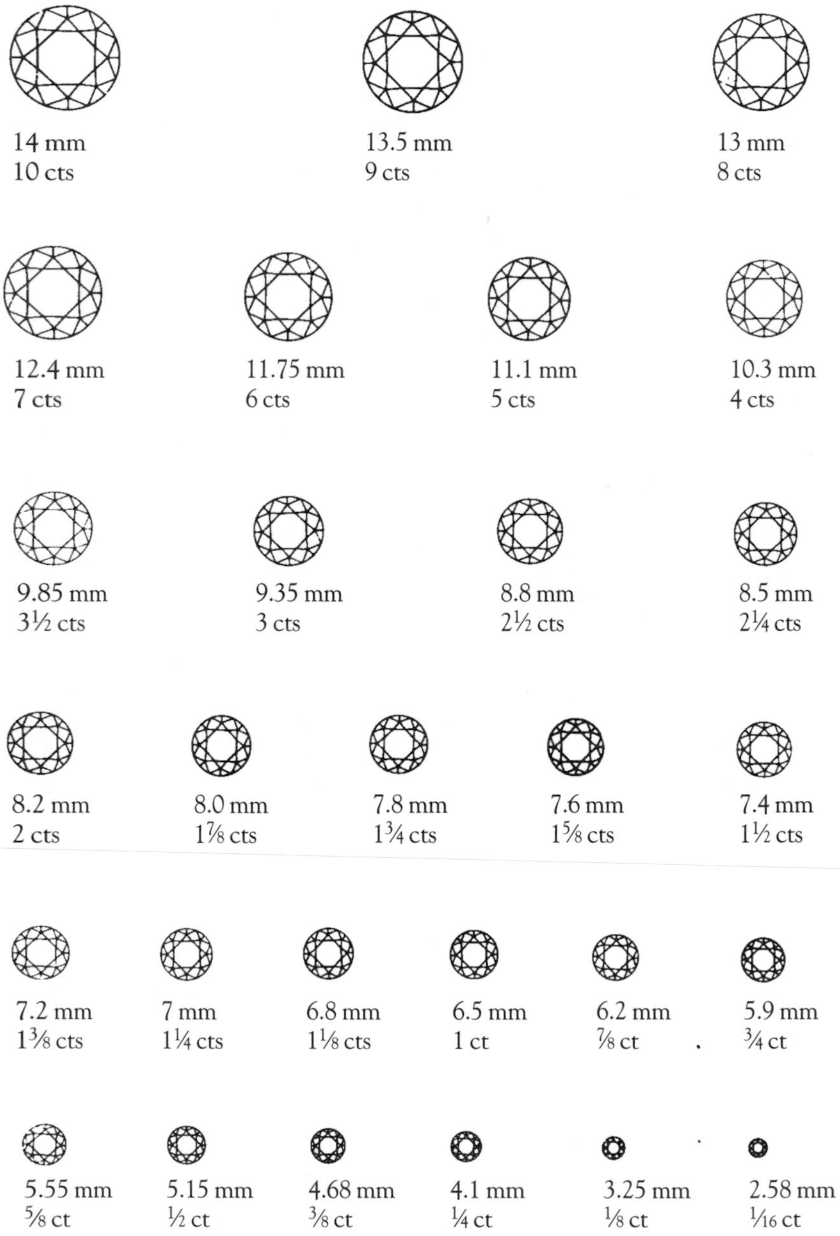

14 mm
10 cts

13.5 mm
9 cts

13 mm
8 cts

12.4 mm
7 cts

11.75 mm
6 cts

11.1 mm
5 cts

10.3 mm
4 cts

9.85 mm
3½ cts

9.35 mm
3 cts

8.8 mm
2½ cts

8.5 mm
2¼ cts

8.2 mm
2 cts

8.0 mm
1⅞ cts

7.8 mm
1¾ cts

7.6 mm
1⅝ cts

7.4 mm
1½ cts

7.2 mm
1⅜ cts

7 mm
1¼ cts

6.8 mm
1⅛ cts

6.5 mm
1 ct

6.2 mm
⅞ ct

5.9 mm
¾ ct

5.55 mm
⅝ ct

5.15 mm
½ ct

4.68 mm
⅜ ct

4.1 mm
¼ ct

3.25 mm
⅛ ct

2.58 mm
1/16 ct

Furthermore, stones of the same quality weighing exactly one carat will sell for *much* more than stones weighing 90 to 96 points. Thus, if you want a one-carat stone of a particular quality, but you can't afford it, you may find you can afford it in a 95-point stone—and a 95-point stone will give the impression of a full one-carat stone when set. You might be able to get your heart's desire after all.

As you will see, the price of a diamond does not increase proportionately; there are disproportionate jumps. And the larger and finer the stone (all else being equal in terms of overall quality), the more disproportionate the increase in cost per carat may be. A top-quality two-carat stone will not cost twice as much as a one-carat stone; it could easily be *three* times as much. A top-quality five-carat stone would not be five times the cost of a one-carat stone; it could easily be as much as ten times what a one-carat stone might cost.

Diamonds are generally weighed before they are set, so the jeweler can give you the exact carat weight, since you are paying a certain price per carat. Remember, also, that the price per carat for a fine stone weighing 96 points is much less than for one weighing one carat or more. So it is unwise to accept any "approximate" weight, even though the difference seems so slight.

As you can see here, it is also important when buying a diamond to realize that since carat refers to weight, the manner in which a stone is cut can affect its apparent size. A one-carat stone that is cut shallow will appear larger in diameter than a stone that is cut thick (heavy). Conversely, a thick stone will appear smaller in diameter.

Furthermore, if the diamond has a thick girdle, the stone will appear smaller in diameter. If this girdle is faceted, it tends to hide the ugly, frosted look of a thick girdle, but the fact remains that the girdle is thick, and the stone suffers because it will appear smaller in diameter than one would expect at a given carat weight. These stones are therefore somewhat cheaper per carat.

❖ What Does *Spread* Mean?

The term *spread* is often used in response to the question "How large is this diamond?" But it can be misleading. Spread refers to the size the stone *appears* to be, based on its diameter. For example, if the diameter of the stone measures the same as what you see in the diamond sizes charts (see pages 77 and 78), which represent the diameter of a perfectly proportioned stone, the jeweler might say it "spreads" one carat. But this does not mean it *weighs* one carat. It means it *looks* the same size as a perfectly cut one-carat stone, but it is cut thinner to look larger than its true weight.

CHAPTER 10

Tips on Getting the Diamond You Really Want, within Your Budget

If you have an unlimited budget, you may feel it's important to have a large stone of the finest quality available—a "D" Flawless with an ideal make. But for most of us who must work within a limited budget, selecting the correct stone and the correct ring is a matter of learning how to juggle, and discovering what factors will best meet our needs, emotional as well as financial.

In diamonds, go for color and sparkle first. If you have a limited budget, you have to compromise on something—either the size, color, clarity grade (flaw grade), or liveliness. Of these four factors, one can see size, color, and liveliness. In terms of what most people notice on the finger, the clarity grade is the *least* important in our opinion. Personally, on a limited budget we would choose a stone with the best possible color and the liveliest personality.

What most people don't understand is that even in SI$_2$ stones, flaws are not really noticeable when the stone is being worn and, in most cases, can't be seen at all without using a magnifier. In fact, if you take a well-cut one-carat D/Flawless diamond and hold it next to a well-cut one-carat D/SI$_2$ diamond, you will not see any difference with the naked eye. Contrary to what many think, it is not the clarity grade that determines how lively and brilliant a diamond will be, but its cut and proportioning. And you may feel much more sparkling yourself if you can spend $8,000 for a diamond (D/SI$_2$)

that could look like a $30,000 (D/IF) diamond to anyone without a magnifier!

The stone's brilliance and liveliness is as important as its color. After all, that's what sets the gem apart from glass and cheap imitations. A well-cut diamond has more sparkle—more brilliance and "fire"—than any other gem. But the key to the sparkle is in its being well cut. We have seen diamonds that were so badly cut that they had no life at all. In fact, one might just as well be looking at a piece of glass.

For this reason, we prefer stones with very fine makes (see chapter 6). Stones that are cut to look a little larger than they actually are can also be pretty, but when they are cut *too spread*, they will be lifeless. In our opinion, we'd rather buy a stone that's cut exceptionally well—a stone that really dances before the eye—even though it costs more. Because it does cost more, we would consider lowering the color grade a little in exchange for the best possible "make," or coming down in size a little. As you shop around, be sure to pay attention to the way a stone is cut. Ask to see stones with "ideal" makes. You'll soon be able to spot differences in brilliance and liveliness. Then your eye will help you find the right balance for your own budget.

A small difference in points can make a big difference in dollars. The cost of a diamond increases significantly when it reaches the full, 1-carat weight. However, try to find a diamond that weighs 90 points (there are 100 points to a carat, so a 90-pointer is 9/10 of a carat). When set, few can see the difference between a 90-point diamond and one that is a full 1-carat stone. The difference, however, is very noticeable in dollars. Where a fine 1-carat diamond (G/VS$_1$ quality) might sell for $9,000, the same quality stone weighing 90 points might cost only $7,500. The money you save could pay for a beautiful diamond-studded wedding band!

If you are considering a diamond in the 2-carat range, the difference is even greater. While a full 2-carat diamond in the quality described above might cost $30,000, a diamond weighing 1.90 carats might cost only $24,000—saving you $6,000.

One word of caution: Be careful that you aren't sold a stone that is too "spread" (a term used to describe a stone that is cut to look larger than its real weight). We've seen stones weighing 90 points that are actually LARGER in dimension than a full 1-carat stone that is cut well; we've seen stones weighing 1.90 carats that are actually larger in dimension than a well-cut 2-carat stone. These stones usually lack the brilliance and sparkle of a well-made stone. You may be pleased with their size, but make sure you are pleased with the sparkle. After all, if you're paying for a diamond, you deserve a stone that shows its full beauty.

What to consider when selecting the color grade. D-color is the rarest and most expensive color in white diamonds. There are very few diamonds that receive this very high grade. Diamonds graded from D through H on the GIA scale are graded in the "white" range by other grading systems and, when mounted, will appear white. I and J colors are called "slightly tinted" by other systems and you may see some yellowish or brownish tint in the stone's body color. K and L may also be called "tinted white," and you can more easily see the tint. M through Z may also be called "tinted color" or "off-white" and appear yellowish or brownish white.

The difference in cost between D- and E-color, however—even though both are considered "white" diamonds—can be significant. In a 1-carat diamond, the cost of a D/Flawless could be $30,000, while the same stone if it were E-color might only be $20,000; a 1-carat stone D/VS$_1$ might retail for $14,000, while the same stone in E-color might cost only $11,000.

It is important to remember that when a diamond is set, it is extremely difficult to tell the difference between colors D, E, and F without comparing them immediately next to each other. For those on a budget, selecting a diamond with colors E, F, or G rather than D might enable you to best meet all your expectations—a "white" diamond with lots of sparkle in a pleasing size.

The color of your setting can make your diamond appear whiter. If you are on a limited budget, keep in mind that if you feel you can't afford a diamond as white as you would like and still have the size and sparkle that's important, setting the stone in white gold or platinum may make the stone appear whiter than it really is. Less white diamonds (through colors L and M) can actually look whiter in a white gold or platinum setting—the whiteness of the metal is reflected into the diamond and masks the yellow, making the stone appear whiter. Yellowish tinted diamonds (M–Z) usually look whiter in a yellow gold setting, where the contrast with the bright yellow of the setting masks the yellowish tint of the diamond and often makes it appear whiter.

Flaws may mar the beauty of your diamond ring less than you think. On a budget, they may add beauty! As we discussed in chapter 8 on flaw grading, flaws cannot normally be seen in a mounted diamond with the naked eye until the classification I_1! And even in stones classified as "I," flaws are normally not immediately visible when the stone is set, especially when being worn. So, while it's important to know what the flaw grade is to be sure you are paying the correct price, this is the factor you can stretch the farthest without affecting the beauty of the stone you select. It's one area in which juggling can dramatically affect the budget while not affecting the sparkle. Therefore, we normally recommend trying to meet your personal preferences regarding the other three factors first. The price difference between Flawless and Internally Flawless, and each successive grade, can be dramatic. As we mentioned earlier, a 1-carat D/IF might well cost $30,000 and a 1-carat D/SI$_2$ only $8,000. Looking at the stones without using a loupe, the D/SI$_2$ would look like the D/IF!

Consider shapes other than round. While the round brilliant-cut diamond is considered by most to be the cut that best reveals the diamond's maximum beauty, it normally looks smaller than diamonds cut in other shapes. Today women are showing an increased interest in other shapes. In comparison to the round, pear-shaped diamonds and marquise-shaped diamonds look larger.

Consider a design that uses several small stones rather than one large diamond. As we discussed in greater depth in the preceding chapter, many beautiful designs use several small diamonds rather than one large diamond. These designs offer a beautiful way to keep the budget down. The smaller the diamond, the lower the price-per-carat. For example, a 1-carat round brilliant-cut diamond set in a solitaire ring might cost $5,000, while a ring containing three stones having a total weight of one carat (each stone weighing 1/3 carat) might sell for only $2,500; or a diamond band containing seven diamonds with a total weight of one carat (with each stone weighing only 1/7 carat) might cost only $1,500. As you can see, the solitaire, while it is the most popular style among brides-to-be, is also the most expensive.

Look around at the innovative designs available in multi-stone rings. These offer an alternative that can create a very important and individual look.

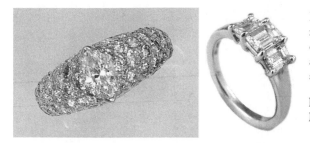

Left: An illusion setting. A half-carat marquise-shaped diamond center stone, cradled in a diamond pavé dome, appears larger than it would in a classic solitaire design and costs less too.

Right: A classic three-stone ring costs less than a large, single-stone ring.

Illusion settings. Certain settings create an *illusion* that the diamond is larger than it is (see chapter 22).

Bold designs in gold and platinum add importance and distinctiveness to smaller diamonds. New designs reflecting today's more independent woman have had a major impact on the engagement ring and wedding band market. Using wider, innovative designs in metal can create a very impressive look, using a smaller diamond (under one carat) as well as larger stones.

Listen to your heart as well as your head. The most important consideration in the selection of your ring is how you feel about it. You want to feel a thrill; you want to feel excited; you want it to be your choice. If you really prefer yellow gold, don't let someone talk you into platinum; if you really prefer the pear shape, don't let someone talk you into round.

One of our clients was torn between two diamonds—one had the finest possible color (D) and she knew it was the "better" stone. The other was a little larger and it wasn't quite as white (F-color), but it had a magnificent make and the sparkle was really dazzling. She decided on the slightly larger stone, even though it was F-color, because she was honest with herself and her fiancé—she really preferred a stone that was a little larger, and she was constantly drawn back to that stone because of its "personality." The other diamond was a "rarer" stone, colorwise, which made it more expensive on a per-carat basis, but it wasn't the one she really felt excited about. She made the right choice in going with her heart and not her head!

CHAPTER 11

How to Read a Diamond Grading Report

Today, few fine diamonds over one carat are sold without a diamond grading report (or certificate, as they are also called) from a respected laboratory. Reports issued by the GIA/Gem Trade Laboratory are the most widely used in the United States and in many countries around the world, but reports from other laboratories (see the appendix) are also highly respected.

A grading report does more than certify the stone's genuineness; it fully describes the stone and evaluates each of the critical factors affecting quality, beauty, and value. Grading reports can be very useful for a variety of reasons. The information they contain can provide verification of the "facts" as represented by the seller and enable one to make a safer decision when purchasing a diamond. Another important function of reports is to verify the identity of a specific diamond at some future time—if, for example, it has been out of one's possession for any reason. For insurance purposes, the information provided on the report will help ensure replacement of a lost or stolen diamond with one that is truly "comparable quality."

Reports aren't necessary for every diamond, and many beautiful diamonds used in jewelry are sold without them. But when considering the purchase of a very fine diamond weighing one carat or more, we strongly recommend that the stone be accompanied by a report from one of the laboratories listed in the appendix, even if it means having a stone removed from its setting (no reputable lab will issue a report on a mounted diamond), and then reset. If you are considering a stone that lacks a report, it is easy for your jeweler or an appraiser to obtain one.

The availability and widespread use of these reports can, when properly understood, enable even those without professional skills to make valid comparisons between several stones and more informed buying decisions. The key is found in *knowing how to read the reports properly.*

Don't Rely on the Report Alone

Reports can be an important tool to help you understand differences affecting rarity and price. But we must caution you not to let them interfere with what you *like* or really want. Remember, some diamonds are very beautiful even though they don't adhere to established standards. In the final analysis, use your own eyes and ask yourself how you *like* the stone. We had a customer who was trying to decide between several stones. Her husband wanted to buy her the stone with the "best" report, but she preferred another stone which, according to what was on the reports, wasn't as "good." They decided against the "best" stone and bought the one that made her happiest. The important thing is that they knew exactly what they were buying and paid an appropriate price for that specific combination of quality factors. In other words, they made an *informed* choice. The reports gave them assurance as to the facts and greater confidence that they knew what they were really comparing.

Improper Use of Reports Can Lead to Costly Mistakes

As important as diamond grading reports can be, they can also be misused and lead to erroneous conclusions and costly mistakes. The key to being able to rely on a diamond report—and having confidence in your decision—lies in knowing how to read it properly.

When trying to decide between two diamonds accompanied by diamond grading reports, buyers all too often make a decision by comparing just two factors evaluated on the reports—*color* and *clarity*—and think they have made a sound decision. This is rarely the case. No one can make a sound decision based on color and clarity alone. In fact, when significant price differences exist between two stones of the same color and clarity, you will find that often the cheaper stone is *not* the same quality, nor the better value.

Color and clarity provide only part of the total picture and differences in price usually indicate differences in quality that you may not see or understand. With *round* diamonds, *all* the information you need is on the report, but you need to understand what all the information means before you can make valid comparisons.

Properly used, diamond grading reports can give you a more *complete* picture, enable you to make sounder comparisons, and determine who is offering good value. Reading reports may seem complicated at first, but if you take time to learn, and seek the help of a knowledgeable jeweler, you'll be amazed at how much more interesting—and unique—you'll find each diamond will become!

Before beginning, however, we must offer one important word of caution: *Don't make a purchase relying solely on any report without making sure the report matches the stone, and that the stone is still in the same condition described.* Always seek a professional gemologist, gemologist-appraiser, or gem-testing laboratory (see chapter 28) to confirm that the stone accompanying the report is, in fact, the stone described there, and that the stone is still in the same condition indicated on the report. We know of instances where a report has been accidentally sent with the wrong stone. And, in some cases, deliberate fraud is involved.

Laser Inscription and Ion Beam Technology

Today, some laboratories are routinely providing a laser inscription of the number of the report along the girdle edge of diamonds on which they are issuing reports. This offers some means of ensuring that the stone and report do, in fact, match. If the diamond you are considering does not have a laser inscription, an independent gemologist can confirm that the stone and report match. Should you wish to have the report number inscribed on the girdle, a jeweler or gemologist can make arrangements with a lab for a nominal charge. European Gemological Laboratory, International Gemmological Institute, and the Gemological Institute of America are among the companies providing laser inscription services. In addition to lasering, the International Gemmological Institute will soon offer a new service that uses ion beam technology to mark a diamond in an innovative manner that is non-invasive and does not mar the diamond in any way. This new technology can also be used to apply a "brand" mark that will be visible only with a special viewer, thus making it more difficult to counterfeit branded diamonds. It will be more difficult to falsify or eradicate such marks as a result of the process itself, so this technology may ultimately replace laser inscriptions.

❖ How to Read a Diamond Grading Report

- *Check the date issued.* It is very important to check the date on the report. It's always possible that the stone has been damaged since the report was issued. This sometimes occurs with diamonds sold at auction. Since diamonds can become chipped or cracked with wear, one must always check them. For example, you might see a diamond accompanied by a report describing it as D/Flawless. If this stone were badly chipped *after the report was issued,* however, the clarity grade could easily drop to VVS, and in some cases, even lower. Needless to say, in such a case value would be dramatically reduced.

- *Who issued the report?* Check the name of the laboratory issuing the report. Is the report from a laboratory that is known and respected? If not, the information on the report may not be reliable. In the United States, respected laboratories that issue diamond reports include the Gemological Institute of America "Gem Trade Laboratory" (GIA/GTL), American Gemological Laboratories (AGL), American Gem Society (AGS), Gem Quality Institute, and International Gemmological Institute (IGI). Respected European labs issuing diamond reports include the Belgian Diamond High Council (HRD), Gemological Laboratory Gubelin (Swiss), and Schweizerische Stiftung fur Edelstein-Forschung (SSEF-Swiss). See the appendix for additional information on these and other laboratories.

Whichever report you are reading (see pages 99–102 for sample reports), all will provide similar information, including:

- *Identity of the stone.* This verifies that the stone is a diamond. Some diamond reports don't make a specific statement about identity because they are called *diamond* reports and are only issued for genuine diamonds. If the report is not called a "diamond grading report," then there must be a statement attesting that the stone described is a genuine diamond.
- *Weight.* The exact carat weight must be given.
- *Dimensions.* Any diamond, of any shape, should be measured and the dimensions recorded as a means of identification, especially for insurance/identification purposes. The dimensions given

on a diamond report are very precise and provide information that is important for several reasons. First, the dimensions can help you determine that the diamond being examined is, in fact, the same diamond described in the report, since the likelihood of having two diamonds with exactly the same carat weight and millimeter dimensions is slim. Second, if the diamond has been damaged and recut since the report was issued, the millimeter dimensions may provide a clue that something has been altered, which might affect the carat weight as well. Any discrepancy between the dimensions that you or your jeweler get by measuring the stone, and those provided on the report, should be a red flag to check the stone very carefully.

Finally, the dimensions on the report also tell you whether the stone is *round* or *out-of-round*. Out-of-round diamonds sell for less than those that are more perfectly round. Roundness is explained below in greater detail.

- **Proportioning, finish, girdle thickness, culet, color, and clarity.** These are covered individually on the following pages.

Round, Brilliant-Cut Diamonds Are "Well-Rounded"

In round diamonds, the stone's *roundness* will affect value, so it is determined very carefully from measurements of the stone's diameter, gauged at several points around the circumference. For a round diamond, the report will usually give two diameters, measured in millimeters and noted to the hundredth: for example, 6.51 rather than 6.5; or 6.07 rather than 6.0, and so on. These indicate the highest and the lowest diameter. Diamonds are very rarely perfectly round, which is why most diamond reports will show two measurements. Recognizing the rarity of truly round diamonds, some deviation is permitted, and the stone will not be considered "out-of-round" unless it deviates by more than the established norm, which, in a 1-carat stone, is approximately 0.10 millimeter. As the size of a diamond increases, the tolerances also increase. In a 2-carat diamond, the tolerance would be approximately 0.12 millimeter; in a 3-carat, 0.14 millimeter; in a 4-carat, 0.16 millimeter; in a 5-carat, 0.17 millimeter; in a 10-carat, 0.21 millimeter; and so on. Slightly higher differences than those shown here will not affect value very much, especially on stones over 2 carats. To determine how much a diamond deviates from being perfectly round, simply subtract the smaller millimeter dimension from the higher dimension. To calculate the acceptable tolerance on a particular stone, average the high and low diameters and multiply that number by 0.0154. In a 1-carat stone, if the difference is 0.10 or less, the stone is considered "round." If the difference is greater, it is "out-of-round."

Depending on the degree of out-of-roundness, price can be affected by 10 to 15 percent, or much more if the stone is noticeably out-of-round. The greater the deviation, the lower the price should be.

Dimensions for Fancy Shapes

While the dimensions for fancy shapes are not as important as they are for round diamonds, there are length-to-width ratios that are considered "normal" and deviations may result in price reductions of 15 percent or more. The following reflect acceptable ranges:

Pear	1.50:1 to 1.75:1
Marquise	1.75:1 to 2.25:1
Emerald	1.30:1 to 1.60:1
Oval	1.35:1 to 1.70:1

To better understand what this means, let's look at a pear-shape diamond as an example. If its report showed the length to be 15 millimeters and the width to be 10 millimeters, the length-to-width ratio would be 15 to 10, or 1.50:1. This would be acceptable. If, however, the dimensions were 30 millimeters long by 10 wide, the ratio would be 30 to 10, or 3:1. This would be unacceptable; the ratio is too great, and the result is a stone that looks much too long for its width. A pear-shape diamond with an unacceptable length-to-width ratio should sell for at least 10 percent less than another pear-shape diamond. *Note:* A long pear shape is not necessarily bad, and some people prefer a longer shape, but it is important to understand that such stones should sell for less than those with "normal" lengths. Always keep in mind the length-to-width ratio of fancy cuts, and adjust the price for stones that are not in the "acceptable" range.

❖ Evaluating Proportioning from the Report

As we discussed earlier, good proportioning is as critical to a diamond as it is to the man or woman who wears it! The proportioning—especially the depth percentage and table percentage—is what determines how much brilliance and fire the stone will have.

The information provided on diamond reports pertaining to proportions is critically important for *round, brilliant-cut diamonds*. Unfortunately, it is only of minimal use with fancy shapes. For fancies, you must learn to rely on your own eye to tell whether or not the proportioning is acceptable: Are there differences in brilliance across the stone? Or flatness? Or dark spots such as "bow ties" resulting from poor proportioning (see chapter 6)?

Evaluating the proportioning of a diamond is as critical as evaluating the color and clarity grades. Diamonds that are cut close to "ideal" proportions and stones with "excellent" makes can easily cost 15 to 25 percent more than a diamond cut with average proportions; diamonds with poor makes sell for 10 to 20 percent less; very badly proportioned stones can be priced as much as 25 to 40 percent less than one with average proportions. As you can see, *the difference in cost between one diamond with "ideal" proportioning and another with "poor"—even where the color and clarity are the same— could be 40 percent or more.* The information on a diamond report can help you evaluate the proportioning and know whether or not you should be paying more, or less, for a particular stone.

"Depth Percentage" and "Table Percentage" Key to Beauty

To determine whether or not a round stone's proportioning is good—which is so critical to its beauty—look at the section of the report that describes *depth percentage* and *table percentage*. The depth percentage represents the depth of the stone—the distance from the table to the culet—as a percentage of the width of the stone. The table percentage represents the width of the table as a percentage of the width of the entire stone. These numbers indicate how well a round stone has been cut in terms of its proportioning, and must adhere to very precise standards. Your eye may be able to see differences in sparkle and brilliance, but you may not be able to discern the subtleties of proportioning. The percentages on the report should fall within a fairly specific range in order for the stone to be judged acceptable, excellent, or poor.

We will not discuss how one calculates these percentages, but it is important for you to know what the ranges are, as outlined in the charts on page 95.

Some reports also provide information about the *crown angle*. The crown angle tells you the angle at which the crown portion has been cut. This angle will affect the depth and table percentage. Normally, if the crown angle is between 34 and 36 degrees, the table and depth will be excellent; between 32 and 34, good; between 30 and 32 degrees, fair; and less than 30 degrees, poor. If the exact crown angle is not given, it is probably considered acceptable. If not, there is normally a statement indicating that the crown angle exceeds 36 degrees, or is less than 30 degrees. But once again, use your own eye to determine whether or not you like what you see. We've seen diamonds that are very beautiful despite having angles that are not within the norm.

Depth Percentage

A round diamond cut with a depth percentage between 58 and 64 percent is normally a lovely, lively stone. You should note, however, that girdle thickness will affect depth percentage. A high depth percentage could result from a thick or very thick girdle, so when checking the depth percentage on the diamond report, check the "girdle" information as well.

Stones with a depth percentage over 64 percent or under 57 percent will normally be too deep or too shallow to exhibit maximum beauty and should sell for less. If the depth percentage is too high, the stone will also look smaller than its weight indicates. If the depth percentage is exceptionally high, brilliance can be significantly reduced and a darkish center may also be produced. If the depth percentage is too *low,* brilliance will also be significantly affected. We've seen diamonds that were so shallow, that is, stones with such low depth percentages, that they had no brilliance and liveliness at all. When dirty, such stones look no better than a piece of glass.

We avoid stones with depth percentages over 64 percent or under 57 percent. If you are attracted to such stones remember that they should sell for much less per carat.

Depth Percentage Guidelines	
DEPTH PERCENTAGE	EFFECT ON PRICE
Ideal—approximately 58 to 60%	20 to 30% more*
Excellent—60+ to 62%	10 to 20% more*
Good—62 to 64%	———
Fair—64 to 66%	15 to 25% less
Poor—over 66% or less than 57%	20 to 40% less

*For *round* diamonds, combined with the right table percentage and fine overall cutting.

Table Percentage

Round stones cut with tables ranging from 53 to 64 percent usually result in beautiful, lively stones. Diamonds with smaller tables usually exhibit more *fire* than those with larger tables, but stones with larger tables may have more *brilliance.* As you will see, table width affects the stone's personality, but deciding which personality is more desirable is a matter of personal taste.

Table Percentage Guidelines	
TABLE PERCENTAGE	EFFECT ON PRICE
Ideal—from 53 to 58%	20 to 30% more*
Excellent—up to 60% (up to 62% in stones under ½ carat)	10 to 20% more*
Good—to 64%	———
Fair—over 64 to 70%	15 to 30% less
Poor—over 70%	30 to 40% less

*For *round* diamonds, combined with the right depth percentage and fine overall cutting.

Finish

Under *finish* on the diamond report you will find an evaluation of the stone's *polish and symmetry.* Polish serves as an indicator of the care taken by the cutter. The quality of the stone's polish is a factor that cannot be ignored in evaluating the overall quality of a diamond, as well as its cost and value. As with a pair of fine leather shoes, the better the polish, the brighter the surface luster!

Polish can be described on the report as *excellent, very good, good, fair,* or *poor.* The price-per-carat should be less on stones with "fair" or "poor" polish. Cost per carat is usually more for stones that have "very good" or "excellent" polish.

Symmetry describes several factors: (1) how the facet edges align with one another; (2) whether or not the facets from one side of the diamond match corresponding facets on the opposite side; and (3) whether or not facets in the top portion of the diamond are properly aligned with corresponding ones in the bottom portion. When the symmetry is described as "fair"—or worse—something is usually out of line.

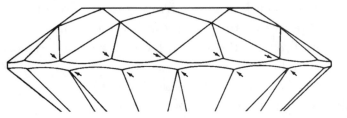

Misalignment of crown and pavilion

When evaluating symmetry, the most important area to check is the alignment of the crown (top) to the pavilion (bottom). If it is not good, it will make a visual difference in the beauty of the stone, and correspondingly in its price. To check for proper alignment here, simply look at the stone from the side to see whether or not the facets just above the girdle align with the facets just beneath the girdle.

When the top and bottom facets don't line up, it indicates sloppy cutting, and, more important, diminishes the overall beauty of the diamond. This will reduce price more than other symmetry faults.

How Does the Girdle Affect Value?

The girdle is another important item described on diamond grading reports. The report will indicate whether or not the girdle is polished, or faceted, and how thick it is. Girdle thickness is very important for two reasons: (1) it affects *value* and (2) it affects the stone's *durability.*

Girdle thickness ranges from extremely thin to extremely thick. Diamonds with girdles that are excessively thin or thick normally sell for less than other diamonds. An extremely thin girdle increases the risk of chipping. Remember that despite their legendary hardness, diamonds are brittle, so a very thin edge poses a greater risk.

If a diamond has an extremely thick girdle, its cost should also be reduced somewhat because the stone will look smaller than another diamond of the same weight with a more normal girdle thickness. This is because extra weight is being consumed by the thickness of the girdle itself (see chapter 6).

There are some cases in which a very thick girdle is acceptable. Shapes that have one or more points, such as the pear shape, heart, or marquise, can have thick to very thick girdles in the area of the points and still be in the acceptable range. Here the extra thickness in the girdle helps protect the points themselves from chipping.

Generally, a diamond with an extremely thin girdle should sell for less than one with an extremely thick girdle because of the stone's increased vulnerability to chipping. However, if the girdle is much too thick (as in some older diamonds), the price can also be significantly less because the stone can look significantly smaller than other stones of comparable weight.

The Culet

The culet looks like a point at the bottom of the stone, but it is normally another facet—a tiny, flat, polished surface. This facet should be *small or very small.* A small or very small culet won't be noticeable from the top. Some diamonds today are actually pointed. This means that there really is no culet, that the stone has been cut straight down to a point instead. The larger the culet, the more visible it will be from the top. The more visible, the lower the cost of the stone. Stones described as having a large or "open" culet as in old-European or old-mine cut diamonds (see chapter 6) are less desirable because the appearance of the culet causes a reduction in sparkle or brilliance at the very center of the stone. These stones normally need to be recut, and their price should take the need for recutting into consideration. Normally the cost is determined by the estimated amount of weight loss resulting from the recutting and can be anywhere from 5 to 25 percent. For the same reasons, a chipped or broken culet will seriously detract from the stone's beauty and significantly reduce the cost.

Color and Clarity Grades

The color and clarity grades found on a diamond report are the items with which most people are familiar, and we have already discussed them in detail in chapters 7 and 8. They are important factors in terms of determining the value of a diamond, but as the preceding discussion has shown, they do not tell the whole story.

A Word about Fluorescence

Fluorescence (see chapter 7), if present, will also be indicated on a diamond grading report. It will be graded *weak, moderate, strong,* or *very strong.* Some reports indicate the color of the fluorescence (blue, yellow, white, and so on). If the fluorescence is moderate to very strong and the color is not indicated, you should ask the jeweler to tell you what color the stone fluoresces. A stone with strong yellow fluorescence should sell for less since it will appear more tinted when worn in daylight or fluorescent lighting. The presence of blue fluorescence will not detract and in some cases may be considered a bonus, since it may make the stone appear whiter than it really is when seen in daylight or fluorescent lighting. However, if the report shows a *very strong* blue fluorescence, be sure to view the stone in daylight or fluorescent light to see whether or not there is an oily or murky appearance to the diamond. If so, it should sell for less; if not, then value should not be affected.

Pay Attention to the Full Clarity Picture Provided

The placement, number, type, and color of internal and external flaws will be indicated on a diamond report, and may include a plotting—a diagram showing all the details. Be sure you carefully note *all* the details in addition to the cumulative grade. Remember, the *placement* of imperfections can affect value (see chapter 8).

A reliable diamond grading report *cannot* be issued on a *fracture-filled diamond,* so GIA and most other labs will not issue a report on stones that have been clarity-enhanced by this method. The diamond will be returned with a notation that it is filled and cannot be graded. Reports *are* issued on stones that have been clarity-enhanced by laser (see chapter 8). Remember, however, that no matter what the clarity grade, a lasered stone should cost less than another with the "same" grade.

A Final Word about Reports

Diamond grading reports provide a very useful tool to aid in comparing diamonds and evaluating quality and value. But the key to their usefulness is proper understanding of how to read them, and how to look at the stone. Those who take the time to learn and understand what they are reading and, therefore, what they are really buying, will have a major advantage over those who do not.

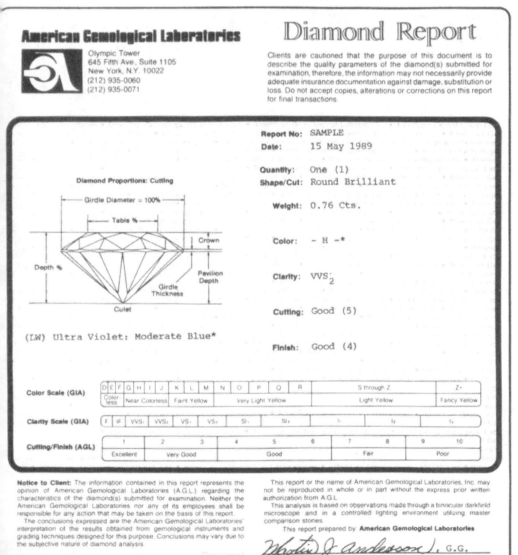

GIA GEM TRADE LABORATORY

A Division of GIA Enterprises, Inc.
A Wholly Owned Subsidiary of the Nonprofit Gemological Institute of America, Inc.

10012345

580 Fifth Avenue
New York, New York 10036-4794
(212) 221-5858
FAX: (212) 575-3095

5355 Armada Drive
Carlsbad, California 92008-4699
(760) 603-4500
FAX: (760) 603-1814

FEB 02 1998

DIAMOND GRADING REPORT

THE FOLLOWING WERE, AT THE TIME OF THE EXAMINATION, THE CHARAC-
TERISTICS OF THE DIAMOND DESCRIBED HEREIN BASED UPON 10×
MAGNIFICATION (FULLY CORRECTED TRIPLET LOUPE AND BINOCULAR
MICROSCOPE), DIAMONDLITE AND MASTER COLOR COMPARISON
DIAMONDS, ULTRAVIOLET LAMPS, MILLIMETER GAUGE, CARAT BALANCE,
PROPORTIONSCOPE, AND ANCILLARY INSTRUMENTS AS NECESSARY.

RED SYMBOLS DENOTE INTERNAL CHARACTERISTICS (INCLUSIONS).
GREEN SYMBOLS DENOTE EXTERNAL CHARACTERISTICS (BLEMISHES).
SYMBOLS INDICATE TYPE, POSITION AND APPROXIMATE SIZE OF
CHARACTERISTICS. DETAILS OF FINISH ARE NOT SHOWN. DIAGRAM MAY
BE APPROXIMATE.

KEY TO SYMBOLS
- ○ CRYSTAL
- ⌒ FEATHER
- · PINPOINT
- ⌃ NATURAL

SHAPE AND
CUTTING STYLE .. ROUND BRILLIANT
   Measurements .... 6.90 - 6.97 X 4.20 MM.
   Weight .... 1.25 CARATS

PROPORTIONS ...
   Depth .... 60.6 %
   Table .... 61 %
   Girdle .... MEDIUM TO SLIGHTLY THICK, FACETED
   Culet .... VERY SMALL
   FINISH
      Polish .... VERY GOOD
      Symmetry ...... VERY GOOD

CLARITY GRADE .. VS1

COLOR GRADE ... F

   Fluorescence ..... NONE

COMMENTS:
   "GIA 10012345" has been inscribed on the girdle of this diamond.

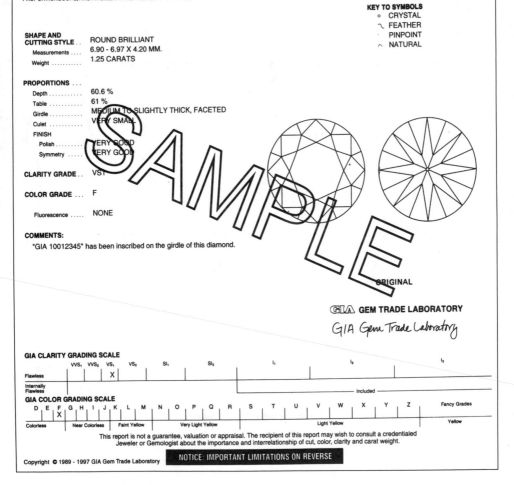

ORIGINAL

GIA GEM TRADE LABORATORY

GIA Gem Trade Laboratory

GIA CLARITY GRADING SCALE

	VVS₁	VVS₂	VS₁	VS₂	SI₁	SI₂	I₁	I₂	I₃
Flawless			X						
Internally Flawless							— Included —		

GIA COLOR GRADING SCALE

D	E	F	G	H	I	J	K	L	M	N	O	P	Q	R	S	T	U	V	W	X	Y	Z	Fancy Grades
	X																						
Colorless			Near Colorless				Faint Yellow				Very Light Yellow						Light Yellow						Yellow

This report is not a guarantee, valuation or appraisal. The recipient of this report may wish to consult a credentialed
Jeweler or Gemologist about the importance and interrelationship of cut, color, clarity and carat weight.

Copyright © 1989 - 1997 GIA Gem Trade Laboratory   **NOTICE: IMPORTANT LIMITATIONS ON REVERSE**

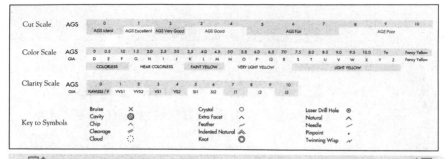

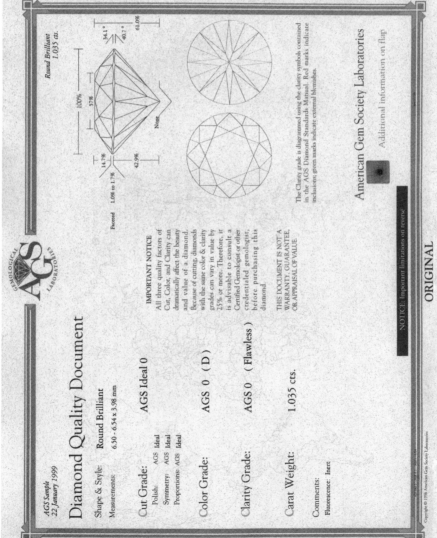

AGS Sample
22 January 1999

Diamond Quality Document

Shape & Style: Round Brilliant
Measurements: 6.50 - 6.54 x 3.98 mm

Cut Grade: AGS Ideal 0
Polish: AGS Ideal
Symmetry: AGS Ideal
Proportions: AGS Ideal

Color Grade: AGS 0 (D)

Clarity Grade: AGS 0 (Flawless)

Carat Weight: 1.035 cts.

Comments:
Fluorescence: Inert

IMPORTANT NOTICE

All three quality factors of Cut, Color, and Clarity can dramatically affect the beauty and value of a diamond. Because of cutting, diamonds with the same color & clarity grades can vary in value by 25% or more. Therefore, it is advisable to consult a Certified Gemologist or other credentialed gemologist, before purchasing this diamond.

THIS DOCUMENT IS NOT A WARRANTY, GUARANTEE, OR APPRAISAL OF VALUE.

Round Brilliant
1.035 ct.

Faceted 1.0% to 1.7%

The Clarity grade is diagrammed using the clarity symbols contained in the AGS Diamond Standards Manual. Red marks indicate inclusions green marks indicate external blemishes.

American Gem Society Laboratories

Additional information on flap

NOTICE: Important limitations on reverse

ORIGINAL

DIAMOND CERTIFICATE

issued by the

EGL · USA

EUROPEAN GEMOLOGICAL LABORATORY ™

Independent educational organization.
Institute for certification of diamonds and precious stones.

Natural Diamond Report

Certificate   US 18409101D

This examination has been carried out
using the current gemological procedures of E.G.L.

WEIGHT	**1.04 CT**
Shape and cut	**ROUND BRILLIANT**
Measurements	**6.55 - 6.50 x 3.95 mm**
PROPORTIONS	
Depth:	**60.00%**
Table:	**59.00%**
Crown:	**13.50%**
Pavilion:	**43.50%**
Girdle:	**THIN TO MEDIUM FACETED**
Culet:	**SMALL**
FINISH	
Polish:	**VERY GOOD**
Symmetry:	**VERY GOOD**
CLARITY GRADE	**VS2**
COLOR GRADE	**D**
Fluorescence:	**FAINT**
Comments:	

October 11, 2002

EUROPEAN GEMOLOGICAL LABORATORY™
EGL USA

The characteristics of the diamond in this report were based on the information gained from utilizing a variety of gem testing instruments. The following instruments were used as required to complete our examination: 10x magnification with a fully corrected loupe and binocular microscope, millimeter gauge, computer aided non-contact measuring device, spectroscope systems, ProportionScope, electronic balance, master color comparison diamonds, long-wave and short-wave ultraviolet light sources, fiber optic illumination, daylight balanced lighting and other instruments. The diagram is an approximate representation of the type and relative position of internal and external characteristics. Red symbols indicate internal characteristics and green symbols indicate external characteristics.

ORIGINAL This report is supplied at the request... issued for his exclusive use. The re... at the time of examination of the stone. It is not a guarantee, va... kind. E.G.L. has made no representation or warranty regarding... described. Since diamond grading is not an exact science th... best professional opinion of this company. E.G.L. is in no ca... which could occur by repeated expertise and/or use of other... criteria other than those chosen by E.G.L.

ADDITIONAL TERMS AND CONDITIONS ON REVERSE

CHAPTER 12

Comparing Diamond Prices

All too often people look for easy answers to complex problems. Many would like to have a simple list of diamond grades and corresponding prices, by size. Unfortunately, market conditions are constantly changing, and, more important, significant differences in price often result from subtle differences in quality not readily discernible to anyone but the professional (see chapter 11 on reading diamond grading reports). Therefore, it is not possible to provide a simple answer to this complex problem.

But that does not mean we cannot provide you with useful information. We can offer some general guidelines that will help you understand the *relative* effects of each of the four primary factors that are used to determine the value of diamonds. They are not intended as hard price lists of what you should be paying in a jewelry store. Keep in mind that these prices are for *unmounted* stones. Fine settings can add substantially to the price, especially rings designed by award-winning artists.

Extreme differences between the prices given on the following pages and a price you might be quoted for a diamond should be examined carefully; if the price is much *lower,* be sure to have the quality checked by an independent laboratory or appraiser to be sure the quality is what it has been represented to be (see the list of appraisers and laboratories in the appendix); if the price is *much* higher, check to be sure the seller is offering good value by comparison shopping in your community.

Having said this, note that the prices given here are for round, brilliant-cut diamonds with "good" proportioning (stones with *"excellent"proportioning* will sell for *more;* stones with *poor proportioning* can sell for *much less*). Diamonds having *"fancy"* shapes (shapes other than round) normally sell for anywhere from 5 to 15 percent less. However, if a particular shape is in very high demand, the price can be higher than it is for round stones. Well-cut marquise-shaped diamonds were selling for more than round diamonds in the late 1980s, but changes in fashion have affected their popularity and price.

Finally, before relying too heavily on the prices listed in this chapter, be sure to read chapter 11 on how to read and understand diamond grading reports. This will give you additional input on how to adjust diamond prices according to the more subtle factors that affect quality and value. Then be sure to have the facts verified by a qualified gemologist-appraiser (see chapter 28).

RETAIL PRICE GUIDES*

Notice both the tremendous price fluctuation among stones of the same size due to differences in the flaw grades and color grades, and the disproportionate jumps in cost *per carat*, depending upon size.

$$\frac{\text{PRICE PER CARAT}}{\text{PRICE PER STONE}} \text{ U.S. Dollars}$$

COLOR GRADE   **½ CARAT (.50+)**

FLAW (CLARITY) GRADE

		D	E	F	G	H	I	J	K
IF†		11,400	9,800	8,400	7,800	7,000	6,400	5,750	4,500
		5,700	4,900	4,200	3,900	3,500	3,200	2,875	2,250
VVS$_1$		9,600	8,800	7,800	7,600	6,800	6,300	5,500	4,250
		4,800	4,400	3,900	3,800	3,400	3,125	2,750	2,125
VVS$_2$		8,800	8,200	7,400	7,200	6,200	6,000	5,250	4,000
		4,400	4,100	3,700	3,600	3,100	3,000	2,625	2,000
VS$_1$		7,600	7,400	7,000	6,600	6,100	5,500	5,000	3,750
		3,800	3,700	3,500	3,300	3,050	2,750	2,500	1,875
VS$_2$		7,000	6,800	6,600	6,000	5,600	5,250	4,500	3,625
		3,500	3,400	3,300	3,000	2,800	2,625	2,250	1,813
SI$_1$		6,500	6,300	6,150	5,750	5,500	4,750	4,250	3,500
		3,250	3,150	3,075	2,875	2,750	2,375	2,125	1,750
SI$_2$		6,000	5,750	5,500	5,250	4,500	4,250	4,000	3,250
		3,000	2,875	2,750	2,625	2,250	2,125	2,000	1,625
I$_1$		4,250	4,000	3,750	3,500	3,250	2,875	2,625	2,500
		2,125	2,000	1,875	1,750	1,625	1,438	1,313	1,250

COLOR GRADE   **¾ CARAT (.70+)**

FLAW (CLARITY) GRADE

		D	E	F	G	H	I	J	K
IF†		13,800	11,200	10,400	9,600	8,400	7,400	6,700	6,250
		10,350	8,400	7,800	7,200	6,300	5,550	5,025	4,688
VVS$_1$		11,200	10,800	9,600	8,800	7,800	7,000	6,300	6,000
		8,400	8,100	7,200	6,600	5,850	5,250	4,725	4,500
VVS$_2$		10,400	9,600	8,800	7,800	7,200	6,400	5,900	5,750
		7,800	7,200	6,600	5,850	5,400	4,800	4,425	4,313
VS$_1$		9,400	8,800	8,200	7,600	7,000	6,200	5,700	5,500
		7,050	6,600	6,150	5,700	5,250	4,650	4,275	4,125
VS$_2$		8,600	8,200	7,800	7,200	6,600	6,000	5,500	5,250
		6,450	6,150	5,850	5,400	4,950	4,500	4,125	3,938
SI$_1$		7,800	7,600	7,000	6,600	6,300	5,700	5,400	5,000
		5,850	5,700	5,250	4,950	4,725	4,275	4,050	3,750
SI$_2$		7,000	6,600	6,000	5,900	5,800	5,500	5,300	4,750
		5,250	4,950	4,500	4,425	4,350	4,125	3,975	3,563
I$_1$		6,500	6,000	5,250	5,125	5,000	4,250	4,125	3,250
		4,875	4,500	3,938	3,844	3,750	3,188	3,094	2,438

* Prices compiled from *The Guide*, Gemworld International, Inc.

† The price difference between FL and IF stones is approximately 5–8% in D–F colors and 1–2% in G–J colors; there is no cost difference in stones of colors below J.

RETAIL PRICE GUIDES*

Notice both the tremendous price fluctuation among stones of the same size due to differences in the flaw grades and color grades, and the disproportionate jumps in cost *per carat*, depending upon size.

$$\frac{\text{PRICE PER CARAT}}{\text{PRICE PER STONE}} \text{ U.S. Dollars}$$

COLOR GRADE — **Light 1-CARAT (.90+)**

FLAW (CLARITY) GRADE		D	E	F	G	H	I	J	K
	IF†	16,200	13,000	11,800	10,800	9,800	8,000	7,000	6,400
		14,580	11,700	10,620	9,720	8,820	7,200	6,300	5,760
	VVS₁	12,800	12,000	11,000	9,800	9,200	7,800	6,800	6,200
		11,520	10,800	9,900	8,820	8,280	7,020	6,120	5,580
	VVS₂	12,200	11,200	10,200	9,200	8,800	7,400	6,600	6,100
		10,980	10,800	9,180	8,280	7,920	6,660	5,940	5,490
	VS₁	11,200	10,200	9,600	9,000	8,400	7,200	6,400	6,000
		10,080	9,180	8,640	8,100	7,560	6,480	5,760	4,500
	VS₂	10,000	9,400	9,000	8,600	7,800	7,000	6,100	5,800
		9,000	8,460	8,100	7,740	7,020	6,300	5,490	5,220
	SI₁	9,000	8,600	8,200	7,800	7,000	6,600	6,000	5,700
		8,100	7,740	7,380	7,020	6,300	5,940	4,500	5,130
	SI₂	8,200	7,800	7,400	7,000	6,200	6,100	5,800	5,250
		7,380	7,020	6,660	6,300	5,580	5,490	5,220	4,725
	I₁	6,500	6,250	6,000	5,750	5,500	4,750	4,500	4,000
		5,850	5,625	5,400	5,175	4,950	4,275	4,050	3,600

COLOR GRADE — **1-CARAT (1.00+)**

FLAW (CLARITY) GRADE		D	E	F	G	H	I	J	K
	IF†	28,000	19,200	17,200	13,800	12,200	10,000	8,400	7,400
		28,000	19,200	17,200	13,800	12,200	10,000	8,400	7,400
	VVS₁	18,400	17,000	14,000	12,600	11,200	9,200	8,200	7,200
		18,400	17,000	14,000	12,600	11,200	9,200	8,200	7,200
	VVS₂	17,000	14,200	13,000	12,000	10,800	9,000	8,000	7,000
		17,000	14,200	13,000	12,000	10,800	9,000	8,000	7,000
	VS₁	13,800	13,400	12,600	11,600	10,400	8,600	7,600	6,800
		13,800	13,400	12,600	11,600	10,400	8,600	7,600	6,800
	VS₂	12,800	12,000	11,800	11,000	9,800	8,400	7,500	6,400
		12,800	12,000	11,800	11,000	9,800	8,400	7,500	6,400
	SI₁	11,400	10,800	10,200	9,600	9,400	7,600	7,400	6,000
		11,400	10,800	10,200	9,600	9,400	7,600	7,400	6,000
	SI₂	10,000	9,600	9,200	8,400	8,200	7,000	6,400	5,600
		10,000	9,600	9,200	8,400	8,200	7,000	6,400	5,600
	I₁	6,400	6,100	6,000	5,900	5,800	5,500	5,400	5,300
		6,400	6,100	6,000	5,900	5,800	5,500	5,400	5,300

*Prices compiled from *The Guide*, Gemworld International, Inc.
† The price difference between FL and IF stones is approximately 5–8% in D–F colors and 1–2% in G–J colors; there is no cost difference in stones of colors below J.

RETAIL PRICE GUIDES*

Notice both the tremendous price fluctuation among stones of the same size due to differences in the flaw grades and color grades, and the disproportionate jumps in cost *per carat,* depending upon size.

$$\frac{\text{PRICE PER CARAT}}{\text{PRICE PER STONE}} \quad \text{U.S. Dollars}$$

COLOR GRADE — 2-CARAT (2.00+)

FLAW (CLARITY) GRADE

	D	E	F	G	H	I	J	K
IF†	44,400	33,400	29,200	23,200	19,600	15,000	12,600	10,400
	88,800	66,800	58,400	46,400	39,200	30,000	25,200	20,800
VVS₁	32,800	29,200	23,600	21,200	17,000	14,400	12,200	10,000
	65,600	58,400	47,200	42,400	34,000	28,800	24,400	20,000
VVS₂	29,200	24,600	21,600	19,200	16,200	13,800	11,800	9,800
	58,400	49,200	43,200	38,400	32,400	27,600	23,600	19,600
VS₁	24,600	22,000	19,800	18,400	15,400	13,600	11,000	9,000
	49,200	44,000	39,600	36,800	30,800	27,200	22,000	18,000
VS₂	20,000	19,200	18,600	17,400	14,400	12,600	10,000	8,800
	40,000	38,400	37,200	34,800	28,800	25,200	20,000	17,600
SI₁	16,800	16,400	15,400	14,800	13,000	11,200	9,000	8,200
	33,600	32,800	30,800	29,600	26,000	22,400	18,000	16,400
SI₂	13,200	13,000	12,800	12,000	11,000	9,400	8,000	6,400
	26,400	26,000	25,600	24,000	22,000	18,800	16,000	12,800
I₁	8,200	7,800	7,400	7,000	6,800	6,600	6,200	5,800
	16,400	15,600	14,800	14,000	13,600	13,200	12,400	11,600

COLOR GRADE — 3-CARAT (3.00+)

FLAW (CLARITY) GRADE

	D	E	F	G	H	I	J	K
IF†	67,600	47,800	40,800	31,400	25,000	19,800	15,400	13,600
	202,800	143,400	122,400	94,200	75,000	59,400	46,200	40,800
VVS₁	48,000	41,000	31,800	25,800	22,400	17,800	14,200	12,600
	144,000	123,000	95,400	77,400	67,200	53,400	42,600	37,800
VVS₂	41,400	31,800	27,200	23,200	20,600	17,000	13,800	12,000
	124,200	95,400	81,600	69,600	61,800	51,000	41,400	36,000
VS₁	32,200	26,800	23,600	22,200	19,000	15,600	12,600	11,200
	96,600	80,400	70,800	66,600	57,000	46,800	37,800	33,600
VS₂	26,400	23,800	22,400	19,800	17,000	13,800	11,400	10,200
	79,200	71,400	67,200	59,400	51,000	41,400	34,200	30,600
SI₁	21,200	20,200	18,800	17,000	14,200	12,400	10,600	9,400
	63,600	60,600	56,400	51,000	42,600	37,200	31,800	28,200
SI₂	16,200	15,200	14,200	13,400	12,600	11,200	9,600	8,200
	48,600	45,600	42,600	40,200	37,800	33,600	28,800	24,600
I₁	11,800	11,000	10,200	9,600	9,000	8,000	7,600	6,400
	35,400	33,000	30,600	28,800	27,000	24,000	22,800	19,200

*Prices compiled from *The Guide,* Gemworld International, Inc.
† The price difference between FL and IF stones is approximately 5–8% in D–F colors and 1–2% in G–J colors; there is no cost difference in stones of colors below J.

RETAIL PRICE GUIDE FOR FANCY-COLOR DIAMONDS *

Prices are per carat in U.S. dollars.

FANCY YELLOW			
Wt.	**FL–VVS**	**VS**	**SI**	**I₁**

FANCY YELLOW				
Wt.	**FL–VVS**	**VS**	**SI**	**I₁**
3/4 ct	6,000–7,000	5,750–6,500	5,000– 6,250	4,250–5,000
1 ct	8,000–9,000	6,800–7,200	6,400–7,000	5,600–6,000
2 ct	12,000–12,600	10,400–12,000	10,000–11,600	8,000–9,000
3 ct	13,000–14,000	12,000–13,000	10,400–12,000	9,200–9,800
4 ct	14,000–16,000	13,000–15,000	12,000–13,000	10,000–11,000
5 ct	16,000–18,000	15,000–17,000	13,000–15,000	11,000–13,000
FANCY INTENSE YELLOW				
Wt.	**FL–VVS**	**VS**	**SI**	**I₁**
3/4 ct	9,000–11,000	8,000–10,000	6,600–8,000	6,000–7,000
1 ct	11,400–15,400	11,000–15,000	10,000–13,600	8,000–10,000
2 ct	16,000–17,800	15,600–17,600	13,600–15,200	10,000–12,400
3 ct	18,000–19,000	17,000–18,000	16,000–17,000	11,000–13,000
4 ct	19,000–23,000	18,000–22,000	17,000–20,000	12,000–14,000
5 ct	23,000–26,000	22,000–26,000	20,000–24,000	13,000–15,000
FANCY LIGHT PINK				
Wt.	**FL–VVS**	**VS**	**SI**	**I₁**
3/4 ct	30,000–34,000	24,000–30,000	18,000–24,000	12,000–16,000
1 ct	36,000–42,000	32,000–40,000	30,000–36,000	22,000–26,000
2 ct	72,000–90,000	70,000–86,000	60,000–80,000	40,000–50,000
FANCY PINK				
Wt.	**FL–VVS**	**VS**	**SI**	**I₁**
3/4 ct	80,000–110,000	70,000–120,000	50,000–80,000	30,000–40,000
1 ct	120,000–160,000	100,000–140,000	80,000–140,000	50,000–70,000
2 ct	200,000–270,000	150,000–200,000	120,000–180,000	60,000–80,000
FANCY BLUE				
Wt.	**FL–VVS**	**VS**	**SI**	**I₁**
3/4 ct	140,000–160,000	100,000–150,000	80,000–100,000	60,000–70,000
1 ct	240,000–280,000	200,000–240,000	170,000–200,000	140,000–180,000
2 ct	350,000–450,000	300,000–400,000	250,000–350,000	100,000–150,000

*Retail prices are based on *The Guide,* Gemworld International, Inc.

CHAPTER 13

False Claims and Costly Bargains

How to Spot Fraud and Avoid Misrepresentation

As you have seen, many factors affect quality and value in diamonds. When you are looking at a stone already set in a ring or other piece of jewelry, it is very difficult, if not impossible, to *see* differences that can dramatically affect cost. For this reason, we urge you to buy any important diamond *unmounted* and to mount it only after all the facts have been verified. But you don't have to be a "gemologist" or fear buying jewelry. If you follow a few simple steps, anyone can buy with confidence.

❖ Four Key Steps to Avoiding Fraud or Misrepresentation

- *The first step is to buy from someone both accessible and knowledgeable.* One of the most important steps is to seek a jeweler who is knowledgeable. You can't be sure of the genuineness and quality of what you are buying if the seller lacks the skill to know for sure what he or she is buying and selling. While you may be tempted to buy a lovely antique engagement ring from an antique show or estate sale—and certainly there are some bargains to be found in such places—you run a higher risk when purchasing in such places because of possible misinformation, unintentional or otherwise. You must weigh the risk versus the potential reward. In addition, before making a final purchasing decision, ask yourself whether or not you will be able to *find* the seller again if what you bought turns out to be other than represented. This is equally true when traveling.
- *Second, ask the right questions.* Don't be afraid to ask direct, even pointed questions. The key to getting complete information

about what you are buying is asking good questions so you can be sure you are aware of important factors affecting quality and value. (To help you ask the right questions, we provide a complete list in chapter 26.)

- *Third, get the facts in writing.* Be sure the seller is willing to put the answers to the questions you ask, and any representations made about the diamond or ring you are considering, *in writing*. If not, we recommend against purchasing from this seller unless there is an unconditional return policy that allows merchandise to be returned within a reasonable period of time, for a full refund (not a store credit). In this case, be sure to follow the next step to be safe.
- *Finally, verify the facts with a gemologist-appraiser.* It's especially important to verify whatever has been put in writing with a professional gemologist-appraiser (see chapter 28). Some unscrupulous dealers are willing to put anything in writing to make the sale, knowing that written assurances or claims about the stone are often sufficient to satisfy buyers' doubts. So this last step may be the most important to ensure you make a wise decision.

In general, you need not worry about fraud or misrepresentation, whether deliberate or unintentional, if you simply follow these four easy steps. They may require a little more time and nominal additional expense, but the end result will be greater knowledge—and assurance—about the ring you choose and your jeweler. And, they may save you from a costly mistake.

❖ Types of Misrepresentation

Beware of Bargains! Diamonds Represented to Be Better Than They Are

Beware of bargains. Most are not. When a price seems too good to be true, it usually is, unless the seller doesn't know its true value (which reflects badly on the seller's expertise).

A large jewelry store in Philadelphia was recently found guilty of misrepresenting the quality of diamonds it was selling. Sales staff consistently represented their diamonds to be several color grades and/or flaw grades better than they actually were. As a result, their prices seemed much more attractive than those of other jewelers. Customers thought they were getting a much better buy from this firm than from others in the area, which was often not the case; since customers didn't know the true quality of the stones they were buying, they couldn't make a fair comparison with what other jewelers were offering. Other jewelers in the area were, in fact, giving better value on stones comparable to what was actually being sold by this "bargain" firm.

Such firms can be found in every city. Many are even willing to put everything in writing, often including a full "appraisal." Such dishonest practices often go undetected because most people assume when a seller is willing to "put it in writing," he or she is properly representing the item. Most buyers never bother to have the facts verified and this can lead to a costly mistake.

Are Wholesale Prices Really Wholesale?

It is natural to be lured by the promise of getting a diamond at a wholesale price: a price significantly below what most retailers charge. We've already discussed some of the pitfalls, but many fall into the trap of believing that even if they don't get exactly what they are told, they will still get it at a price below what they would have paid at a local jewelry store. Yet, this is frequently not the case.

We recently went undercover for one of the TV networks and made a purchase from a diamond dealer touting "wholesale" prices. In addition to misrepresentation of quality, the price we paid for the stone was *double* the stone's *retail* value. We purchased a stone described by the seller to have a color grade of J–K and a clarity grade of SI_2. He gave us an appraisal with all the representations stated clearly in writing. The diamond was actually S-color, and the clarity was no better than "I_2." It was also fracture-filled, despite the fact that he had shown me fracture-filled diamonds, explaining what they were—and supposedly gaining my confidence by so doing—and we had told him explicitly that we did not want a fracture-filled diamond! We paid $3,200 for the stone; the *retail* value was $1,400 to $1,500. We could have purchased this stone from any retail jeweler for less. The moral: don't assume you get a good buy just because you are in a "wholesale" jewelry district.

Scams Involving "Appraisals" Prior to Sale

Beware of jewelers not willing to put the facts in writing, but who offer to let you take the stone, prior to the sale, to an appraiser in the neighborhood. This may be a scam. It is often seen in wholesale districts like New York's famous 47th Street.

The first step in this scam is to build you up with all the reasons why you are going to get an exceptional buy—because the seller "bought it right" (whatever that means), or wants to "pass the savings on to you," or isn't greedy ("I don't care who I sell to at wholesale, after all, a sale is a sale"), and so on. When you find something you are seriously interested in buying, the seller then explains, for a variety of seemingly valid reasons, why he or she will not put any information pertaining to the quality of the stone in writing on the bill of sale. The salesperson then acknowledges that you are wise to want to verify everything and encourages you to get an appraisal prior to making the purchase. Many people are immediately hooked the moment the dealer *suggests* you get it appraised and conclude, erroneously, that since they can get an appraisal if they choose, everything must be in order. So they don't.

Those who decide to follow the salesperson's suggestion and get an appraisal usually face another problem. They don't know an appraiser or certainly not any in the neighborhood. The seller assures you that this is not a problem, however, because there are "lots of good appraisers nearby." (Note that where gem and jewelry appraisers are concerned, this is not the case in most cities. In New York's diamond district, for example, there are only three appraising laboratories that hold recognized credentials, and for these, an appointment is required.) Next, the seller will explain that to reduce any risk for you, and for his own insurance/security reasons, he will have the firm's "bonded guard" accompany you and carry the stone. On the surface, this sounds perfectly reasonable. Now, once you have left the store and are pondering where to go to find an appraiser, the bonded guard comes to your aid and subtly directs you to an appraiser (one "with whom his firm's customers are very impressed"). Upon entering the appraiser's office, a bell alerts the appraiser that someone has entered, and you find yourself in a small waiting room, separated from the "laboratory" by a glass partition with closed blinds; the appraiser looks through the closed blinds to see who has entered his waiting room . . . not only does he see you, the customer, but more importantly, he sees "Mr. Bonded Guard," whom he knows, of course! The appraiser now explains that he needs a couple of minutes to finish something before he can admit you into the lab. While you wait, he simply calls "Mr. Bonded Guard's" firm to learn what you've been told. It should come as no surprise that his "appraisal" will be totally consistent with what you were told by the seller.

One of our clients almost had a similar experience. She went to New York, to a 47th Street firm. She was offered a 5-plus-carat diamond ring at a price that was one-fourth the price most retailers had been quoting for what appeared to be comparable quality. She thought the ring looked very beautiful, and became very excited about being able to get such a bargain. But when she asked the seller to back up his description of the quality of the diamond in writing, he said it was against his store policy since they were not "gemologists." He was willing to guarantee the price, however, assuring her that if she found a diamond of comparable quality at a better price, he would refund the difference. When she insisted that she needed to be sure of the quality of the stone before she would purchase it and wouldn't buy it unless he was willing to put his representations in writing, he suggested she get it appraised before making any decision. She did not know any local appraisers, but, luckily, we were in New York at the time and were able to use a colleague's lab to examine the ring carefully (it was awkward for the seller to refuse to let her have *us* look at it). Not surprisingly, the quality was not as represented. The flaw grade had been misrepresented by *four* grades, and the color had been enhanced *seven grades* by "painting"! (Painted diamonds have a coating that doesn't come off with normal cleaning and may take months or years to wear off. We had to clean the stone chemically to determine it was painted, and reveal its true color!)

In this particular case, given the true quality of the diamond, the price being asked for the ring was certainly not the "steal" it appeared to be. It wasn't a bad price, but other retailers were offering comparable stones at comparable prices, or less.

Many visitors to wholesale diamond districts such as 47th Street are from out of town and don't know a reliable local appraiser. Unscrupulous sellers often count on this because it gives them the opportunity to create a scenario such as those described above. Sometimes, they may even recommend several "reliable" appraisers, but rather than seem too obvious, most suggest *you* choose your own (some even make a fuss about not wanting to know who you choose). They know that you will be accompanied by someone from their own firm, and since it's rarely possible for a buyer to just walk into a reputable appraising firm without an appointment, it is highly likely you will pick an appraiser with whom they have an "arrangement." One of the most important things for you to remember is that *all appraisers are not the same, nor are all appraisers equally competent or reliable* (see chapter 28). Unfortunately, the "reliable appraiser" in this situation often means the *seller* can rely on the *appraiser* to tell the prospective buyers what the seller wants them to hear.

One must always be careful of recommendations from the seller. While legitimate jewelers usually know better than anyone else who the best gemologist-appraisers are in their communities, and their recommendations should be respected, you must still be sure to check the credentials yourself to avoid such scams. Unfortunately, especially in the jewelry districts of major cities, far too many appraisers are not qualified, and some are in collusion with unscrupulous jewelers.

Such practices are overtly dishonest, of course, but all too often they leave honest jewelers in a bad light as a result. In such cases, the dishonest jeweler will appear to be offering the best price, while the honest jeweler—who may actually be offering the best value— falsely appears to be charging "too much."

Finding the right appraiser is an essential step in making sure that you have made a wise purchase and that the quality has been fairly represented. There are many ways in which unsuspecting buyers can be fooled. In general, when selecting a diamond, you need to guard against fraud and misrepresentation in any of the following four areas:

- Weight misrepresentation
- Color alteration and misgrading
- Flaw concealment and misgrading
- Certification—alteration and counterfeit certificates

❖ Weight

Giving "total weight" of *all stones* when more than one is involved, rather than the exact weight of the *main stone,* is one form of misrepresentation often encountered. This is a violation of Federal Trade Commission (FTC) guidelines. In giving the weight, particularly on any display card, descriptive tag, or other type of advertising for a particular ring or other piece of jewelry, the weight of the main stone or stones should be clearly indicated as well as the total weight of all the stones.

Thus, if you purchase a "3-carat diamond" ring with one large center stone and two small side stones (as found in many engagement rings), the center stone's weight should be clearly stated; for example, "The weight of the center stone is 2.50 carats, with side stones that weigh 0.25 carats each, for a total weight of 3.00 carats." There is a tremendous price difference between a single stone weighing 3 carats and numerous stones having a total weight of 3 carats. A single, 3-carat stone of good quality could sell for $50,000, while three carats consisting of numerous stones (even with some weighing a carat or more) of the same quality could sell anywhere from $5,000 to $20,000, depending on how many stones there are and the weight of each one.

When inquiring about the weight of a diamond, be sure to ask the right question: Ask how much it *weighs* rather than how *large* it is. In any case, the answer should provide the *exact* carat weight. Beware when the response includes the word "spread"—"this stone *spreads* one carat." *A stone that spreads one carat does not weigh one carat.* It simply means it looks as large as a one-carat stone in its width.

❖ Color

Failure to Disclose Permanent Treatments

Diamonds can be treated in many ways to improve their color. Some are temporary and others are permanent. Regardless of permanence, any treatment should be disclosed so that you know you are paying an appropriate price.

High-pressure/high-temperture annealing (HPHT). This is a new treatment being used to enhance diamonds. The process can transform very tinted, off-white diamonds (as low as Q–Z colors) into color-less and near-colorless stones—even D, E, and F! It can also be used to create fancy-color diamonds. Fancy colors produced by the HPHT treatment include greenish yellow, yellowish green, and even very rare shades of pink and blue. The change is permanent, but detection requires sophisticated equipment that can be found only in major gem-testing laboratories.

Diamonds treated by HPHT annealing entered the marketplace before the gemological community was aware of the use of this technology on diamonds and before they understood how to distinguish them from natural diamonds. *We recommend that any color-less or near-colorless diamond that has a diamond report issued between January 1996 and June 2000 be examined by a gemologist to determine whether or not it is one of the rare diamond types that respond to this treatment and, if so, that it be resubmitted to a major gem-testing lab (see appendix) for verification.*

Fancy-color diamonds produced by the HPHT annealing process, especially pink and blue diamonds, are more difficult to detect. We highly recommend that fancy-color blue and pink diamonds purchased recently be accompanied by a lab report issued by a major lab, and that if a report already accompanies the stone, that it be resubmitted if the report predates December 2000.

Radiation treatment. Exposing off-color diamonds such as yellowish or brownish tinted stones (and also badly flawed stones in which the flaws would be less noticeable against a colored background) to certain types of radiation can result in the production of fancy-colored stones. This treatment produces rich yellows, greens, and blues, and greatly enhances salability because these colors are very desirable. In and of itself, radiation is not fraud; in fact, it may make a "fancy" color diamond affordable to someone otherwise unable to afford one. But again, just be sure that the stone is properly represented and you know what you are buying, and that you are getting it at the right price—which should be much lower than that of the natural fancy.

Temporary Color Enhancement

Touching the culet, or side, of a slightly yellow stone with a coating of purple ink, such as found in an indelible pencil, neutralizes the yellow, producing a whiter-looking stone. This can be easily detected by washing the stone in alcohol or water. If you have any questions about the color, tactfully request that the stone be washed (in front of you) for better examination. A reputable jeweler should have no objection to this request.

Improving the color by utilizing a sputtering technique (also called "painting" the diamond). This technique is not frequently used, but stones treated in this manner do appear often enough to be worth mentioning. It involves sputtering a very thin coating of a special substance over the stone or part of the stone, usually the back, where it will be harder to detect when mounted. The girdle area can also be "painted" with the substance and create the same effect. The substance, like indelible pencil, also neutralizes the yellow and thereby improves the color by as much as *seven color grades,* but unlike indelible ink, *the substance will not wash off*. It can be removed in two ways: by rubbing the stone briskly and firmly with a cleanser, or by boiling the stone carefully in sulfuric acid. If the stone is already mounted and is coated on the back, using cleanser is not feasible. The sulfuric acid method is the only way. But please note: Using sulfuric acid can be extremely dangerous and must be done only by an experienced person. We cannot overstate the hazards of conducting this test.

Coating the diamond with chemicals and baking it in a small, lab-type oven. This technique also tends to neutralize some of the yellow, thereby producing a better color grade. This coating will be removed eventually by repeated hot ultrasonic cleanings, which will gradually erode the coating. A more rapid removal can be accomplished by the more dangerous method of boiling in sulfuric acid.

Erroneous Color Grading

Mistakes in grading of color may be unintentional (resulting from insufficient training or experience, or simply from carelessness), or they may be deliberate. Once again, you're safer considering the purchase of a stone that has had such important data as color described in a diamond grading report or certificate issued by a reliable gem testing lab. Many jewelry firms now offer diamonds accompanied by grading reports, often issued by respected organizations such as the GIA Gem Trade Lab (the most widely used in the United States). Diamonds accompanied by reports usually cost a little more but provide an element of security as well as credible documentation if you wish to sell this stone at some future time. If the stone you are considering is accompanied by such a report, be sure to verify that the information on the certificate is accurate (see chapter 11).

❖ Clarity Enhancement and Flaw Concealment

Clarity Enhancement

Be especially alert to the possibility that clarity may be enhanced. The two most frequently used techniques are *lasering inclusions* and *filling fractures*. In both cases, dark inclusions or cracks that might normally be visible—in some cases, very visible—are concealed, or become much less noticeable (these techniques are discussed in chapter 8). Be sure to ask whether or not the stone has been lasered or filled.

Flaw Concealment

Where possible, flaws are concealed by their settings. A good stone setter will try to set a stone in such a manner that the setting will help conceal any visible imperfections. For this reason, flaws near or at the girdle will have less negative impact on value than those found in the center of a stone; since most settings cover all or part of the girdle, they are simply less visible here. Indeed, a setting can make a flaw "invisible."

There is nothing fraudulent in using the setting to conceal something in the stone as long as the stone has been properly represented. The only danger is that both the customer and the jeweler may have missed the imperfection if the diamond was purchased already set in the ring.

Can concealment affect value? In most diamonds other than those that have been graded FL or IF, the presence of a minor flaw concealed under a prong will not affect the price significantly. However, given the difference in price between diamonds graded FL or IF and VVS, a minor blemish or inclusion hidden by the setting could result in the stone being improperly graded as FL, for example, rather than VVS. This would have a significant effect on value, especially if the stone has exceptionally fine color. For this reason, FL or IF stones should be *viewed unmounted*.

❖ Certification of Diamonds

As discussed in chapter 11, today most fine diamonds weighing one carat or more are carefully evaluated prior to being set by a respected laboratory and are issued a diamond grading report. Such reports certify the stone's genuineness and also provide important information regarding color grade, flaw grade, weight, cutting and proportioning, and so on. If you are considering the purchase of a very fine diamond weighing one carat or more and it is *not* accompanied by such a report, we would strongly recommend that you or the seller have the stone evaluated by the GIA or another respected laboratory prior to purchase if possible (if not, be sure the seller has put comparable information on the sales receipt; when you confirm everything with a gemologist-appraiser, the appraiser can submit the stone to a lab and obtain the report for you). We recommend getting the report even if it means having a stone that is already set removed from the setting and subsequently reset. Given the significant difference in cost that can result from a grading error in the rarer grades, we believe this procedure is worth the inconvenience and expense.

Unfortunately, the confidence of the public in stones accompanied by certificates has given rise to the practice of altering and counterfeiting them. While you can be relatively sure that "certificated" stones sold by reputable, established jewelry firms are what they claim to be, there are some suppliers and dealers who are seizing opportunities to prey on the unsuspecting.

Altering Certificates

Sometimes information is changed on an otherwise valid certificate; for example, the flaw or color grade may be altered. If you have any question regarding information on the certificate, a phone call to the lab giving them the certificate number and date will enable you to verify the information on the certificate.

Counterfeit Certificates

Producing a certificate from a nonexistent lab is an increasingly common problem. Stones accompanied by fancy "certificates" from impressive-sounding labs *that don't exist* are appearing more and more frequently. If the certificate is not from a recognized lab (see appendix), it should be carefully checked. Check to find out if reputable jewelers in the area have heard of the lab, or if the Better Business Bureau has had any complaints. If the lab seems legitimate, call to verify the information on the certificate, and, if all seems in order, you can probably rest comfortably that it is a legitimate report. In any event, the information provided should be verified by a gemologist to make sure the stone has not been damaged since the report was issued.

Some jewelers may not allow verification of an existing certificate by a little-known lab simply because they've been victims themselves or it isn't worth the inconvenience to them. In this case, you might ask the jeweler to get the stone certificated by one of the recognized labs. Many jewelers today are happy to provide this service. If not, then you must decide how badly you want the stone, how much you feel you can trust the jeweler, and what degree of monetary risk you can afford.

Switching the Stone Described on a Report

In some cases the report is bona fide but the stone has been switched. To protect both the consumer and the lab, some labs are taking advantage of ingenious techniques to ensure against switching. For example, a service called Gemprint™ utilizes laser technology to display a diamond's unique pattern of reflection and then records it photographically. The result is an electronic "fingerprint" of the diamond, which can be used for identification purposes (see chapter 28). In addition, the GIA can now actually *inscribe its report number*, which is visible only under magnification, directly onto the diamond itself, along the girdle. By so doing, one can very easily be sure a specific report was issued for a specific stone (but the inscription is no guarantee that the clarity of the diamond matches the report; it could have been damaged subsequent to the issuance of the report). There is an additional nominal fee for this service.

In the absence of an inscription, one clue to a switched stone might be provided by comparing the carat weight and dimensions given on the report. If the measurements and weight match exactly, the probability is slim that the stone has been switched, provided the report hasn't been altered. But it's always a good idea to contact the lab to confirm the details of the report, and then double-check all the information. If the measurements don't match, a gemologist can determine whether or not the report was issued for the same stone by examining the type and placement of inclusions or blemishes described on the report.

Unfortunately, if the stone has been mounted, it may be difficult to get precise measurements to compare. In this case, if there is any cause for suspicion, you may be taking a risk to buy the stone unless the seller allows you to have the stone removed from the setting and both the report and the stone verified by a qualified gemologist-appraiser. This arrangement requires an understanding in writing that the stone can be returned within a certain time limit.

Always make sure in this situation, for both your protection and the jeweler's, that the jeweler writes down on the bill of sale or memo *all* of the stone's dimensions as best as can be determined: diameter, depth, and weight (or, in shapes other than round, the length and width, depth, and weight). This is to help ensure that you aren't accused of switching the stone after leaving the premises in the event you must return it.

❖ Baiting and Flamboyant Advertising

We've all seen come-on or misrepresentative advertising. Quite simply, it is advertising that lures the buyer into a store or into making a purchase. The Better Business Bureau, in their booklet, "Facts You Should Know about Jewelry," describes these practices very well. (This booklet is available upon request from your local Better Business Bureau.)

❖ Is It a Diamond or a Diamond Impostor?

With the current popularity of antique, heirloom, and estate rings, often purchased from sources other than traditional jewelry stores, we think it is important to talk about diamond imitations, and how to spot them, since they are often found in old rings.

How can you tell if a stone is really a diamond? As we have said many times, unless you are an expert—or consult one—you cannot be sure about the identification of a stone. Nevertheless, there are a few simple tests you can perform that will show up most diamond impostors very quickly. Here are a few things to look for.

Is newsprint readable or observable through the stone? If the stone is a round, modern-cut stone and is unmounted, or mounted in such a way as to allow you to place it table-down over some small newsprint, check whether you can see or read any portion of the lettering. If so, it is not a diamond. Refraction of light within a genuine diamond is such you will not be able to see any of the letters in the newsprint.

Is the stone glued into the setting? Diamonds are seldom glued in; rhinestones often are.

Is the back open or closed? If the stone is a properly set diamond, the back of the setting will usually be open, allowing you to readily see a portion of the pavilion. Some *antique pieces* containing rose-cut or single-cut diamonds may have closed backs, and some of today's finest custom designers may use a closed-back technique. Otherwise, if a piece has a closed back it could be rhinestone, the back being closed to conceal foil applied to the back of the stone to create greater brilliance.

Recently a young woman called and asked if we would examine an antique diamond ring she'd inherited from her great-grandmother. She mentioned that as she was cleaning it, one of its two diamonds had fallen out of the setting, and inside the setting she saw what she described as pieces of "mirror." She added, "Isn't that strange?" Of course, our suspicions were immediately aroused, and upon examination of the piece, they were completely confirmed.

When we saw the ring, we could immediately understand why she felt it was a valuable heirloom. It was beautiful, with a classic design. It held two "diamonds" appearing to be approximately one carat each. The ring mounting was finely worked platinum filigree. But the design of the mounting, which had been common in her great-grandmother's day, made viewing the stones from the side of the ring almost impossible. The top of the stone and the beautiful platinum work were visible, but little more. Furthermore, the back was not completely enclosed; a small, round hole would easily have led to the assumption that the stones were the real thing, since the setting wasn't completely closed, as were most imitations at that time. The "set" diamond appeared to be a well-proportioned "old-mine" cut with very good color. The loose stone, however, with some of the "shiny stuff" still clinging to it, lacked brilliance and fire.

This was one of the finest examples of fraud we had seen in a long time. The "stones" were well cut and proportioned; the mounting was beautifully worked in a precious metal; the stones were held by very small prongs, which was typical of good design at that time. But inside the mounting, backing the stones, was silver foil. They were not genuine diamonds, but foil-backed glass!

The use of silver foil is an effective method to "create" a diamond. It acts as a mirror to reflect light so that the stone appears so brilliant and lively that it can pass as a diamond. The foiling seen today consists of making the back facets into true mirrors and then giving the backs of these mirrors a protective coating of gilt paint. These are then set in jewelry so that their backs are hidden.

It's a sad story but not an altogether uncommon one. We don't know how many more rings as cleverly done as this one exist today, but approximately 5 percent of the antique jewelry we see is set with fake gems. Fine glass imitations (often referred to as "paste") have been with us since the Venetians of the Renaissance period perfected the art of glassmaking; fraud, unfortunately, has been with us since time immemorial. Don't allow yourself to be deluded into believing that something you possess is "genuine" simply because it is "antique" or has "been in the family" for a long time.

How many facets are visible on the top? In cheaper glass imitations only nine top facets are usually visible, as opposed to thirty-three visible top facets in a diamond of "good" simulation. Single-cut or Swiss-cut diamonds (see chapter 4) will also show only nine facets on top, but they will be set in open-back mountings, whereas cheap glass imitations are usually set in closed-back mountings.

Is the cut symmetrical? Since diamond is so valuable and symmetry so important to its overall appearance and desirability, the symmetry of the faceting on a diamond will be very carefully executed, whereas in diamond imitations the symmetry of the facets may be sloppy. For example, the eight kite-shaped facets (sometimes called bezel facets) will often be missing one or more points on the side, or on the top or bottom, showing a small straight edge rather than a point. This is sloppy faceting and can be an important indication that the stone in question is not a diamond, since it indicates that the cutter did not take proper care. It should be noted that some poorer-grade or old-cut diamonds may also show sloppiness.

Are the crown and the pavilion of the stone properly aligned? While occasionally a diamond may show partial misalignment, imitations are frequently and often badly misaligned.

Are the facet edges or faces scratched, chipped, or worn? Diamond imitations include some stones that are very soft and/or brittle, such as zircon, GGG (a man-made imitation), Fabulite (a man-made diamond simulation also known as Wellington Diamond), and glass. Due to their lack of hardness and, in the case of zircon, brittleness, these imitations show wear easily, and one can often detect scratches or chips on the facet edges or faces that would not be seen in diamond. The edges are somewhat more vulnerable, and scratches or chips may be more easily seen there, so check the edges first. Then check the flat faces for scratches. Check areas that would be most exposed and areas around the prongs, where a setter might accidentally have scratched the stone while setting it.

Zircon, a stone found in nature that is often confused with cubic zirconia (CZ), a man-made imitation, is hard but very brittle, so it will almost always show chipping at the edges of the facets if the stone has been worn in jewelry for a year or more. Glass and Fabulite will also show scratches after minimal exposure to handling and wear. Fabulite further differs from diamond in its fire; it will show even *more* fire than diamond, but with a strong bluishness to it.

In addition, with a very good eye or the aid of a magnifier, you can examine the lines or edges where the facets come together in these imitation materials. In diamond, these facet edges are very sharp because of the stone's spectacular hardness. In most imitations, however, since the stone is so much softer, the final polishing technique rounds off these edges, and that sharpness is absent.

Some diamond look-alikes, however, are more durable and resistant to noticeable wear. These include colorless synthetic spinel, colorless synthetic sapphire, colorless quartz, YAG (another man-made imitation), and CZ. While these may scratch or chip over time with regular wear, scratches or chips are not as numerous and will be less noticeable.

❖ An Important Word about Cubic Zirconia and Its Latest Rival—Synthetic Moissanite!

Diamond imitations have been made for hundreds of years, but the latest are much more convincing than previous attempts. Two of the most recent—cubic zirconia and synthetic moissanite—have been mistaken for diamond and merit some special discussion.

Cubic Zirconia

Cubic zirconia (CZ) is considered by most people to be the best diamond imitation available, so good that many people, even jewelers, have mistaken it for diamond. Shortly after its appearance, several well-known Washington, D.C., jewelers found themselves stuck with CZ instead of the one-carat diamonds that had actually been in their inventory. The crooks were very clever. A well-dressed couple would arrive at the diamond counter and ask to see various one-carat round, brilliant-cut loose diamonds. Because of their fine appearance and educated manner, the jewelers relaxed their guard. The couple would then leave, not making a purchase decision just then, but promising to return. When the jewelers went to replace their merchandise, something didn't seem quite right. Upon close examination, the jewelers discovered that the "nice couple" had pocketed the genuine diamonds and substituted CZ!

CZ is almost as brilliant as diamond, has even greater fire (which masks its lesser brilliance), and is relatively hard, giving it good durability and wearability. CZ is also being produced today in fancy colors—red, green, blue, and yellow. Although it makes a nice diamond "alternative," it is normally not considered a choice for the engagement ring. Most jewelers today test their diamond inventory with electronic diamond testers and are unlikely to sell a CZ as diamond, but since there have been cases where a CZ ring has been inadvertently mixed in with genuine diamond rings, we will take a moment to discuss how you can make sure *you* know what you are buying.

How Can You Spot a CZ?

It is unlikely you will need to check for CZ if buying your diamond from a reputable jeweler, but if you are considering an antique or heirloom ring from some other source, keep in mind that the original stone may have been replaced with a CZ; we often encounter imitations in old pieces.

Some of the tests already discussed may help you detect a CZ. The following, however, may eliminate any remaining doubt.

If a stone is unmounted, or if it can be easily removed from the setting, have it weighed. If you are familiar with diamond sizes (see pages 77 and 78), you can estimate the diamond carat weight by its diameter. A loose stone can be weighed on a scale, which most jewelers and many antique dealers have handy, and you can determine how much it should weigh if it is truly a diamond. If the weight is much *greater* than the diamond weight should be, based on its diameter, then it is *not* a diamond. A CZ is approximately 75 percent heavier than a diamond. So a CZ that looks like a 1-carat diamond in terms of its size will weigh 1 3/4 carats; a CZ that looks like a 1/4 carat diamond in terms of size will weigh approximately 40/100 carat.

Look at the girdle. If the girdle is frosted, a subdued whiteness resembling slightly wet or oiled frosted glass will indicate CZ. Unfortunately, looking at girdles to differentiate between the appearance of frosted CZ and frosted diamond girdles requires considerable experience.

Use an electronic diamond tester. There are pocket-size diamond testers for under $175 that will tell you whether or not you have a diamond; most retail jewelers have them readily available. If you follow the instructions, they are easy to use. A diamond tester will instantly tell you that CZ is not a diamond. Most won't tell you what you have if it's not diamond, but only confirm whether or not it *is* diamond.

If after these tests you have some questions, take the stone to a qualified gemologist with lab facilities for positive identification.

Synthetic Moissanite—A "Sparkling" Newcomer That Fools Electronic Diamond Testers

The newest diamond imitation to enter the market is *synthetic moissanite*. It is not yet widely available, but several jewelry store chains now sell it and production is increasing. Its major advantage over CZ is its hardness; moissanite is much harder than CZ and other natural gemstones, although its hardness is still not comparable to diamond. It is also similar to diamond in brilliance, but it has a much more "fiery" appearance than diamond because its dispersion (ability to divide white light into its rainbow colors) is much higher than diamond. In terms of its color range, truly "colorless" stones (D–F) are not expected to become available in the foreseeable future; most are in the slightly tinted range (K–M), but stones may soon become available in the G to J range. This tint, combined with extremely high dispersion, gives synthetic moissanite a distinctive appearance that easily distinguishes it from diamond to the trained eye. For this reason, some think that CZ remains a better imitation, and CZ is much more affordable than synthetic moissanite.

A serious problem posed by synthetic moissanite is that *it fools electronic diamond testers;* when tested, electronic diamond testers erroneously indicate "diamond"! So it is very easy to understand how a jeweler might inadvertently buy and then sell moissanite as diamond, and we know of cases where this has recently happened.

Synthetic moissanite is a convincing diamond imitation that many find attractive. However, at this time, it could easily be mistaken for diamond—and couples must guard against buying it inadvertently as diamond. Fortunately, despite its ability to fool electronic diamond testers, a gemologist can quickly and easily separate it from diamond with simple tests because it exhibits characteristics not seen in diamond. In most cases, it can be quickly identified using only a jeweler's 10x loupe.

❖ Avoid "Bargains"—And Avoid Costly Mistakes

Take time to do your homework first, to learn what to look for and what questions to ask. Keep our recommended four-step procedure in mind, then shop carefully and compare stones being offered by several fine jewelers in your community. This will give you a chance to get a clearer sense of what something should legitimately sell for, decide whether or not something sounds "too good to be true," and make sounder decisions about which jeweler is asking a *fair* price. And remember: No one gives away a valuable gem. There are very few "steals" and even fewer people truly qualified to know a "steal" when they see one.

Comparison of Diamond & Diamond Look-Alikes

Name of Stone	Hardness (MOHS' Scale 1–10) 1 = Soft, 10 = Hardest	Read-through*	Degree of Disperson (Fire, Flashes of Color Observed)	Wearability
Diamond	10 (Hardest natural subtance in existence)	None, if properly cut	High; lots of fire and liveliness	Excellent
Strontium titanate (also known as "Fabulite" or "Wellington Diamond")	5–6 (Soft)	None, if properly cut	Extremely high; too high (much more than diamond); shows lots of blue flashes	Poor—scratches and wears badly
Cubic zirconia (CZ)	8.5 (Hard)	Slight	Very high; lots of life	Very good
Gadolinium gallium garnet (GGG; produced very briefly)	6.5 (Somewhat soft)	Moderate	High; almost identical to diamond	Fair—scratches easily; wears badly; sunlight causes brownish discoloration
Yttrium aluminum garnet (YAG; used extensively)	8.5 (Hard)	Strong	Very low; almost no visible display of fire	Good
Synthetic rutile (shows yellowish color)	6.5 (Soft)	None	Extremely high; lots of life—but strong yellowish flashes	Poor; scratches easily and shows excessive wear
Zircon	7.5 (Moderately hard)	Moderate	Good; lively	Fair—hard but brittle, so chips easily and shows wear equivalent to much softer stones
Synthetic sapphire	9 (Very hard)	Very strong	Very low; little life or display of color flashes	Very good
Synthetic spinel	8 (Hard)	Very strong	Low; little "life"	Very good
Glass	5–6.5 (Soft)	Very strong	Variable—low to good depending on quality of glass and cut	Poor; susceptible to scratches, chipping, and excessive wear
Synthetic moissanite	9.25 (Very hard)	None	Extremely high; much too high for diamond; higher than CZ	Excellent

*This technique—the ability and ease with which one can read print while looking through the stone—is reliable only when looking at round, brilliant-cut stones (although it is *sometimes* useful for ovals and some fancy cuts).

PART FOUR

Colored Gemstones in Engagement and Wedding Rings

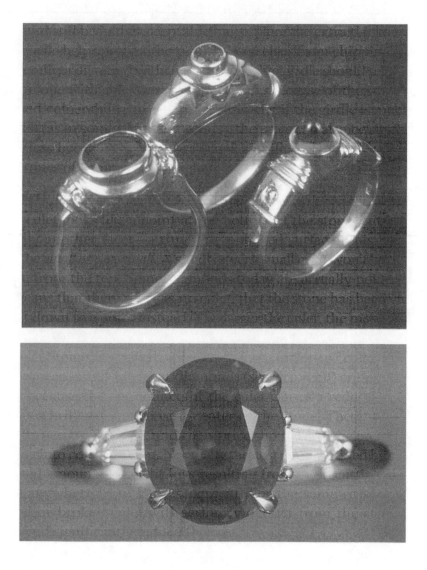

CHAPTER 14

The Allure of Colored Gemstones in Betrothal Rings

Fascination with colored gemstones dates back to the very beginning of civilization. Long before the discovery of diamonds, the blue sapphire evoked visions of heaven; the red of ruby was a reminder of the very essence of life. As early as Roman times, rings containing colored stones were prized as symbols of power and friendship. In fact, the most powerful—and most beloved—wore rings on every joint of every finger, reflecting the status of their position!

As betrothal rings, colored gemstones also hold an illustrious position. In addition to the beauty of particular colors, certain powers attributed to certain colored gems made them not only beautiful but also meaningful choices. We see many examples of colored stones in engagement and wedding rings, from many centuries ago to the present, used both alone and in combination with diamonds.

Following the discovery of diamonds in South Africa, which made diamonds more widely available and affordable, colored gemstones were briefly ignored during the earlier part of this century. While there have always been people who preferred colored gemstones despite the trends, colored stone engagement rings have only recently re-emerged as a choice for the modern bride. The selection of a sapphire and diamond engagement ring by His Royal Highness Prince Charles for Lady Diana, followed not long thereafter by his brother Prince Andrew's selection of a ruby and diamond engagement ring for Sarah Ferguson, sparked a revival of interest in colored gemstones for the bride-to-be.

While rubies, sapphires, and emeralds have historically been among the most coveted gems, particularly for important

A Renaissance ruby ring

A medieval sapphire ring

occasions, there are many alternatives in colored gems for today's bride, depending on budget and personal preference. Many find birthstones make an attractive choice because of the very personal connection to the bride herself. Keep in mind that most birthstones come in several colors. You may be surprised to learn that the color you associate with your birthstone may be only one of several colors in which the gemstone occurs. For example, most people think garnet is dark red and are surprised to learn it can be emerald green, mandarin orange, yellow, white, purple—virtually every color in the rainbow except blue. If you have discarded the birthstone as a choice because you don't care for its color, check out all the colors in which it may be available before making a decision. Some colors in a particular gem may be rarer and less readily available, and often costlier than better known colors, but your jeweler can work with you to discover your alternatives. One can combine a birthstone with diamonds, blending the symbolism of diamonds with the personal significance of the birthstone for a lovely, deeply meaningful, and often much more affordable ring.

In addition to birthstones, the choice of a particular colored stone may be connected to mystical powers, attributes, or symbolism with which the stone has been historically identified. There is an almost limitless wealth of information about colored gems, enough to stir the imagination of even the greatest cynic.

❖ Love Rings and "Sentimental" Jewelry

Throughout history, colored gemstones set in rings and other jewelry have carried hidden messages. We are seeing similar pieces being produced today. For example, a ring containing diamond, emerald, amethyst, ruby, emerald, sapphire, and topaz, arranged in that order, spells the word "dearest" if one takes the first letter of each word, thus carrying the sentiment that the wearer is more dear than any other to the giver; a ring containing pearl, ruby, emerald, and sapphire spells *"prés,"* which, in French, means "near" and suggests that the wearer is always near to the giver; amethyst, moonstone, opal, ruby, and emerald spells *"amore,"* which is Italian for "love." And so on. Such a ring can create a wonderful, "sentimental" engagement ring.

CHAPTER 15

The Magic and Mystery
of Colored Gems

The world of colored gemstones is endlessly fascinating. Since ancient times, colored stones have been thought to possess certain magical powers or the ability to endow the wearer with certain attributes. And for the couple who wants to create a ring with very personal significance, some of the attributes accorded to the gems described in this chapter might offer a unique way to do just that, by selecting a gem (or gems) with an appropriate "hidden message" or association.

Colored gems, because of the magical powers associated with them, achieved extensive use as talismans and amulets; as predictors of the future; as therapeutic aids; and as essential elements to many religious practices—pagan, Hebrew, and Christian. Emeralds were thought to be good for the eyes; yellow stones were believed to cure jaundice; red stones to stop the flow of blood.

The following is a list of the zodiacal gems passed on from very early history, and the powers or special characteristics attributed to each:

Aquarius (Jan. 21–Feb. 19)	Garnet—believed to guarantee true friendship when worn by an Aquarian
Pisces (Feb. 20–Mar. 20)	Amethyst—believed to protect a Pisces wearer from extremes of passion
Aries (Mar. 21–Apr. 20)	Bloodstone—believed to endow an Aries wearer with wisdom
Taurus (Apr. 21–May 20)	Sapphire—believed to protect from and cure mental disorders if worn by a Taurus
Gemini (May 21–June 21)	Agate—long life, health, and

	wealth were guaranteed to a Gemini if an agate ring was worn
Cancer (June 22–July 22)	Emerald—eternal joy was guaranteed to a Cancer if an emerald was taken with him on his way
Leo (July 23–Aug. 22)	Onyx—would protect a Leo wearer from loneliness and unhappiness
Virgo (Aug. 23–Sept. 22)	Carnelian—believed to guarantee success in anything tried if worn on the hand of a Virgo
Libra (Sept. 23–Oct. 23)	Chrysolite (peridot)—would free a Libra wearer from any evil spell
Scorpio (Oct. 24–Nov. 21)	Beryl—should be worn by every Scorpio to guarantee protection from "tears of sad repentance"
Sagittarius (Nov. 22–Dec. 21)	Topaz—protects the Sagittarian, but only if the Sagittarian always shows a topaz
Capricorn (Dec. 22–Jan. 20)	Ruby—a Capricorn who has ever worn a ruby will never know trouble

The preceding list of zodiac signs is from a Hindu legend, but there are others. An old Spanish list, probably representing an Arab tradition, ascribes the following stones to the various signs of the zodiac:

Aquarius—Amethyst	Taurus—Ruby and diamond
Leo—Topaz	Scorpio—Garnet
Pisces—[indistinguishable]	Gemini—Sapphire
Virgo—Magnet (lodestone)	Sagittarius—Emerald
Aries—Crystal (quartz)	Cancer—Agate and beryl
Libra—Jasper	Capricorn—Chalcedony

It was believed that certain planets influenced stones, and that stones could therefore transmit the powers attributed to those planets. A further extension of this belief can be seen in the practice of engraving certain planetary constellations on stones. For example, a stone engraved with the two bears, Ursa Major and Ursa Minor, would make the wearer wise, versatile, and powerful. And so it went. And from such thought came the belief in birthstones.

❖ The Evolution of Birthstones—A Natural Choice For a Very Personal Engagement Ring

The origin of the belief that a special stone was dedicated to each month and that the stone of the month possessed a special virtue or "cure" that it could transmit to those born in that month goes back to at least the first century. There is speculation that the twelve stones in the great breastplate of the Jewish High Priest may have had some bearing on this evolution. In the eighth and ninth centuries, the interpreters of Revelation began to ascribe to each of those stones attributes of the twelve apostles. The Hindus, on the other hand, had their own interpretation.

But whatever the reason, one fact is clear. As G. F. Kunz points out in *The Curious Lore of Precious Stones*, "there is no doubt that the owner of a ring set with a birthstone is impressed with the idea of possessing something more intimately associated with his or her personality than any other stone, however beautiful or costly. The idea that birthstones possess a certain indefinable, but nonetheless real, significance has long been present, and still holds a spell over the minds of all who are gifted with a touch of imagination and romance." And as a choice for the engagement ring stone, we also find birthstones among the traditions, offering a very personal alternative to diamond or other colored gemstones.

❖ Present-Day Birthstones

The following is the list of birthstones adopted in 1952 by major jewelry industry associations.

Month	Birthstone	Alternate Stone
January	Garnet	
February	Amethyst	
March	Aquamarine	Bloodstone
April	Diamond	
May	Emerald	
June	Pearl	Moonstone or Alexandrite
July	Ruby	
August	Sardonyx (Carnelian)	Peridot
September	Sapphire	

October	Opal	Tourmaline
November	Topaz	Citrine
December	Turquoise	Lapis lazuli, Zircon

Besides the lists of birthstones and zodiacal or talismanic stones, there are lists of stones for days of the week, for hours of the day, for states of the union, for each of the seasons, even anniversaries!

Anniversary Gift List

1. Gold jewelry
2. Garnet
3. Pearl
4. Blue Topaz
5. Sapphire
6. Amethyst
7. Onyx
8. Tourmaline
9. Lapis Lazuli
10. Diamond jewelry
11. Turquoise
12. Jade
13. Citrine
14. Opal
15. Ruby
20. Emerald
25. Silver Jubilee
30. Pearl Jubilee
35. Emerald
40. Ruby
45. Sapphire
50. Golden Jubilee
55. Alexandrite
60. Diamond Jubilee

❖ The Importance of Color and Its Mystical Symbolism in Gems

The wide spectrum of color available in the gemstone realm was not lost on our forebears. Not only did strong associations with specific stones evolve, but also associations of color with personal attributes. Over time, a fairly detailed symbolism came to join color with character. Those attributes, as they have come down to us, include:

Yellow	Worn by a man, denotes secrecy (appropriate for a silent lover); worn by a woman, generosity.
White (colorless)	Signifies friendship, integrity, and religious commitment for men; purity, affability, and contemplation for women.

Red	On a man, indicates command, nobility, lordship, and vengeance; on a woman, pride, haughtiness, and obstinacy.
Blue	On a man, indicates wisdom and high magnanimous thoughts; on a woman, jealousy in love, politeness, vigilance.
Green	For men, signifies joyousness, transitory hope, decline of friendship; for women, unfounded ambition, childish delight, and change.
Black	For men, means gravity, good sense, constancy, and strength; for young women, fickleness and foolishness, but for married women, constant love and perseverance.
Violet	For men, signifies sober judgment, industry, and gravity; for women, high thoughts and spiritual love.

❖ What Colored Stones Are Available Today?

Today, gems are worn primarily for their intrinsic beauty and are chosen primarily for aesthetic reasons. Choice is dictated more by personal color preferences, economics, and fashion than by any special attributes attached to the gems themselves. The world of colored gems today offers us an almost endless choice. New gems have been discovered and are being made available through the major jewelry companies. If you like red, there are rubies, garnets, red tourmalines, red spinels, and even *red* emerald and red diamonds; if you prefer blue, there are sapphires, iolite, blue spinel, blue topaz, blue tourmaline, tanzanite, and even blue diamonds. For those who prefer green, there are emeralds, tsavorite (green garnet), green zircons, green tourmalines, green sapphires, peridots, and even green diamonds.

❖ Select a Durable Colored Stone
For Your Engagement Ring

In selecting a colored stone for your engagement ring, it is important to choose a stone that is durable and to avoid those that are especially fragile. After all, you want your engagement ring to last a lifetime. Some gems, such as emerald, a gem with a reputation for being fragile, might not make the best choice as an engagement ring for a very active woman if she is going to wear it every day. Unless you can afford a very fine emerald, one that is relatively free of inclusions that might make it more vulnerable to breakage, you may want to consider a more durable green gemstone such as tsavorite (green garnet), which is also a rare and beautiful gem, with the added benefit that it is more durable, yet more affordable, than emerald. If emerald is the "gem of her dreams," and nothing else will do, be sure to choose a design that offers special protection for the stone.

These distinctive engagement ring settings will suit fragile stones and more active lifestyles.

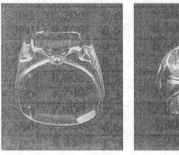

❖ Colorful Choices—A Guide to Popular Gems

The following chart shows what stones are available in various colors. Chapter 19 describes the stones and provides important information particular to each.

Now you will know what to ask the jeweler to show you—and don't forget to do a lot of shopping, looking, and asking questions; this is the only way you will develop an eye for the particular stone you are seeking and feel more confident about your own ability to see quality differences and understand how they might affect the cost.

Gem Alternatives by Color

Color Family	Popular Name of Stone	Gem Family
Red (from red to shades of pink)	*Ruby*—red, bluish red to orange-red	Corundum
	Garnet—several red color varieties	
	Pyrope—brownish red to red	Garnet
	Almandine—violet to pure red, orangy red-brown to brownish red	Garnet
	Rhodolite—red to violet	Garnet
	Malaya—brownish red to orange-red	Garnet
	Spinel—red to brownish red and pink	Spinel
	Pink sapphire—pinkish red	Corundum
	Zircon—brownish red to deep, dark red	Zircon
	Rubellite—red to violet-red and pink	Tourmaline
	Morganite—pink to orange-pink	Beryl
	Kunzite—violet-pink to pink-violet	Spodumene
	Red "Emerald"—red to bluish red to orange-red	Beryl
	Topaz—pink to violet-pink	Topaz
	Pink tourmaline—all shades of pink	Tourmaline
Orange	*Padparadsha sapphire*—pinkish orange	Corundum
	Topaz—brownish orange and yellow-orange	Topaz
	Spinel—brown to orange	Spinel
	Zircon—orange to golden brown	Zircon
	Garnet—a couple of orange varieties	
	Hessonite—orange-brown	Garnet
	Malaya—pink orange to brownish red	Garnet
	Spessartite (Mandarin)—yellow-orange to red-orange	Garnet
	Tourmaline—orangy brown, yellow-orange	Tourmaline
	Morganite—pale orange to orangy pink	Beryl

Color Family	Popular Name of Stone	Gem Family
Yellow	*Sapphire*—yellow	Corundum
	Beryl—golden yellow	Beryl
	Chrysoberyl—yellow, yellow-green, yellow-brown	Chrysoberyl
	Citrine—yellow to yellow-brown	Quartz
	Topaz—yellow to orangy yellow to sherry yellow	Topaz
	Tourmaline—yellow to greenish yellow to brownish yellow to orangy yellow	Tourmaline
	Grossularite—yellow to greenish yellow to brownish yellow	Garnet
	Andradite—honey yellow to greenish yellow	Garnet
	Zircon—yellow to yellow-brown	Zircon
Green	*Emerald*—yellowish green to bluish green	Beryl
	Tourmaline—several green color varieties	
	Verdelite—all shades of green	Tourmaline
	Chrome—rich green to slightly yellow-green	Tourmaline
	Paraiba—light to deep green to blue-green	Tourmaline
	Peridot—yellow-green to green	Peridot
	Zircon—green to yellow-green to gray-green	Zircon
	Alexandrite—daylight: bluish to blue-green; artificial light: violet-red	Chrysoberyl
	Sapphire—yellow-green to blue-green to gray-green	Corundum
	Garnet—a couple of green varieties:	
	Demantoid—yellow-green to emerald green	Garnet
	Tsavorite—yellowish green to bluish green	Garnet

COLOR FAMILY	POPULAR NAME OF STONE	GEM FAMILY
Blue	*Sapphire*—cornflower blue to greenish blue to inky blue	Corundum
	Tanzanite—violet-blue	Zoisite
	Spinel—gray-blue, greenish blue, true pastel blue	Spinel
	Aquamarine—light pastel to deep pastel blue to blue-green	Beryl
	Topaz—light pastel to deep pastel blue to blue-green	Topaz
	Zircon—pastel blue	Zircon
	Water sapphire—violet-blue	Iolite
	Tourmaline—a couple of blue color varieties	Tourmaline
Violet	*Amethyst*—lilac to violet to reddish purple to brownish purple	Quartz
	Sapphire—lilac to purple to violet	Corundum
	Rhodolite—red-violet to violet-red	Garnet
	Spinel—grayish violet to pure purple	Spinel
	Morganite—pinkish lavender to lavender	Beryl
	Tourmaline—light lilac to deep purple	Tourmaline

Art Deco period replicas provide heirloom feeling.

CHAPTER 16

Determining Value in Colored Gems

The mention of the word *gemstone* instantly conjures up exotic images of dazzling gemstones in overflowing treasure chests or fabulous crown jewels or important museum collections. It conjures up images of dazzling color and shimmering brilliance. But the term *gemstone* or *gem* is often used carelessly to describe almost any stone. In fact, most stones are not "gems." Even among that rare group often described as "the *precious* three"—ruby, sapphire, and emerald—we find stones that are not "gems." So what is the definition of a gem?

No one has come up with a universally accepted definition, but most agree that a gemstone is a mineral (or in some cases, an organic material) that posseses unusual *beauty, durability,* and *rarity.* And we would add one more factor: it must have cachet. That is, it must possess mystery, mystique, and glamour—those things that bring it into the world of our dreams and make us yearn to possess it.

While somewhat subjective, and not without some exceptions, the first three criteria are always at the heart of how we classify stones and determine whether or not they are gems. The first, and perhaps the most important, is beauty. If it isn't beautiful, why would anyone want to possess it? But beauty alone is not enough. A gem must also be sufficiently durable to withstand the normal wear and tear of use, to stand the test of time. This is at the heart of why gemstones figure in so prominently as heirlooms: they are durable. It is their durability that is the key to a gem's ability to retain its beauty and allure, to be passed on from generation to generation. And finally, we must consider the rarity factor, the most important in terms of valuation. Generally speaking, the rarer the gem, the more costly, and vice versa.

❖ The Four C's of Colored Gems

We've already discussed the Four C's to consider in choosing a diamond (see chapter 5), but colored gems have four C's of their own: color, color, color, and color! This statement may sound like an exaggeration, but not so much as you might think.

Generally speaking, the finer and rarer the color, the less impact cutting, clarity, and carat weight have on the value of the gem. On the other hand, the more common the color, the more impact these other factors will have.

❖ The Importance of Color

When we discuss color, we are not talking simply about "hue" (the specific color, such as red, blue, or green). Color science, and the evaluation of color, is a very complex area. But if you understand the various elements that must be factored into the evaluation of color, you can begin to look at colored gems in a totally different light.

Color is affected by many variables that make accurate evaluation difficult. Color is affected primarily by light—the type of light and its intensity. In addition, evaluating the color of a gem can be very subjective in terms of what is considered pleasing and desirable. Unlike diamond, there is no standardization for colored gemstones, although there are several systems for color grading and grading of colored gemstones in general, which are understood and used by gemologists. Efforts are ongoing to try to develop a universally recognized system for grading colored gemstones, but until that day arrives, nothing can replace the value of a trained eye, coupled with years of experience in the colored gemstone field.

❖ Key Elements in Describing Color

The color we see in gems is always some *combination* of the pure spectral colors—which range from pure red to pure violet—coupled with varying degrees of brown, white, black, and gray. These latter colors, in combination with the spectral colors, affect the *tone* of the color seen and make the classification of color more difficult. For example, if there is white present with red, you will have a lighter tone of red; if there is black, you will have a darker shade. Depending upon the degree of gray, white, black, or brown, an almost infinite number of color combinations can result.

Several elements are examined when we describe and evaluate color. They include the following:

- Hue—the precise spectral color (red, orange, yellow, green, blue, violet, indigo); to what extent is there any undertone of another color
- Intensity—the brightness or vividness (dullness or drabness) of the color
- Tone—how light or dark the stone is
- Distribution—the even (or uneven) distribution of the color

Both intensity and tone of color can be significantly affected by the proportioning of the cut. In other words, a good lapidary (gem cutter) working with a fine stone will be able to bring out its inherent beauty to the fullest, making it very desirable. A poor cutter may take the same rough material and create a stone that is not really desirable, because a poor cut will significantly reduce the vividness and alter the depth of color, usually producing a stone that is much too dark to be attractive.

In general, stones that are either very pale or very dark sell for less per carat. There seems to be a common belief that the darker the stone, the better. This is true only to a point. A rich, deep color is desirable, but not a depth of color that approaches black. You must shop around and continue to train your eye to differentiate between a stone with a nice depth of color and a stone that is too dark.

As a general rule, the closer a stone's color is to the pure spectral hue—that is, having no "undertone" of any other color diluting its purity—the better the color is considered to be; the closer it comes to a pure hue, the rarer and more valuable. For example, envision a color spectrum with absolutely pure color wedges from red to violet; if we are considering a green stone, the closer it comes to the pure green shown on a spectrum, the better; the stronger any undertone of another color such as blue or yellow, the less rare and less costly.

When considering the purchase of a colored gemstone, it is even more important to shop around to develop an eye for all the variables of color—hue, intensity, tone, and distribution. Some stones simply exhibit a more intense, vivid color than other stones (all else being equal), but only by extensive visual comparison can you develop your own eye.

Let's discuss the ruby, for example. Fine red rubies from Burma are perhaps the most coveted in the world, primarily because of their color. While not truly a "pure" red, fine Burmese rubies come closest to being a pure red. The tone may vary, however, from very light to very dark. As with most stones, the very light stones and the very dark stones sell for less per carat. Historically, Burmese rubies have been the most highly prized and the most expensive because of the desirability of their color and their scarcity.

Thai rubies can vary tremendously in hue and tone, going from a light to dark red with differing degrees of a blue undertone, giving them a purplish cast that sometimes makes them resemble garnet, a much cheaper stone. Some shades of Thai ruby are very expensive, others are much less expensive, but they are all less expensive than fine Burmese rubies because of the color difference.

African rubies have a tint or undertone of brown or orange, which makes them also much cheaper than the Burmese reds, but more valuable than the Thai ruby, depending on the color of the Thai ruby and how much brown might be present in the African ruby.

Ceylon (Sri Lanka) rubies are also very popular but are often on the light side; many are more accurately "pink sapphire." (Sapphire and ruby are the same stone, physically and chemically. The red variety is called ruby, while the equally popular blue—and all other colors—is called sapphire.)

Next, let's look at emeralds. Some of the finest emeralds today come from Colombia. The Colombian emerald is the color of fresh, young, green grass—an almost pure, spectral green with a faint tint of either yellow or blue. The finest emerald from Colombia has a rich, deep green (do not confuse with "dark" green) with a very faint undertone of blue; this color is considered the finest and most valuable color for emerald and the reason that Colombian emerald is so highly sought and prized.

Another source of fine emerald is Zambia. Zambian emerald is also a nice shade of green, but it has a bluer undertone that produces a slight darkening effect, which makes the color less valuable than that found in the finest Colombian. However, it usually has fewer flaws than the Colombian and cuts a more lively stone. Therefore, some of these Zambian stones, depending on depth of color, compare very favorably to fine Colombian emeralds aesthetically, while costing less per carat. Also, keep in mind that not all Colombian emeralds have fine color; today many Zambian emeralds have a color that surpasses many of the Colombian emeralds currently being mined.

❖ Lighting and Environment Affect the Color You See

The color of a stone can be drastically affected by the kind of light and the environment (color of wallpaper, color of shirt, fluorescent light, etc.) in which the examination takes place.

If examined under a fluorescent light, for example, a ruby may not show its fullest red because fluorescent lights are weak in red rays, which will cause the red in the ruby to be diminished and to appear more purple-red in body color. The same ruby examined in daylight or under incandescent light (such as an ordinary electric lightbulb), which is not weak in red rays, will appear a truer, fuller red. The same ruby will look even redder if examined against a piece of yellow-orange paper. Loose rubies are often shown in little envelopes, called "parcel papers," that have a yellow-orange liner to enhance the red color to the fullest.

Another example of color being affected by the type of light in which it is observed can be seen in the gem alexandrite. Alexandrite can be a bluish green gem in daylight or under daylight-type fluorescent light, and a deep red or purple-red under incandescent light.

The most important thing to keep in mind before buying a colored gem is this: *Look at the particular gem you are considering in more than one type of light!* Examine it outside in sunlight; look at it under a normal houselamp (lamp or light with normal lightbulbs); view it in shade or under the long fluorescent tubes that light most office buildings today. Most stores will have both fluorescent lighting and incandescent "spot" lights. Windows can provide daylight light. Perhaps a "broom closet" is available to give you the effect of lamplight at home in the evening. Also be sure to examine colored gems *in the type of lighting environment you will most often be wearing them.* In the case of the engagement ring, since it will be worn all the time, it is important to make sure you like the color of the stone in *all* lights.

❖ A Word about Color Distribution or Zoning

A stone showing *zones* of color

Even though zoning doesn't really describe color, it is very important in evaluating color. In some stones, color isn't always evenly distributed but may exist in zones—adding color to colorless areas surrounding the zone. This is frequently observed in amethyst, ruby, and sapphire. These zones may be noticed by looking through the side of the stone, moving it slowly, while tilting it and rotating it.

Sometimes a stone in the rough is colorless, or nearly so, but has a spot or layer of color. If the cutter cuts the stone so that the culet is in the color spot, the whole stone will appear that color. If there is a layer and the cutter cuts the stone so that the layer lies in a plane nearly parallel to the table, the whole stone will look completely colored. Evenness of color and complete saturation of color are very important in determining the value of colored gems.

❖ A Word about Color-Change Stones

Some stones exhibit a very strange phenomenon when viewed in different types of light: they change color completely. These stones are called color-change gems. There are color-change spinels, color-change sapphires, color-change garnets, and even color-change tourmalines! In these gem families, however, the color change phenomenon is rare. The gem alexandrite, on the other hand, *always* exhibits a color change, and its value is based largely on the degree of change. There are even color-change synthetics, such as the inexpensive synthetic color-change sapphire that is often misrepresented and sold as genuine alexandrite. Alexandrite is a bluish green gem in daylight or under daylight-type fluorescent light, and a deep red or purple-red under incandescent light.

❖ What is Fluorescence?

Fluorescence, a form of luminescence, is a property that some gemstones have that causes the stone to show a distinct color when exposed to ultraviolet rays produced by an ultraviolet lamp. The color of a stone viewed under ultraviolet

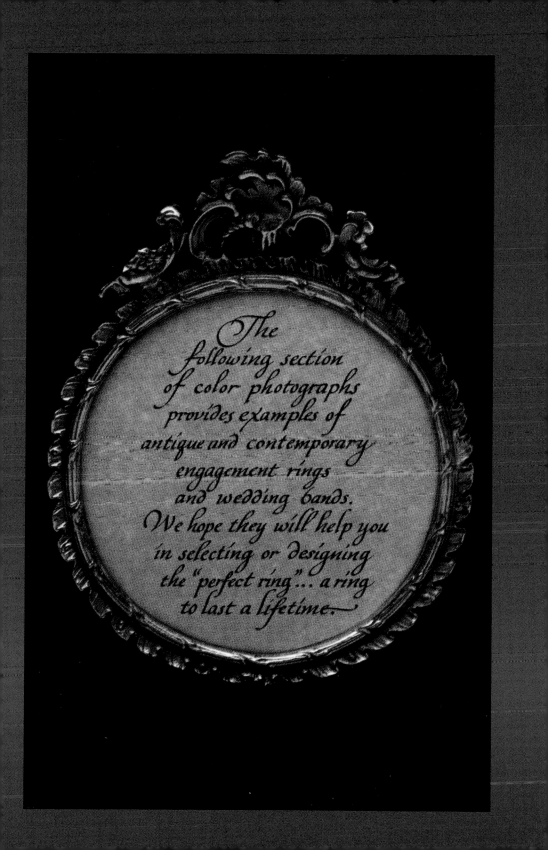

The
following section
of color photographs
provides examples of
antique and contemporary
engagement rings
and wedding bands.
We hope they will help you
in selecting or designing
the "perfect ring"... a ring
to last a lifetime.

Antique Betrothal Rings

Sforza Marriage Ring, 15th c.

Table-cut Diamond Ring, 15th c.

Hogback Diamond Ring, 15th c.

Fede Ring, 15th c.

Fede-type Gimmel Ring, 17th c.

Fancy Color Pink Diamond Ring, 17th c.

from the 15th to the 19th Century

Bali Ring,
late 19th c.

Ring set with
uncut diamond crystals, 15th c.

The Bottom of an
Intricately Enamelled
16th c. Ring

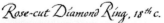

Table-cut Ring
17th c.

Gimmel Ring, 16th c.

Rose-cut Diamond Ring, 18th c.

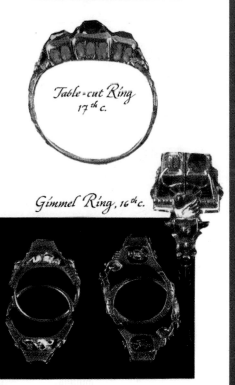

Antique and Heirloom Rings and Reproductions Move into the Limelight

Art Deco style captures the feeling of the 1920s.

Modern details coupled with engraved shanks create a lovely blend of old and new.

Art Deco style reflected in distinctive use of colored stones.

A Renaissance style is artistically presented in this new collection.

18th-century table-cut diamond ring with ornate shoulders.

Art Deco ring with rare *vivid* yellow diamond flanked by trapezoid-cut white diamonds descending into baguette- and square-cut diamonds.

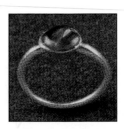

13th-century bezel-set cabochon sapphire and gold ring.

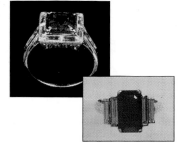

Mid-19th-century *natural* pearl and diamond ring.

Art Deco rings: emerald framed by baguettes; emerald-cut ruby flanked by straight baguette diamonds. Both classic designs of the period.

This new sapphire and diamond line recreates early 20th-century feeling.

This new collection evokes the lacy feeling of the Edwardian period (1901–1914), beautiful with or without an engagement ring.

Rings reminiscent of Great-Grandmother's, these intricate reproductions reflect detailing seen in the late 19th and early 20th century.

Some Classic Designs for Diamond and Colored Gemstone Engagement Rings

Interesting use of *princess*-cut stones for contemporary yet classic feeling.

Creative use of side stones and color adds interest and character.

Radiant-cut yellow diamond flanked by *trapezoid* side stones.

Classic emerald cut with traditional tapered *baguettes*.

Tiny diamonds and delicate metalwork delight the eye.

Natural color sapphire using three tapered baguettes scrolled across the shoulder.

Three elegant designs for colored gemstones

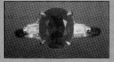

Sapphire accented by *bullet*-shape diamonds.

Sapphire with *half-moon* cut diamonds.

Classic Tiffany-style
six-prong ring.

Variations of the classic "solitaire"

Solitaire with a "twist."

Classic, yet
bold, with
diamond set in
partial bezel.

Classic multi-stone ring designs

Engagement rings and complementary gem-studded wedding bands: Prong-set 3-stone ring with 7-stone bar-set wedding band; solitaire with round diamonds channel-set in shank with channel-set diamond band.

Larger center stone
creates a soft
tapered effect.

Contrasting gold
adds distinction.

Ring with three
unusual *cushion*-cut
diamonds.

Design inspired
by color and
shape.

Oval and emerald-cut diamonds
accent colored center stones.

Unusual prong design lends
grace to 5-stone ring.

Winning Styles
from Leading Jewelry Designers

Tina Segal

Steven Kretchmer

Cornelius Hollander

Scott Kay

William Richey

George Sawyer

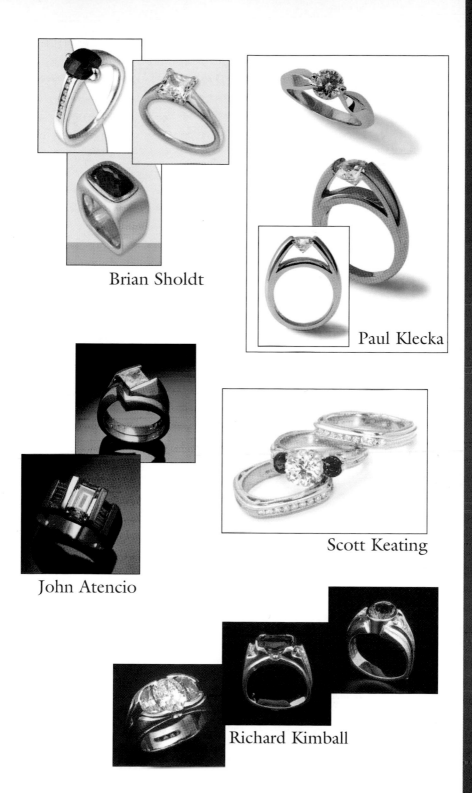

Brian Sholdt

Paul Klecka

John Atencio

Scott Keating

Richard Kimball

Winning Styles
from Leading Jewelry Designers

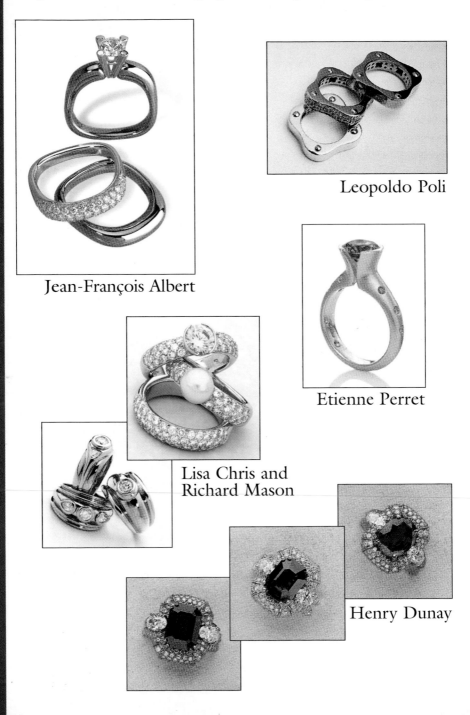

Jean-François Albert

Leopoldo Poli

Etienne Perret

Lisa Chris and
Richard Mason

Henry Dunay

Cathy Waterman

Whitney Boin

William Schraft

Haig Tacorian

Robin Garin

Martin Gruber

Chris Correia

Wedding Bands . . .
A Symbol of Endless Love

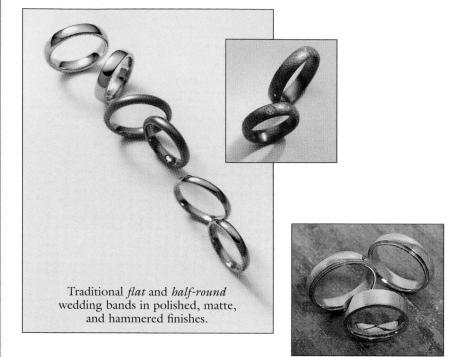

Traditional *flat* and *half-round*
wedding bands in polished, matte,
and hammered finishes.

Traditional flat band and
bands with beveled edges,
in contrasting matte and
polished finishes.

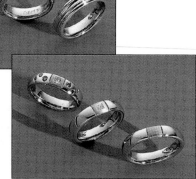

Modern gold bands combining
yellow and white, with and
without diamonds.

Wedding bands in a range
of widths, using diamonds in
varied sizes and colors.

Above left: Use of
baguette-cut diamonds in
channel setting.
Center: Emerald-cut
diamonds in bar-set band.
Both encircle the finger.
Right: Bar-set diamonds set
across top of finger.

Popular diamond wedding band classics are
available in every shape and may be channel-set,
bar-set, or prong-set. Equally popular for
important anniversary gifts.

New collection creates an
elegant, sophisticated look as a
wedding or anniversary ring.

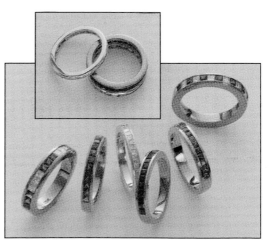

Elegant band with
round bar-set
diamonds encircling
the finger.

Classic use of colored stones, with or without diamonds,
are popular choices for wedding bands, anniversary
bands, and to commemorate the birth of a child.

Designer Wedding Bands

Richard Landi

Craig Drake

Etienne Perret

Haig Tacorian

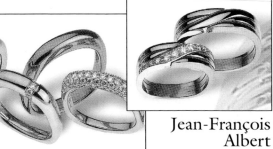

Jean-François
Albert

Chris Correia

Susan Michel

Steven Kretchmer

George Sawyer

Brian Sholdt

Michael Good

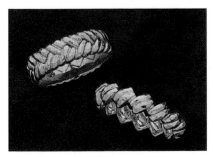

Henry Dunay

Whitney Boin

Popular Diamond Shapes...
Old & New

Sparkling, Classic *Brilliant* Cuts

Oval

Trilliant

Pear

Marquise

Round

Heart

New Heights in *Step* Cuts

Step-cut **trapezoids** are a nice complement to classic **emerald cut.**

Step-cut **half-moons** add a distinctive touch to new **Crisscut**®.

Elegance is easily achieved with the **Royal Asscher**® which often stands alone.

A square brilliant **radiant** cut.

The startlingly simple and luminous **Context**® cut.

Tiffany's new square **Lucida**™.

The whimsical **Lily Cut**®.

Above left: **Quadrillion**™ princess cut.
Above: Ring using Quadrillions to set off the round center stone.

Above left: **Spirit Sun**®, a revolutionary sixteen-facet diamond with pointed crown that achieves greater brilliance and reflectivity.
Above right: **EightStar**®, a "super ideal" cut exhibiting eight perfectly aligned arrows.

rays can be a more intense shade of the stone's normal body color or an altogether different color. If you have ever visited a museum and seen common, drab-colored rocks suddenly light up in psychedelic colors when the room is darkened and the "black light" (a type of ultraviolet light) is turned on, then you have seen this phenomenon known as "fluorescence." These minerals appear to be a certain color when seen in normal light, but when viewed under pure ultraviolet wavelengths, they reveal altogether different colors.

Ultraviolet rays are all around us. They are present in daylight (sunburn is caused by certain ultraviolet wavelengths) and in those long tubes that give us "fluorescent" light (but a different wavelength is emitted that is not harmful and does not cause sunburn). An *ultraviolet lamp* produces only ultraviolet radiation—long-wave ultraviolet and short-wave ultraviolet—and a gemstone's reaction to ultraviolet radiation can be an important key to gemstone identification and treatment detection.

Fluorescence is one of nature's most interesting phenomena to observe. However, ultraviolet radiation and its ability to stimulate fluorescence in gemstones is really not difficult to understand. You simply need to know that there is visible light and invisible light all around us. Light travels in waves, and the length of those waves determines whether they are *visible* or *invisible,* and what color we actually see. Some light waves are too short to be visible to humans; some are too long to be visible. The colors we see—red, orange, yellow, green, blue, and violet—have wavelengths that occur in a range visible to the human eye. Ultraviolet has wavelengths that go beyond violet, and are outside our visible range, so they are invisible to us.

Rays produced by an ultraviolet lamp are too short for us to see, but when they strike certain gems, properties within those gems *change the length of the invisible wavelengths into longer wavelengths so that they become visible.* When this happens, colors appear that were not visible before viewing with the ultraviolet lamp. When a gemstone produces colors that can be seen only with the ultraviolet lamp, we say it *fluoresces* or it has *fluorescence.* Some stones fluoresce only under long-wave ultraviolet radiation, some only under short-wave, and some fluoresce under both wavelengths but show a stronger reaction under one wavelength than the other. Whether or not a stone fluoresces, the particular colors in which it fluoresces, and the wavelength under which it fluoresces—long-wave or short-wave—is important to note and will be indicated on any colored gemstone report.

Fluorescence Can Affect the Color Seen in Different Lighting Environments

As mentioned earlier, fluorescence is an important key to the identification of many gemstones and can also be indicative of certain types of treatment. But even more important, it can affect the color we see in daylight and a stone's color trueness in all types of lighting. This is the case with Burmese ruby, for example. One of the characteristics that make ruby of Burmese origin so desirable is its fluorescence. Burmese rubies fluoresce red under short-wave, and very strong red under long-wave, whereas most Thai rubies have a very weak to inert fluorescence and this can affect the color we perceive in different lighting environments. Thai rubies and Burma rubies will both show a nice red color in "incandescent" light (a warm light in which any red stone looks great), but a Thai ruby will look much *less* red in daylight, whereas the Burma ruby—which fluoresces a good red under all ultraviolet wavelengths—will still show a good red in daylight because of the ultraviolet radiation present naturally in daylight!

❖ Clarity

As with diamonds, clarity refers to the absence of internal flaws or inclusions. Flawlessness in colored stones is even rarer than in diamonds. However, while clarity is important, and the cleaner the stone the better, flawlessness in colored stones does not usually carry the premium that it does with diamonds. Light, pastel-colored stones will require better clarity because the flaws are more easily visible; in darker-toned stones the flaws may not be as important a variable because they are masked by the depth of color.

The type and placement of flaws are more important considerations in colored stones than the presence of flaws in and of themselves. For example, a large crack (called a "feather") that is close to the surface of a stone can be dangerous because it weakens the stone's durability and breaks the light continuity. Also, it may show an iridescent effect that could detract from its beauty. (Iridescence usually means that a fracture or feather breaks through the surface some-where on the stone.) Such a flaw would certainly reduce the stone's value. But if the fracture is small and positioned in an unobtrusive part of the stone, it will have a minimal effect on its durability, beauty, and value. Some flaws actually help a gemologist or jeweler to identify a stone. There are also certain types of flaws that are characteristic of specific gems and specific localities and, again, may detract only min-imally from the value. In some cases, the presence of a particular flaw may provide positive identification of the exact variety or origin and actually cause an increase in the per-carat value. We should note, how-ever, that a very fine colored gem that really is flawless will probably bring a disproportionately higher price-per-carat because it is so rare.

❖ Types of Inclusions (Flaws) Found in Colored Gems

There are numerous types of flaws (inclusions) found in colored gems. Since certain ones are found in some gems but not in others, they provide the gemologist with an important means of positive identification in many cases. For anyone interested in learning more about flaws in colored gems, *Gem Identification Made Easy, 2nd Edition* (GemStone Press, Woodstock, Vt., 1998) provides over 70 color pho-tographs of inclusions seen under magnification and explanations on how to use basic pocket-size instruments to detect them and identify gemstones. (See appendix, "Selected Readings.")

If the flaws weaken the stone's durability, affect color, are easily noticeable, or are too numerous, they will significantly reduce the value. Otherwise, they may not affect price to any great extent at all. And in some cases, if they provide positive identification and proof of origin, they may actually have a positive effect on price, increas-ing the cost rather than reducing it (as with Burmese rubies and Colombian emeralds). And in the case of flawless colored stones, be-cause they are so rare, they may bring a disproportionately higher price-per-carat.

Again, as a consumer it is important to shop around and become familiar with the stone you wish to purchase and to train your eye to discern what is acceptable and what is not.

❖ Terms Used to Describe Optical Effects in Faceted and Nonfaceted Gems

The physical characteristics of colored stones are often described in terms of the way light travels through them, their unique visual effects, and the way they are cut. Here are a few terms you need to know:

- *Transparent.* Light travels through the stone easily, with minimal distortion, enabling one to see through it easily.
- *Translucent.* The stone transmits light but diffuses it, creating an effect like frosted glass. If you tried to read through such a stone, the print will be darkened and obscured.
- *Opaque.* The stone transmits no light; you cannot see through it even at a thin edge.

❖ Special Optical Effects

- *Adularescence.* A billowy, movable cloud effect seen in some stones, such as moonstone; an internal, movable sheen.
- *Asterism.* Used to describe the display of a star effect (four- or six-rayed) seen when a stone is cut in a nonfaceted style (star ruby, garnet, and sapphire.)
- *Chatoyancy.* The effect produced in some stones (when cut in a cabochon style) of a thin, bright line across the stone that usually moves as the stone is moved from side to side; sometimes called a *cat's-eye* effect.
- *Iridescence.* A rainbow color effect produced by a thin film of air or liquid within the stone. Most iridescence seen in stones is the result of a crack breaking the surface. This detracts from the value, even if it looks pretty.
- *Luster.* Usually refers to the surface of a stone and the degree to which it reflects light. Seen as the shine on the stone. Diamond, for example, has much greater luster than amethyst. Pearls are also evaluated for their luster, but pearls have a softer, silkier-looking reflection than other gems. The luster in pearls is often called orient.
- *Play of color.* Used frequently to describe the fire seen in opal, or the multiple flashes or pattern of color.

❖ Cut

Colored gems can be *faceted* or cut in the *cabochon* or unfaceted style. Generally speaking, the preference in the United States until recently was for faceted gems, so the finest material was usually faceted. However, this was not always the case in other eras and other countries; in Roman times, for example, it was considered vulgar to wear a faceted stone. Preference also varies with different cultures and religions, and the world's finest gems are cut in both styles. Don't draw any conclusions about quality based solely on style of cut.

Cabochon. A facetless style of cutting that produces smooth rather than faceted surfaces. These cuts can be almost any shape. Some are round with high domes; others look like squarish domes (the popular "sugarloaf" cabochon); others are "buff-topped," showing a somewhat flattened top.

Many people around the world prefer the quieter, often more mysterious personality of the cabochon. Some connoisseurs believe cabochons produce a richer color. Whatever the case, today we are seeing much more interest and appreciation for cabochons around the world and more beautiful cabochons than have been seen in the market in many years.

Cabochon cut
Note the smooth top of this *sugarloaf* cabochon.

Faceted. A style of cutting that consists of giving the stone many small faces at varying angles to one another, as in various diamond cuts. The placement, angle, and shape of the faces, or facets, is carefully planned and executed to show the stone's inherent beauty—fire, color, brilliance—to fullest advantage. Today there are many "new" faceted styles, including "fantasy" cuts that combine rounded surfaces with sculpted backs.

❖ The Importance of Cut

The cutting and proportioning of colored stones does *not* carry the premium that it does with diamonds; in diamonds, it is the brilliance and liveliness that makes the stone beautiful and desirable (since it is essentially color*less*), and it is the cutting that determines how lively and brilliant the stone will be. With colored gemstones, the color itself is what draws you to it, and the differences in color affect differences in cost more than any other single factor. In colored stones, cutting is important, but not in the same way as with diamonds. In colored gems, cutting is important for the following reasons and in this order of importance:

- Cutting affects the *depth of color seen*
- Cutting affects the *size* of the colored gem
- Cutting affects the *liveliness* of the stone

If the inherent color of a colored stone is good to begin with, a good cut will enhance its natural beauty to the fullest and allow it to exhibit it finest color and liveliness. If we take the same material and cut it poorly, its natural beauty will be lessened, causing it to look too dark, too light, or even "dead."

The deeper a stone is cut, the deeper the color will appear; the shallower, the paler. And, of course, it follows that if a stone is cut *less* deep, it will appear *larger in size* for its weight than another that must be cut much deeper to show a comparable color. This is important to understand because the depth of the cut thus impacts not only on the color seen in the finished gem, but also on its size. A gem with an inherently rich, deep, uniform color throughout the rough, for example, requires less depth in the cutting to "face up" a fine color; a stone with a weaker, or perhaps less well-distributed color, must be cut deeper in order to exhibit a color comparable to the first stone in this example. The less deep the stone must be cut to reveal a fine color, the larger it will look for its weight; the deeper it must be cut, the smaller it will appear for its weight.

The depth of the cut also affects the brilliance and liveliness of the finished stone. Even so, *the cutter will always cut the stone to get the best color possible.* In many cases, this means cutting the stone deeper than it should be cut to get the best brilliance, or in some cases, more shallowly than would be ideal in terms of brilliance. Here again, the better the color, the less impact "brilliance" has on value; the less fine the color, the more important its brilliance, which will add character and personality to the stone to help compensate for the less fine color.

In many cases, the problem is that the cutter wants to get the biggest stone from the rough and cuts a stone with fine color overly deep to get a heavier stone; these stones may appear overly dark when finished and actually sell for less per carat than if they had been cut more shallowly; such stones can often be re-cut into more beautiful stones, with a greater value per carat, so that the value remains the same (sometime even more) even though it may weigh less after recutting.

Generally speaking, however, when we examine a colored stone that looks lively to our eye and has good color—not too dark and not too pale—we can assume that the cut is reasonably good. If the stone's color is poor, or if it lacks liveliness, we must immediately examine it for proper cut. If it has been cut properly, we can assume the basic material was poor. However, the material may be very good and the cutting poor; in such cases, it may be possible to recut the stone into a beautiful gem.

While most people don't wish to become involved in recutting a stone, and this is something you probably wish to avoid when shopping for a lovely stone for your engagement ring, it may be useful to know if you are working with an "heirloom" stone—one passed down through the family—or are considering an estate piece. If such is the case, a fine jeweler, gemologist-appraiser, or local lapidary club member can steer you to someone who can tell you whether or not you can improve the appearance of a stone, and its value, by recutting it.

❖ Cutting and Proportioning in Colored Stones— A Few Considerations

To help you make a wiser choice when considering a colored gemstone, it might be useful to ask yourself the following questions:

Is the shade pleasing, and is the stone lively and brilliant? If the answer is yes to both considerations, then the basic material is probably good, and you must make a decision based on your own personal preferences and budget.

Is the color too light or too dark? If so, and if the cut looks good, the basic uncut material was probably too light or too dark. Consider purchasing it if it is personally pleasing, but only if the price is right (significantly lower than stones of better color). This is something you should be able to determine after spending some time shopping around for the particular stone in which you are interested, paying attention to differences in "tone."

Is its brilliance even, or are there dead spots or flat areas? If the brilliance is not uniform, or the stone looks dead or flat, it may be the result of poor cutting, poor material, or the wrong cut for the particular stone. For example, tourmaline cut in a traditional emerald-cut may look flat, while special faceting on the back can add tremendous brilliance. Such stones should sell for much less. If the color is wonderful, and the overall personality of the stone still appeals to you, however, it may be more affordable and still make an attractive engagement ring.

Is the stone cut so shallow that its wearability is reduced? If the stone is cut too shallow, too thin, it may not be feasible to wear it in a ring.

Will this stone be prone to collecting dirt or grease? This is an important consideration for you because an engagement ring will be worn daily. In shallowly cut *pastel or light-colored stones,* such as aquamarine, zircon, amethyst, and topaz, *the apparent body color and brilliance are diminished considerably if grease or dirt collects on the back side.* This is often the case with a ring worn daily and subjected to cooking, dishwashing, cosmetic application, bath oils, etc., and these stones will need to be frequently cleaned.

❖ Weight

All gems are weighed in carats, except pearls and coral. (Pearls and coral are sold by the grain, momme, and millimeter. A grain is 1/4 carat; a momme is 18.75 carats.) Normally, the greater the weight, the greater the value per carat, unless we reach unusually large sizes—in excess of 50 carats—after which size may become prohibitive for use in a ring and price-per-carat may drop because such large sizes are more difficult to sell (unless it is a rare stone in that size).

Also, remember again not to confuse weight with size. Some stones weigh more than others; the density (specific gravity) of the basic material is heavier. A 1-carat ruby will have a different size than a 1-carat emerald or a 1-carat diamond. Some stones are readily available in large sizes (over 10 carats), such as tourmaline. For other stones—precious topaz, emerald, alexandrite, demantoid and tsavorite garnets, ruby, and red beryl—gem material in sizes over 5 carats may be very rare and considered large, and will command a disproportionately higher price. With these stones a 10-carat stone can command any price—a king's ransom. A 30-carat blue diamond was sold in 1982 for $9 million; imagine what it might bring today!

Scarcity of certain sizes among the different colored stones affects the definition of "large" in the colored-gem market. A fine 5-carat alexandrite or ruby is a very large stone; an 18-carat tourmaline is a nice size stone. As with diamonds, stones under 1 carat sell for less per carat than stones of 1 carat or more. But here it becomes more complicated. The definition of "large" or "rare" sizes differs tremendously, as does price, depending on the stone. For example, an 8-carat tourmaline is an average-size stone, fairly common, and will be priced accordingly. A 5-carat tsavorite is extremely rare and will command a price proportionately much greater than a 1-carat stone. Precious topaz used to be readily available in 20-carat sizes and larger, but today even 10-carat stones of very fine color are practically nonexistent and their price has jumped tremendously.

Keep in mind also that *the depth of the cut will affect the size you see.* A 2-carat stone that has been cut very deep will look much smaller than one that is cut less deep. In fact, we've seen 1-carat stones that look larger than 2-carat stones that are cut too deep.

❖ Colored Gemstone Certificates

Systems for grading colored gemstones are not yet established worldwide. As a result, certificates or grading reports for colored gemstones vary widely in the information provided. Reports for colored stones have a more limited value in some respects than diamond reports, which are widely relied on to describe and confirm diamond quality using precise, universally accepted standards. Nonetheless they are *very* important.

Today's new-type synthetics, newly discovered gemstone materials, and increased use of treatments are creating a need for reports that verify *identity* (the type of gem), *genuineness* (whether it is synthetic or not), whether *natural* or *treated*, and, if treated, the *type* and *degree of treatment.*

If considering the purchase of any expensive colored gemstone today, especially gems of unusual size or exceptional quality and rarity, we recommend obtaining a report from a recognized laboratory (see appendix). The most widely recognized reports for colored gemstones include those issued in the United States by American Gemological Laboratories (AGL), Gemological Institute of America (GIA) Gem Trade Laboratory, and American Gem Trade Association (AGTA) Gemological Testing Center; in Switzerland, leading firms are Laboratory Gübelin and Schweizerische Stiftung für Edelstein-Forschung (SSEF); in the United Kingdom, the Gemmological Association and Gem Testing Laboratory of Great Britain; in

Belgium, Hoge Raad voor Diamant (HRD).

At the least, colored gemstone reports should identify the gemstone and verify whether it is natural or synthetic. You can also request a *grading report,* which will provide, in addition to identity, a full description of the stone and a rating of the color, clarity, brilliance, and other important characteristics. Just keep in mind that there is no universally accepted grading system, so each lab uses its own. Nonetheless, they provide important information pertaining to the stone's quality. This information is always useful for insurance purposes and can also be helpful if you are comparing several stones with an eye toward purchase. Also, depending on the information the gemologist can obtain from the gemstone during examination, some laboratories will indicate country of origin, if requested. The AGL, the AGTA Lab, SSEF, and Laboratory Gübelin will indicate origin when possible; GIA will not indicate country of origin.

Treatment disclosure is essential. Whether or not a gem has been treated and, if so, the degree of treatment, affect value and durability as well as appearance. Furthermore, it is important to know whether or not the treatment is permanent and whether it necessitates special care. Regardless of the type of report, treatment information should be included. *"Quality" or "origin" reports that omit information related to treatments are insufficient to make sound decisions.*

In the past few years we have begun to see "treatment" or "enhancement" reports. These reports confirm identity and genuineness and also include important information pertaining to treatments. They indicate whether or not the color and clarity have been enhanced. In addition, they include the degree of enhancement—such as faint, moderate, extensive, or a similar description. In some cases, the report will indicate the type of treatment or filler if there are sufficient gemological data, but sometimes these data are not available without very sophisticated equipment that many labs do not have. An "enhancement" report alone is often sufficient to make a purchase decision, since your own eye may be able to provide the rest of the information you need—especially if you have taken sufficient time to look at and compare lots of stones.

Fees for colored gemstone reports vary depending on the type of gem; the type of report requested; and the time, skill, and gemological equipment necessary to perform conclusive tests. An estimate can usually be obtained by making a telephone call to the laboratory. When you are considering a colored gemstone that is accompanied by a report, keep in mind the different types of reports available. Also keep in mind that the information provided on the report is only as reliable as the gemologist performing the evaluation, so be sure the report is issued by a respected laboratory; if in doubt, check with one of the labs listed in the appendix to see if they are familiar with the laboratory in question. Next, ask yourself what the report is really telling you—is it confirming identity and genuineness only? If so, remember that *quality* differences and treatments have the greatest effect on value. A genuine one-carat ruby, sapphire, or emerald can sell for $10 or $10,000 or more, depending on the quality of the particular stone and whether or not it has been treated. *Being genuine doesn't mean a stone is valuable.*

Take time to look at many stones, ask questions, and make comparisons. In this way you can develop a good eye and an understanding of the differences that affect quality rating, beauty, and value.

❖ A Note on Gemstone Prices

Here we do not provide a guide to colored gemstone pricing, because there is no universal grading system, and very subtle differences in color and clarity can affect prices significantly. It is especially important to become familiar with the gemstone you seek and compare prices among gemstones of comparable quality to develop your own eye for quality differences and their impact on cost. Be sure to ask the questions we suggest in chapter 26. For comparative price *ranges* see *Colored Gemstones: The Antoinette Matlins Buying Guide.*

American Gemological Laboratories

Olympic Tower
645 Fifth Avenue
New York, N.Y. 10022
(212) 935-0060
(212) 935-0071

Colored Stone Certificate

CERTIFICATE NO: CS SAMPLE

DATE: 25 February 1993

IDENTIFICATION: Natural Sapphire, Kashmir*

SHAPE AND CUT: Cushion Antique Mixed Cut

CARAT WEIGHT: 2.24 Cts.

MEASUREMENTS: 8.61 x 6.08 x 4.65 mm.

COLOR GRADE: 4/85*

Color Rating/Tone 4/80-85

Color Scan $B_{70}V_{15}G/Gy_{15}$

Light Source Duro-Test: Vita Lite

COMMENTS: *Total quality integration rating: Excellent. *Based on available gemological information, the origin of this material would be classified as Kashmir. *No significant gemological evidence of heat induced appearance modification present. *Faint to moderate color zoning?, texture and moderate dichroic effect1 present.

CLARITY GRADE: MI_1^*

PROPORTIONS: Good (4)

Depth % 76.5%

Brilliancy % Range: 50-90%
Average: 80%

Finish Very Good - Good (3-4)

NOTE: All color determinations are subject to the color temperature of the light source and the color sensitivity of the observer.

The quality and commercial desirability of any color is determined by examining the interrelationships of all factors indicated under Color Grade. Conclusions may vary due to the subjective nature of colored stone analysis.

This report prepared by: **American Gemological Laboratories, Inc.**

Martin J. Anderson, G.G.

© 1978 American Gemological Laboratories, Inc. /F1977 A.H.D. Analytics Inc.

Color Rating (AGL)

1	2	3	4	5	6	7	8	9	10
Excellent		Very Good		Good		Fair		Poor	

Clarity Scale (AGL)

Fl	I1	I2	I3	VI1	VI2	I1	I2	I3	
Free of incl.	Lightly Included		Moderately Included			Highly Included			

Tone (AGL) (1 = Colorless, 100 = Black)

0	5	10	15	20	25	30	35	40	45	50
	V-Light		Light			Light-Med			Medium	

D1	D2	E1			
Excessively Included					

Proportions/Finish (AGL)

1	2	3	4	5	6	7	8	9	10
Excellent		Very Good		Good		Fair		Poor	

55	60	65	70	75	80	85	90	95	100
Medium		Medium-Dark				Dark-Vy Dark		

Girdle Diameter = 100%

Table %

Crown

Pavilion Depth

Girdle Thickness

Culet

Depth %

Proportions: Cutting

Note that this report provides all of the important information that one needs: identification, enhancement and quality information.

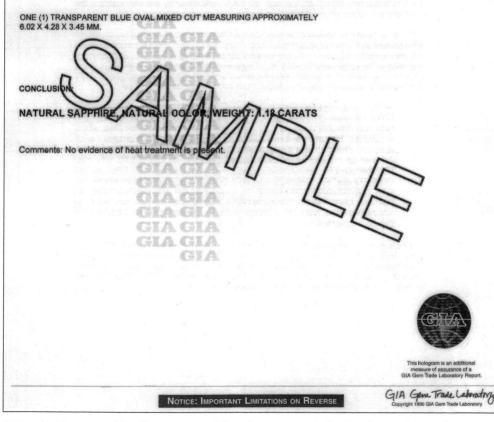

10348435

IDENTIFICATION REPORT

APR 08 1998

This Report is not a guarantee, valuation or appraisal. Its contents represent the opinion of the GIA Gem Trade Laboratory at the time of grading, testing, examination and/or analysis. The recipient of this Report may wish to consult a credentialed jeweler or gemologist about the information contained herein.

At the time of the examination, the characterization of the item(s) described herein was based upon the following as applicable: magnification, millimeter gauge, non-contact measuring device, electronic carat balance, color comparators, standardized viewing environment and light source, ultraviolet lamps, refractometer, dichroscope, spectroscope, polariscope, specific gravity liquids, ultraviolet-visible and infrared spectrometers, X-ray fluorescence spectrometer, gamma-ray spectroscopy systems, beta radiation scintillation detector, radiation survey meter, X-ray luminescence equipment, X-ray powder diffraction camera, X-radiographic equipment, and ancillary instruments as necessary.

ONE (1) TRANSPARENT BLUE OVAL MIXED CUT MEASURING APPROXIMATELY
6.02 X 4.28 X 3.45 MM.

CONCLUSION:

NATURAL SAPPHIRE, NATURAL COLOR, WEIGHT: 1.18 CARATS

Comments: No evidence of heat treatment is present.

This hologram is an additional measure of assurance of a GIA Gem Trade Laboratory Report.

NOTICE: IMPORTANT LIMITATIONS ON REVERSE

GIA Gem Trade Laboratory
Copyright 1996 GIA Gem Trade Laboratory

GIA colored gemstone identification report. Note the comments indicating that no clarity enhancement is present, but there is no information regarding overall quality.

AGTA GEMOLOGICAL TESTING CENTER

RUBY IDENTIFICATION REPORT

Date: SAMPLE
Report No. SAMPLE

The item described below has been examined by at least two professional staff gemologists of the AGTA Gemological Testing Center. The results of the examination are presented here subject to the limitations printed on the reverse of this report

Item Description: Loose Stone

Number of gems examined: 1
Color: Red
Transparency: Transparent
Weight (ct): 2.94
Dimensions (mm): 9.29 x 6.86 x 5.00

Shape: Oval
Cut: Mixed, Brilliant Crown
Enhancement: None, no indications of enhancement by heat[1]

Result: NATURAL RUBY

Origin: BURMA (MYANMAR)[2]

Comments: [1]It is rare for a ruby to have not been enhanced by heat. [2]The data obtained during the examination of this stone indicates that the probable geographic origin is as stated (see below for testing techniques).

The reverse of this page is an integral part of the report. It contains important information that may help in the interpretation of the information on this side.

Garry Du Tolt

Kenneth Scarratt

For and on behalf of the
AGTA GEMOLOGICAL TESTING CENTER

Tests Carried Out to Establish the Identity of the Ruby Described Herein							
Refractive index ☒	Specific gravity ☐	Hand spec ☒	Microscope ☒	Polariscope ☐	FTIR ☐	Others ☒	
Radiography ☐	Raman ☐	UVMS/NIR ☐	Image spec ☐	XRD ☐	EDXRF ☒		

American Gem Trade Association Gemological Testing Center, 18 East 48 th Street, Suite 1002, New York, NY 10017, USA
Tel: 212.752.1717 Fax: 212.750.0930

A sample AGTA report that provides identification, country of origin, and information indicating the ruby is *not* treated.

CHAPTER 17

Colored Gemstone Treatments

There is a wide variety of natural gemstones from which to choose today, but many gemstones sold have been treated in some way. Virtually *all* rubies, sapphires, and emeralds sold worldwide are now routinely treated in some way to enhance their appearance. Generally speaking, they are properly priced, and there is nothing wrong with purchasing a treated gemstone as long as you understand what you have and pay the appropriate price for it.

❖ Gemstone Treatment Is Routine Today

For hundreds of years mankind has been enhancing natural colored gems. In most cases the jewelry trade finds these practices acceptable because the prevailing attitude is that these treatments simply continue the process that Mother Nature started; all gems are exposed to heat, and many to radiation, as they are forming in nature. Today certain gems are routinely heated or exposed to some type of radiation to change or enhance their color and clarity, and pricing is based on the assumption that enhancement has occurred.

For an engagement ring, some prefer a gem that is not treated. Such gems are very rare today and are much costlier. Most are sought by collectors and connoisseurs. Nonetheless, they exist, and very fine jewelers may assist you in locating such a gemstone. If the color of a gem is very fine, however, and is represented to be *natural*, it should be accompanied by a laboratory report confirming this fact. Some of the best sources for fine, natural-color gems are major estate pieces that sometimes re-enter the market when well-known international auction houses such as Antiquorum, Christie's, or Sotheby's hold their "Magnificent" or "Important" jewelry sales. If considering a ring from one of these auction salons, however, be sure to ask the department head about treatments, and if you are seeking a natural gemstone, we advise you not to bid on any item unless there is a laboratory report that explicitly states whether or not the gemstone has been treated in any way.

Whether from an auction house or another source, fine rare gems with natural color will normally be accompanied by a gem testing report verifying that fact. Without a report, or any representation to the contrary, assume that the color of any gemstone sold today has been enhanced in some manner. When buying any expensive rare gem represented to have natural color, be sure it is accompanied by a report from a respected gem testing lab that verifies this fact, or make the purchase contingent upon getting a report.

❖ Types of Treatments Used Routinely to Enhance Colored Gemstones

While it is not really necessary for you to know the type of treatment with which a stone has been treated, it may be helpful to have an idea of the most routine treatments used. Here we will briefly discuss them, but keep in mind that in addition to these treatments, there are also treatments that are not considered "acceptable" within the trade. These will be discussed in the following chapter.

Heating. Subjecting certain gems to heating procedures is a practice that is hundreds of years old and is accepted within the jewelry industry as long as the change induced is *permanent*. Most sapphires and rubies are heated. The treatment may lighten, darken, or completely change the color, and simultaneously improve the clarity and improve the overall brightness of the stone. A skilled gemologist or gem testing laboratory can usually determine whether or not the color of these gems has been altered through heating techniques by examining the stone's inclusions under the microscope. Sapphire and ruby, for example, can withstand high temperatures, but often the heat causes small crystal inclusions present inside the stone to melt (improving the clarity) or explode. These altered inclusions then provide the evidence of heating.

It may be easy to determine that a stone *has* been heated, but it is sometimes impossible to know for certain that it has not been, that is, that its color is natural. Making this determination can require a high degree of skill and sophisticated equipment, often only available at a major laboratory such as GIA or AGL; even then, it may not be possible to ascertain definitively. Gemologists must carefully examine the internal characteristics of the particular stone. Sometimes they see an unaltered inclusion that would lead to a conclusion that the color is natural; other times they see an altered inclusion that indicates treatment; and sometimes the inclusions that one seeks to make a positive determination, or changes and abnormalities in them, simply are not present. When there is nothing inside the gem to indicate whether it has or has not been heated, we cannot be sure.

Radiation. Radiation techniques are relatively new. Frequently used on a wide range of gemstones, radiation is sometimes combined with heating. The effect is permanent on some stones and accepted in the trade; it is not acceptable on other stones because the color fades or changes back to its original color over a relatively short time. There are still some questions regarding radiation levels and the long-term effects on health. The Nuclear Regulatory Agency has been working to establish standards, and the GIA Gem Trade Laboratory now has a facility with the capability to test gemstones for "acceptable" and "unacceptable" radiation levels.

Oiling. Oiling has been used on emeralds routinely for many years to conceal the fine cracks that commonly occur in emerald as a result of the conditions under which it is formed in nature. These cracks look whitish and therefore weaken the green body color of the emerald; the film of oil that is absorbed by the stone eliminates this whitishness, thus making the cracks themselves "disappear" and simultaneously improving the color. This is an accepted practice and will normally last for many years. However, if the stone is put in a hot ultrasonic cleaner (which is dangerous to emerald and should never be used for any emerald), or any solvent such as paint remover, the oil may be removed from the cracks and the whitish areas become visible again, weakening the color. Should this happen, the emerald can easily be re-oiled and restored to its former appearance.

Fracture filling with epoxy resins. As with diamonds, fractures that break the surface of a colored gem can be filled with a liquid glass or glass-like substance, or with an epoxy-resin type filler. Fillers make cracks less visible and improve a stone's overall appearance.

Epoxy resin treatments are relatively new and involve a process whereby epoxy resin fillers are introduced into the cracks, often sealed in with hardeners. The net effect is the same as oiling an emerald, but epoxy resin makes it more difficult to detect a crack at all. This may be beneficial to the stone but may make accurate grading more difficult.

It is often difficult to determine exactly what type of treatment has been used on emerald, and the extent to which the treatment has improved the appearance of the gemstone, without submitting the stone to a gem testing laboratory with sophisticated equipment.

In the case of an emerald that is being selected for use in an engagement ring, which is usually worn every day, it is important to know whether or not there are potentially dangerous cracks that might affect the emerald's durability. For this reason, we recommend obtaining a gem testing laboratory report that verifies whether or not the emerald has been treated with oil or epoxy resin, and if so, whether or not there are any cracks that reduce the durability or wearability of the stone.

Diffusion treatment. Diffusion is a newcomer to the world of treated gemstones and is already surrounded by controversy. It is used primarily on blue sapphire but may also be used on ruby and fancy-orange or padparadscha sapphire (see chapter 19). Diffusion (sometimes called "deep diffusion" or "surface diffusion") is a process that alters the color of a gem by exposing the surface to certain chemicals (the same used by nature) and heating the gem for a prolonged period of time. The material being treated, however, is usually *colorless* or very pale, and *the beautiful color produced by the treatment is usually confined to the surface of the gem only*. If you sliced a diffused sapphire in half, you would see an essentially colorless stone, with a very narrow rim of blue along its perimeter. This could create a problem if the stone is ever badly chipped or nicked and needs to be recut or polished; the surface color might be removed in the recutting, leaving a colorless sapphire in its place. For this reason, **we do not recommend diffused sapphire for engagement rings,** although the treatment could be repeated, should this happen, to restore the original color. (When repeated on a previously diffused stone, the process requires less time, and the restored color is virtually identical to the original.)

A new process now allows color to penetrate into more of the stone, but at this time "deep" diffusion simply means the color penetrates a little deeper than in the earliest diffused stones, and color is still confined to the surface. Fortunately, the presence of diffused sapphire in the jewelry market should not cause alarm because this treatment can be detected by major gem-testing labs. Surface-diffused blue sapphires have been found mixed in parcels with non-diffused sapphires, and some may inadvertently have been set in jewelry and sold. So it is important to buy any fine blue sapphire only from a knowledgeable, reputable jeweler. We also recommend making the sale contingent on the stone not being diffused, and take it to a gemologist for verification. You or your jeweler can also submit the stone to a recognized gem-testing lab. If you find the stone is diffused, you should have no problem exchanging it, getting a reduced price, or obtaining a refund.

Diffused sapphires offer beautiful stones at very affordable prices (about one-sixth the normal cost), but since some care must be exercised with wear, we feel it is not as good a choice for the engagement ring as other choices might be.

❖ Affordable Beauty

Since many natural gemstones are so rare and costly today, the introduction of treated gemstones has provided a way for more people to be able to acquire a lovely gem at an affordable price. The most important consideration here, as in all purchases of gemstones, is to know exactly what you are buying. While some fraudulent practices involving treated stones certainly exist (see chapter 18), the selling of treated gemstones is perfectly legitimate so long as all the facts are disclosed, the type of treatment used for enhancement is acceptable in the trade, and all important representations are stated on the bill of sale. With these safeguards you can be reasonably secure about the purchase you are contemplating and enjoy the fine color and beauty of a treated stone for many years to come.

❖ A Word about Synthetics

Scientific advances and new technology have resulted in a whole world of *synthetic* gemstone materials, but it's important to understand that a synthetic is not an imitation. Technically, the term "synthetic" indicates that the material is made by man *using the same chemical ingredients found in natural products;* in other words, using Mother Nature's recipe. This means that a synthetic gemstone will have essentially the same physical, chemical, and optical properties observed in natural gemstones. From a practical standpoint, this also means that they will respond to various gem-identification tests the same way as natural stones. This can make them difficult to distinguish from the natural gem.

An imitation is also made by man, but not with nature's recipe, so it is very different physically and chemically from the gem it is imitating, and very easy to separate from the natural gem with standard gem identification techniques. For example, a glass "gem" is an imitation. Red glass could imitate ruby, but it resembles ruby only *in color.* A quick examination with a simple jeweler's loupe would reveal telltale signs that it is glass, and any gemological test would clearly corroborate this conclusion.

Today there are numerous synthetic gems, but they are not all produced the same way. Some are produced inexpensively, and although they are made with nature's recipe, they don't really look like the natural gem. They are made quickly, by a process very different from nature's ("flame fusion"). These are often confused with imitations because of their unnatural appearance and low cost. This type of synthetic is widely available today and has been made for almost one hundred years.

In recent years, technological advances have enabled scientists to create environments that come much closer to duplicating what is found in nature. As a result, crystals can actually be "grown" in laboratories, creating a product that very closely resembles the natural gem. These are called "flux-grown," "created," or "laboratory-grown" synthetics.

Unfortunately, synthetic stones are sometimes mixed with parcels of natural gems and are inadvertently sold for natural gemstones. The abundance of synthetic materials simply provides another reason to be sure to have the identity of your gemstone verified by an independent gemologist-appraiser.

CHAPTER 18

Fraud and Misrepresentation in Colored Gems

As stated previously, the occurrence of misrepresentation and fraud in jewelry transactions is low. Most jewelers are reputable professionals in whom you can place your trust. However, in the colored-gem market more misrepresentation occurs than in the diamond market, primarily because of the scientifically more complex nature of colored stones. So it is even more important for you to be aware of the deceptive practices you might encounter when buying a colored gem, both to protect yourself from the less obvious scams, and to better understand the importance of dealing with a reliable jeweler.

Take care to be sure that your gemstone is what it is represented to be. When buying an expensive colored gem, we cannot over-emphasize the importance of seeking verification from a qualified gemologist—preferably one with extensive experience in the colored gem market.

❖ Misrepresenting Synthetic as Natural

Today it is easy to find that a synthetic has been misrepresented as natural, especially in antique and estate pieces, but also in new jewelry. Synthetic gems have been manufactured for many years. Good synthetic sapphires, rubies, and spinels have been made since the early 1900s. Very good synthetic emeralds began to be produced commercially in the 1940s. These synthetics, while they looked like the real thing to the average consumer and were very attractive because of their affordable price, could be readily distinguished from the real thing by a competent jeweler.

Today, this may not be the case, particularly with ruby and emerald. While the older techniques for producing these synthetics are still used, as we mentioned earlier, new sophisticated methods have enabled the production of synthetic rubies and emeralds that are not readily discernible, because they do not possess the familiar characteristics common to the older type synthetics with which the dealer and jeweler are so familiar. In addition, many synthetics are mixed in with parcels of natural stones today and get inadvertently set into jewelry.

It is essential for anyone who is buying a fine gemstone to have an experienced gemologist verify authenticity—particularly with fine rubies, emeralds, and sapphires. Thousands of dollars may be at stake, for a jeweler can easily and *innocently* represent a synthetic as genuine because he or she bought it as genuine.

❖ Fracture Filling

As with diamonds, fractures that break the surface of a colored gem can be filled with a liquid glass or glasslike substance. The filler makes the crack less visible and improves the stone's overall appearance. A coloring agent can also be added to the filler to simultaneously improve the stone's overall color. Selling a fracture-filled gem without disclosure is not an accepted trade practice. To do so knowingly constitutes fraud, but it's being done nonetheless. Be especially careful where fine rubies are concerned.

❖ Dyeing

Dyeing has been practiced since ancient times. The gems most frequently dyed are jade, coral, lapis, and to a lesser degree, poor-quality star rubies, star sapphires, and emeralds.

❖ Simulated Stones

These should not be confused with synthetics. A simulated stone is usually a very inexpensive man-made stone, such as glass. These stones simulate the stone's color only and are very easily differentiated from the genuine. There are glass simulations of all the colored stones, and glass and plastic simulated pearls, turquoise, and amber are among the most common.

❖ Look-Alike Substitution

This practice involves misrepresenting a more common, less expensive stone for another rarer, more expensive gem of similar color. Today, with so many gems available in every color, both deliberate and accidental misrepresentation can occur.

❖ Foil-Backed Stones

This technique is not frequently encountered in modern jewelry, but anyone interested in antique jewelry should be aware of it. It is seen with both nonfaceted and faceted stones, set usually in a closed-back mounting. This technique involves lining the inside of the setting with silver or gold foil to add brilliance and sparkle (as with foil-backed glass imitating diamond), or with colored foil to change or enhance color by projecting color into the stone. Always be apprehensive when considering a piece of jewelry that has a closed back. While relatively common in antique jewelry, foil backing is also seen in modern jewelry.

We recently examined a heavy, yellow gold cross set with five fine, flawless emeralds that appeared to have exceptionally fine green body color. The stones were set "in the gold" so that the backs of the stone couldn't be seen. Our suspicions were aroused, because the emeralds were all flawless and the color was so uniformly fine. Upon closer examination it became clear that the green body color was projected into the stones by a fine emerald green foil backing, placed between the stone and the back side of the mounting. The stones were probably not even emerald, but near-colorless aquamarines. Since both aquamarine and emerald belong to the same mineral family (beryl—emerald is the name given to the rare green variety of beryl, while we call the more common blue variety aquamarine), an inexperienced jeweler or gemologist using standard, basic procedures to identify the stones could have erroneously identified them as fine emeralds.

❖ Composite Stones

Composite stones are exactly what the term implies—stones composed of more than one part. Composites come in two basic types. Doublets are composite stones consisting of two parts, sometimes held together by a colored bonding agent. Triplets are composite stones consisting of three parts, usually glued together to a colored middle part.

Doublets

Doublets are especially important to know about because, while widely used in antique jewelry before the development of synthetics, they are making a comeback today and reappearing throughout the jewelry market.

In antique pieces, the most commonly encountered doublet, often referred to as a *false doublet,* consisted of a red garnet top fused to an appropriately colored glass bottom. With the right combination, any colored gem could be simulated by this method. Garnets were used for the top portion of these false doublets because they possessed nice luster and excellent durability and were readily available in great quantity, which made them very inexpensive.

Another form of the doublet is made from two parts of a colorless material, fused together with an appropriately colored bonding agent. An "emerald" (sometimes sold as "soudé" emerald) can be made, for example, using a colorless synthetic spinel top and bottom, held together in the middle (at the girdle) by green glue. Red glue or blue glue could be used to simulate ruby or sapphire.

True doublets are created by fusing two *genuine* stone parts together with an appropriately colored glue to create a "larger" gem of better color than the original components. For example, we sometimes see emerald doublets composed of two parts of genuine *pale green*

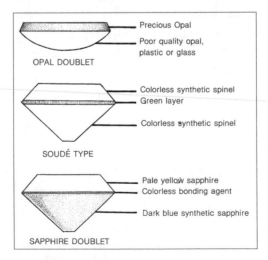

OPAL DOUBLET — Precious Opal / Poor quality opal, plastic or glass

SOUDÉ TYPE — Colorless synthetic spinel / Green layer / Colorless synthetic spinel

SAPPHIRE DOUBLET — Pale yellow sapphire / Colorless bonding agent / Dark blue synthetic sapphire

Composite stones (also called assembled stones)

emerald, fused with deep green glue to create a large, deep green "gem" emerald.

A clever version of a true doublet that we sometimes still encounter is a "sapphire" doublet composed of two pieces of genuine pale yellow sapphire fused together with blue glue. This creates an especially convincing "fine blue sapphire." The same techniques are used to make ruby doublets, although they don't look as convincing. And the same basic procedures can produce emerald doublets, using beryl instead of sapphire.

It is alarming to see the large number of ruby and sapphire doublets now being sold as genuine that consist of genuine tops—usually nearly colorless or a very inexpensive greenish brown color—fused to a synthetic sapphire or ruby bottom. Unfortunately, these are often mixed in with parcels of natural gems and are then set into jewelry and inadvertently sold as genuine by reputable firms.

Opal doublets also occur, usually consisting of a thin top layer of genuine opal cemented to a base that can be either a poorer grade of opal or some other substance altogether. The most commonly encountered opal doublets are those made to look like the precious black opal. This doublet is usually composed of a translucent or transparent top that is cemented by black cement to a bottom portion of cheaper opal or other material that acts as a support. Please note that the tops of these "black opal" doublets are usually not genuine black opal, though they certainly look like it.

Opal doublets are also made by cementing a thin piece of fine opal to a larger piece of less fine opal to create a larger overall appearance. The doublets can be identified by observing the *join* of the two pieces at the girdle; you can see the dark line of the cement between the two pieces.

Because so many doublets are flooding the market, those who love sapphire, ruby, and emerald must be particularly careful and buy only from reputable jewelers. We know a woman who paid $16,000 recently for a "genuine" emerald ring from a jeweler on New York's 47th Street. It contained a soudé emerald doublet and was worth only a couple hundred dollars for the gold and diamonds in the setting. Luckily, this woman had all the right information on the bill of sale, discovered the error in time, and was able to return the ring and get her money back from the seller.

There is nothing wrong with buying a doublet as long as you know what you are buying and pay a fair price. Normally doublets are not sought as a stone for engagement rings, but you must be careful not to buy one unknowingly. Be sure to verify all the facts by having it examined by a gemologist.

Triplets

Triplets are frequently encountered in the opal market and have substantially replaced opal doublets. The triplet is exactly like the opal doublet except that it has a cabochon-shaped colorless quartz cap (the third part) that covers the entire doublet, giving the delicate doublet greater protection from breakage and providing greater luminescence (brightness) to the stone.

With careful examination a competent jeweler or gemologist should be able to easily differentiate a doublet or triplet from the natural. We should note, however, that detection of an opal doublet may be very difficult if it is set in a mounting with a rim (bezel set) covering the seam where the two pieces are cemented together. It might be necessary to remove the stone from its setting for positive identification. Because of opal's fragile nature, removal must be performed only by a very competent bench jeweler (a jeweler who actually makes or repairs jewelry), and he may agree to do so only at your risk, not wanting to assume responsibility for any breakage. In the case of a black opal worth several thousand dollars, it is well worth the additional cost and inconvenience to be sure it is not a doublet worth only a few hundred dollars. Always be apprehensive when buying a "flat-topped opal" that is bezel set.

CHAPTER 19

Popular Colored Gemstones

Here we would like to provide an alphabetical listing of colored gemstones, including birthstones, which might make especially good choices for an engagement ring.

❖ Alexandrite

Alexandrite makes a wonderful choice for a "changeable woman" who loves red and green. Alexandrite is a fascinating, transparent gem that appears grass green in *daylight* and raspberry red under *incandescent light*. It is a variety of chrysoberyl reputedly discovered in Russia in 1831 on the day Alexander II reached his majority—hence the name. In Russia, where the national colors also happen to be green and red, it is considered a stone of very good omen. It is also considered Friday's stone or the stone of "Friday's child," and is one of the birthstones for June.

Alexandrite is a relatively recent gem. Nonetheless, it has definitely come into its own and is presently commanding both high interest and high prices. It is brilliant, durable, and very wearable. Availability is good in small sizes, but it has become relatively scarce in sizes above two carats. A fine three-carat stone can easily cost $25,000 today, or more. Larger stones of fine quality command even higher prices. Alexandrite is normally cut in a faceted style, but some cat's-eye type alexandrites, found in Brazil, are cut as a cabochon to display the eye-effect. These are usually small; the largest we've seen was approximately three carats.

Prior to 1973, there were really no good synthetic alexandrites. While some synthetics were frequently sold as alexandrite, they really didn't look like the real thing but were hard to differentiate since so few had ever seen the real thing. However, they are easy for a gemologist to spot. In 1973 a very good synthetic alexandrite was produced that is not easy to distinguish from the real thing. While a good gemologist today can tell the synthetic from the genuine, when these synthetics first appeared on the market many were mistaken for the real thing. So be especially careful to verify the authenticity of your alexandrite, since it might have been mistakenly identified years ago and passed along as the real thing to you today.

❖ Amethyst

Amethyst, a transparent purple variety of a mineral known as "quartz," is one of the most popular of the colored stones. Recognized in contemporary times as the birthstone of February, it was once believed to bring peace of mind to the wearer. It was also believed to prevent the wearer from getting drunk, and if the circle of the sun or moon was engraved thereon, it was thought to prevent death from poison! Available in shades from light to dark purple, it is relatively hard, fairly brilliant, and overall a good, versatile, wearable stone, available in good supply even in very large sizes (although large sizes with deep color are now becoming scarce). Amethyst is probably one of the most beautiful stones available at a moderate price, although one must be careful because "fine" amethyst is being produced synthetically today. Amethyst may fade from heat and strong sunshine, but if you guard your amethyst from these conditions, it will retain its color indefinitely.

❖ Aquamarine

To dream of aquamarine signifies the making of new friends; to wear aquamarine earrings brings love and affection (perhaps a nice anniversary gift?). Aquamarine, a universal symbol of youth, hope, and health, blesses those born in March. (Prior to the fifteenth century it was thought to be the birthstone for those born in October.)

Aquamarine is a member of the important beryl family, which includes emerald, but aquamarine is less brittle and more durable than emerald. Aquamarine ranges in color from light blue to bluish green to deep blue, which is the most valuable and desirable color. (We suggest you avoid a shallow-cut stone, since the color will become paler as dirt accumulates on the back and must be kept especially clean). It is a very wearable gem, clear and brilliant, and, unlike emerald, is available with excellent clarity even in very large sizes. Long considered a beautiful and moderately priced gem, it is now entering the "expensive" classification for stones in larger sizes with a good deep blue color.

One must be careful not to mistake blue topaz for aquamarine. While topaz is a beautiful gem, it is usually much less expensive since it is usually treated to obtain its desirable color. For those who can't afford an aquamarine, however, blue topaz is an excellent alternative—as long as it is properly represented . . . and priced.

Also, note that many aquamarine-colored synthetic spinels are erroneously sold as aquamarine.

❖ Beryl

As early as 1220 A.D. the virtues of beryl were well known to man. Beryl provided help against foes in battle or litigation, made the wearer unconquerable but at the same time friendly and likable, and also sharpened his intellect and cured him of laziness. Today beryl is still considered important but primarily for aesthetic reasons. The variety of colors in which it is found, its wonderful clarity (except for emerald), its brilliance, and its durability (again with the exception of emerald) have given the numerous varieties of beryl tremendous appeal.

The beryl family offers us many beautiful gems: the blue variety is known as *aquamarine,* the pink variety as *morganite* (named after the wealthy twentieth-century philanthropist, J. P. Morgan), a colorless variety as *goshenite,* and the deep green variety as *emerald* (see page 178). There is also a more common variety that occurs in a range of yellow shades that is known simply as *golden beryl* or *yellow beryl.* And another fairly common variety known simply as *green beryl* occurs in a light-to-medium bluish, yellowish, or grayish green. The least well-known is the rarest of all, the red variety, which is also called red "emerald"(see page 180).

Beryl has also been found in many other colors, including lilac, salmon, orange, sea green, as well as colorless. While most of these varieties are not yet available to any but the most ardent "rock hound," they can still be found at very affordable prices (usually under $300 per carat or less).

❖ Citrine

Citrine is a gem that has often been called by other names—quartz topaz, citrine topaz, or topaz—all of which are misleading; the correct name for this yellow variety of the mineral quartz is citrine. It comes in a wide range of "yellow" shades, from pale straw yellow to lemon yellow, from amber brown to reddish-orange. It is a pleasing stone in terms of color and fairly durable. It is slightly softer and less brilliant than the more rare and costly "precious topaz" with which it has often been confused (most "topaz" birthstone jewelry usually contains citrine). It also lacks the subtle color shading, the pinkier yellow or pinkish amber shades that lend to precious topaz a distinctive color difference.

Citrine is a very affordable gem and can make a very lovely ring, especially when designed with diamonds. For someone with a limited budget, citrine offers an attractive choice with which to create a ring that incorporates a personal element (if the birthday is in November, citrine is one of the birthstones for that month), with the romantic symbolism of "preciousness" and "forever" communicated by the diamonds.

❖ Emerald

Emerald is a green variety of the mineral beryl. One of the rarest members of the beryl family, it is one of the most highly prized of all the gems. There is only one member of the beryl family that is rarer—the *red* variety, also known as red "emerald." Aside from being the birthstone for May, it was historically believed to bestow on its wearer faithfulness and unchanging love, and was thought to enable the wearer to forecast events.

Contrary to popular belief, emerald is not soft. It ranks 7 1/2 to 8 on Mohs' scale—an internationally recognized standard that ranks hardness on a scale from 1 to 10, with 1 being the softest and 10 the hardest. It is more fragile than other varieties of beryl and other gems, however, because it is more brittle and under more stress from fractures resulting from the violent geologic conditions under which it formed. This is why it is important to exercise care when you are wearing and handling emerald.

The highest-quality emerald has the color of fresh young green grass—an almost pure spectral green, possibly with a very faint blue

tint. Flawless emeralds are so rare that they are immediately sus-
pect; thus, "flaws" have come to serve as "fingerprints" of genuineness. Connoisseurs seek fine emeralds from Colombia, which is
known for its intensely rich, vivid-colored emeralds. Colombia is
one of the most important emerald sources historically, but other
sources now include Afghanistan, Brazil, India, Pakistan, Russia,
and Zambia. It is also worth noting that a new emerald discovery in
the United States, in Hiddenite, North Carolina, has produced some
major crystals with fine color and clarity. While emeralds from this
source are costly, they may make an especially meaningful choice as
an American gem for a precious engagement ring.

Because of emerald's popularity and value, imitations and synthetics are abundant. Glass (manufactured complete with "flaws"),
doublets, and triplets are also commonplace. Techniques to enhance
color and reduce the visibility of flaws are also frequently used. A
common practice, one that goes back to early Greek times, is to fill
cracks with oil (sometimes tinted green). Oiling emerald is a practice that is accepted by the jewelry industry since it is actually good
for the stone in light of its fragile nature. Oiling hides some of the
whitish flaws, which are actually cracks, by filling them so they become less visible. The oil becomes an integral part of the emerald
unless it is subjected to ultrasonic cleaners or some type of solvent
such as paint remover (be sure she removes her emerald ring before
helping you with any painting chores!).

A good friend of ours took her heirloom emerald ring to her jeweler for a "really good cleaning." Luckily for the jeweler, she never
left the store and was standing right there when the ring was put
into the cleaner and removed. She couldn't believe her eyes. She
was shocked by the loss of color and the "sudden appearance of
more flaws." The ultrasonic cleaner had removed the oil that had
penetrated the cracks, and an emerald several shades lighter and
more visibly flawed emerged. Had she not been there, she would
never have believed the jeweler hadn't pulled a switch. Fortunately,
emeralds can be re-oiled, and the jeweler was able to re-oil hers, and
its former appearance was restored.

Epoxy resin fillers are a recent newcomer, but this treatment is
gaining popularity and is now used on many emeralds mined in
many parts of the world, including Colombia and Brazil. The use of

oil and epoxy resins are considered acceptable practices, but be sure the price reflects the actual quality of the stone.

As with all highly desired gems, the greater the value and demand, the greater the occurrence of fraudulent practices. Examples of almost every type of technique to simulate emerald can be found—color alteration, synthetics, substitutes (of less valuable green stones), doublets or other composites, etc. Therefore, be especially cautious of bargains, deal with reputable jewelers when planning to purchase an emerald, and always have the purchase verified by a qualified gemologist-appraiser.

An American Gem—Red Emerald. Gemologists prefer calling this gem *red beryl* or *bixbite* (after Mr. Bixby, the man who discovered it) rather than red "emerald," but whatever the name, it is a beautiful gem and one of the world's rarest. It would make a wonderful engagement ring choice for those who are seeking a red gem that communicates "rarity" and "preciousness"!

The only known source of gem-quality red beryl is the United States. Before red beryl became available, the rarest variety of beryl was the deep green emerald. The red variety is even rarer, and in an effort to communicate its rarity, preciousness, and value, few object to calling it red "emerald," and physically it more closely resembles emerald than any other member of the beryl family.

Red emerald remains rare in sizes over 2 carats. The world's largest red emerald weighs 8.03 carats; the second largest weighs 4.50 carats. In sizes up to 2 carats, the price of fine-quality red emerald can be comparable to fine ruby, and the price often exceeds that of green emerald. These gems have only recently found their place in the jewelry world but are already being shown in fabulous pieces made by the greatest designers.

❖ Garnet

If your fiancée is loyal, devoted, and energetic, perhaps garnet is the perfect stone for your engagement ring. Red garnets were "known" to promote sincerity, and relieve anger and discord. And if you engrave a well-formed lion image on it, it will protect and preserve health, cure the wearer of all disease, bring honors, and guard from all perils in traveling. All in all, quite a worthwhile stone.

The garnet family is one of the most exciting families in the gem world. A hard, durable, often very brilliant stone available in many colors (greens, reds, yellows, oranges), it offers great versatility. Depending on the variety, quality, and size, lovely varieties of garnet are available from under $20 per carat to more than $10,000 per carat. Garnet is also mistaken for other (usually more expensive) gems. Green garnet, tsavorite, is one of the most beautiful, and all but a few would assume it was an emerald of the finest quality. In fact, it is rarer, more brilliant, and more durable. There is also a rarer green garnet, called demantoid, which costs slightly more than tsavorite but which, although slightly softer, has more fire. These gems offer exciting alternatives to the person desiring a lovely green gem. While still rare and expensive themselves, these gems are far less expensive than an emerald of comparable quality. Garnet also occurs in certain shades of red that have been taken for some varieties of ruby, and in yellow it has been confused with precious topaz. Even a "color-change" variety has been discovered, changing from red to *blue* depending upon the light.

Garnet can be found in almost every color and shade. It is best known in a deep red variety, sometimes with a brownish cast, but it can also be found in fiery orange-red and brilliant wine red shades as well. Other colors include orange, purple, violet, and pink. A non-transparent variety, grossularite, resembles jade and may be mistaken for jade when cut into cabochons or carved.

❖ Jade

Jade has long been revered by the Chinese. White jade (yes, white) was believed by the early Chinese to quiet intestinal disturbances and black jade to give strength and power. A very early written Chinese symbol for king was a string of jade beads, and jade beads are still used in China as a symbol of high rank and authority. Jade is also an important part of the Chinese wedding ceremony (the "jade ceremony" holds a prominent place here), for to the Chinese, jade is considered the "concentrated essence of love."

Jade is not as hard as other gems, but it is still very wearable because it is very tough. It is a translucent to opaque gem, often seen in fine jewelry and also in carvings. There are really two types of jade—jadeite and nephrite—which are really two separate and distinct minerals, differing from one another in weight, hardness, and color range.

Jadeite is the most expensive and most desirable variety. It was the most sought after by the Chinese after 1740. It is not found in China, however, but in Burma. Some fine jadeite also comes from Guatemala. It comes in a much wider range of colors than nephrite: green, mottled green and white, whitish gray, pink, brown, mauve, yellow, orange, and lilac. In fact, it comes in almost every color. But with the exception of green jade (which comes in shades that vary from pale to a beautiful emerald green), colored jade is usually pale and unevenly colored. The most desirable color is a rich emerald green sometimes referred to as imperial jade. Smooth, evenly colored pieces of this jadeite are highly prized. In fact, they can be classed as precious stones today. The mottled pieces of irregular green, often seen carved, are less valuable but are still more rare and valuable than nephrite jade.

Nephrite jade, the old and true Chinese jade, resembles jadeite but is slightly softer (yet slightly tougher and thus, less easily broken) and has a much more limited range of color. It is regularly seen in dark green shades (sometimes so dark as to look black: black jade), usually fashioned in cabochon cut, round beads, or in carvings. Nephrite green is a more sober green than the apple green or emerald green color of good jadeite. It is closer in color to a dark, sage green or spinach green. Nephrite may also be a creamier color, as in mutton fat jade. Any fine Chinese carving that is more than 250 years old is carved from nephrite (jadeite was unknown to the Chinese before 1740).

Nephrite has been found in many countries, including the United States, where in the late nineteenth century Chinese miners panning for gold in California discovered large boulders of nephrite jade that they sent back to China to be cut or carved. It is also common in Wyoming, Alaska, and British Columbia.

Nephrite jade is much more common than jadeite and is therefore much less expensive. But it is a lovely, popular stone and makes lovely jewelry.

One must be careful, however, when purchasing jade. You will often see "Imperial" jade that is nothing more than a cheap jade that has been dyed. Much of it is treated (usually this means dyed or polymer impregnated) to enhance its value. The dyeing, however, may be very temporary. Black jade is usually dyed or very dark green nephrite that looks black. There are also numerous minerals that look like jade and are sold as jade under misleading names, such as "Korean jade" or "new jade," both of which are serpentine (another green stone similar to some varieties of jade, but more common and less expensive). Much of the intricately and beautifully carved jade is actually serpentine, which can be scratched easily with a knife.

Soapstone may also look like jade to the amateur, especially when beautifully carved. This stone is so soft that it can easily be scratched with a pin, hairpin, or point of a pen. (But don't scratch it in a noticeable place and, if it doesn't belong to you, seek permission before performing this test!) It is very much less expensive than comparable varieties of jade, and it is softer and less durable.

Jade is a wonderful stone. Imperial jade is breathtaking. It is no wonder it was "the Emperor's stone." But jade has long been copied, misrepresented, and altered. Be sure to verify its true identity with a gemologist-appraiser to be sure you are buying what you think you are buying. And then enjoy it!

❖ Moonstone (Feldspar)

Moonstone is definitely a good luck stone, especially for lovers. As a gift for lovers the moonstone holds a high rank, for it is believed to arouse one's tender passion and give lovers the ability to foretell their future—good or ill. (But to get this information, the stone must be placed in the mouth while the moon is full.) Perhaps a more important use, however, was in amulets made of moonstone, which would protect men from epilepsy and guarantee a greater fruit-crop yield when hung on fruit trees (it assisted all vegetation).

The name "moonstone" is probably derived from the theory that one can observe the lunar month through the stone—that a small white spot appears in the stone as the new moon begins and gradually moves toward the stone's center, getting always larger, until at full moon the spot has taken the shape of a full moon in the center of the stone.

Moonstone, a birthstone for June, is a member of the feldspar family. It is a transparent, milky white to bluish white variety in which can be seen a billowy, moveable, almost cloud-like white or blue light within the stone's body. It is a popular stone for rings because as the hand moves the effect of the brilliant light/color is more pronounced. The bluer color is the finer and more desirable, but it is becoming rare in today's market, particularly in large sizes.

There are some glass imitations of moonstone, but compared to the real thing they are not very good.

❖ Opal

The opal has suffered from an unfortunate reputation as being an evil stone and bearing an ill omen. There are several explanations for the ominous superstitions surrounding this wonderful gem, but we'd rather mention some of its good properties and leave you with an assurance that the evil association has never been merited and probably resulted from a careless reading of Sir Walter Scott's *Anne of Geierstein*.

Among the ancients, opal was a symbol of fidelity and assurance, and in later history it became strongly associated with religious emotion and prayer. It was believed to have a strong therapeutic value for diseases of the eye, and worn as an amulet it would make the wearer immune from all such diseases as well as increase the powers of the eyes and the mind. Further, many believed that to the extent the colors of red and green were seen, the therapeutic powers of stones of those colors (ruby and emerald) were also to be enjoyed by the wearer—the power to stop bleeding , etc. (when ruby-red is present); the power to cure kidney diseases, etc. (when emerald-green is present). The black opal was particularly highly prized as the luck stone of anyone fortunate enough to own one!

This stone, whose brilliance and vibrant colors resemble the colors of the fall, is certainly appropriate as a birthstone for October. When we try to describe the opal, we realize how insufficient the English language is. It is unique among the gems, displaying an array of very brilliant miniature rainbow effects, all mixed up together.

Its most outstanding characteristic is this unusual, intense display of many colors flashing out like mini-rainbows. This effect is created by opal's formation process, which is very different from that of other gems. Opal is composed of hydrated silica spheres. The mini-rainbows seen in most opals result from light interference created by these spheres. The arrangement of the spheres, which vary in size and pattern, is responsible for the different colors.

Opal is usually cut flat or in cabochon, since there is no additional brilliance to be captured by a good faceting job. Color is everything. The more brilliant the color, the more valuable the gem. It is probably truer of opal than any other stone that the more beautiful the stone and its color, the more it will cost.

The finest of all is the black opal. Black opals are usually a deep gray or grayish black with flashes of incredibly brilliant color dancing around within and about the stone as it is turned. One must be careful when purchasing a black opal, however, to ensure that it is not a *doublet* or *triplet*, a stone composed of two or three pieces of stone glued together, unless that is explicitly stated and the price appropriate for a composite stone. There are many such doublets on the market because of the black opal's rarity, beauty, and extremely high cost (one the size of a lima bean can cost $25,000 today). The black opal doublet provides an affordable option to one who loves them but can't afford a true black opal. But it also offers another opportunity for misrepresentation that can be very costly to the consumer.

Generally speaking, purity of color, absence of dead spots (called "trueness"), flawlessness, and intensity or brilliance of color are the primary variables affecting value. Opals with an abundance of red are usually the most expensive; those strong in blue and green are equally beautiful but not as rare, so their price is somewhat less. Some opals are very transparent and are classified as "jelly," "semi-jelly," or "water" opals.

While there are imitations, for the most part they are still not worth mentioning. The synthetic opal, however, can be very difficult to separate from the natural and is being encountered with increasing frequency. Also, the color of black opals can be improved by treatment, and treated opals are encountered frequently. So let us reiterate yet again—make sure you know what you are getting by checking the facts with a gemologist-appraiser. And as we've mentioned many times, before buying, shop around. This holds truer for opal, perhaps, than any other stone.

One word of caution must also be offered: Opals require special care because some tend to dry and crack. Avoid exposure to anything that is potentially drying. And, immersing an opal in a glass or bowl of water for several hours will help preserve it. *Note:* At one time jewelers recommended periodically wiping opals with an oiled cloth to deposit a light film of oil on the opal's surface. This advice has been proven wrong. *Never rub an opal with oil or immerse it in oil; an oily build-up will destroy the fiery play of color that makes the opal valuable, and, once destroyed, it cannot be restored.*

❖ Peridot

Today's birthstone for August, peridot was also a favorite of the ancients. This lovely, transparent, yellowish green to deep chartreuse stone was quite a powerful gem. It was considered an aid to friendship and was also believed to free the mind of envious thoughts (which is probably why it was an aid to friendship). Because of its yellowish green color, it was also believed to cure or prevent diseases of the liver and dropsy. And, if that's not enough, if worn on the left arm it would protect the wearer from the evil eye.

It is also popular today but probably more for its depth of green color than its professed powers. While not as brilliant as many other gemstones, the richness of its color can be exceptional. It comes in shades from yellowish green to darker, purer green colors. It is still widely available in small sizes but larger sizes are becoming scarce, so prices in larger sizes are now fairly high for good quality material.

Some caution should also be exercised in wearing peridot. It is not a very hard stone and may scratch easily. Also, some less expensive stones that resemble peridot include green sapphire and certain colors of green tourmaline, so you must be sure to verify that you have purchased peridot and not one of these less expensive gemstones.

❖ Ruby

Prized through the ages, even by kings, as the "gem of gems . . . surpassing all other precious stones in virtue," and today's birthstone for July, ruby is the red variety of the mineral corundum. Historically, it has been symbolic of love and passion, considered to be an "aid to firm friendship," and believed to ensure beauty. Its color ranges from purplish or bluish red to a yellowish red. The finest color is a vivid, almost pure spectral red with a very faint undertone of blue, as seen in Burmese rubies, which are considered the finest among ardent collectors. Other sources of fine ruby include Thailand, Vietnam, Cambodia, Kenya, Tanzania, and Azad Kashmir in Pakistan.

The ruby is a very brilliant stone and is also a very hard, durable, and wearable stone. Because of these characteristics, ruby makes an unusually fine choice for engagement rings.

Translucent varieties of ruby are also seen, and one variety exhibits a six-ray star effect when cut as a cabochon. This variety is called "star ruby" and is one of nature's most beautiful and interesting gifts. But, as with so many other beautiful gifts once produced only in nature, today man has also learned to make synthetic star ruby.

Here again, remember that the greater the value and demand, the greater the use of techniques to "improve" or simulate. Again, examples of almost every type of technique can be found—color enhancement, diffusion treatment, synthesis, look-alike substitutes, doublets, triplets, glass-filling and other clarity enhancements, etc. The newest synthetic rubies—the Ramura, Chatham, and Kashan rubies—are so close to natural ruby in every aspect that many are actually passing for genuine, even among gemologists. When verifying the identity and quality of a fine ruby, make every effort to select a gemologist with many years' experience in colored gems and an astute knowledge of the marketplace today.

Here again, be especially cautious of bargains. Deal with reputable jewelers when planning to purchase, and have the purchase double-checked by a qualified gemologist-appraiser. And when considering any very fine ruby, we highly recommend submitting the stone to a major gem testing laboratory for confirmation of identity and whether or not any enhancement techniques have been used.

❖ Sapphire

The "celestial" sapphire, symbol of the heavens, bestower of innocence, truth, good health, and preserver of chastity, is known today as the birthstone of September. Sapphire is corundum. While we know it best in its blue variety, which is one of the most highly prized varieties, it comes in essentially every color (the red variety is ruby). As we mentioned when discussing ruby, sapphire's hardness, brilliance, and availability in so many beautiful colors make it probably the most important and most versatile of the gem families, and an especially good choice for engagement rings.

The finest sapphires are considered to be the blue varieties found in Burma and Kashmir, which are closest to the pure spectral blue. Fine, brilliant, deep blue Burmese sapphires will surely dazzle the eye and the pocketbook, as will the Kashmir, which is a fine velvety-toned deep blue. Many today tend to be too dark, however, because of the presence of too much black and poor cutting (cutting deep for additional weight).

Ceylon sapphires (Ceylon is the old name for Sri Lanka, but it is still used when referring to sapphires) also offer a very pleasing shade of blue, but are a less deep shade than the Burmese or Kashmir, often on the pastel side.

We are also seeing many Australian sapphires. These are often a dark blue, but have a slightly green undertone, as do those from Thailand, and sell for much less per carat. They offer a very affordable alternative to the Burmese, Kashmir, or Ceylon, and can still be very pleasing in their color. Blue sapphires also come from Tanzania, Brazil, Africa, and even the United States (Montana and North Carolina). American sapphires occur in a range of colors and are highly sought by collectors.

With sapphire, country of origin can have a significant effect on price, so if you are purchasing a Burmese, Kashmir, or Ceylon sapphire, that should be noted on the bill of sale.

Like ruby, the blue sapphire may be found in a translucent variety that may show a six-ray star effect when cut into a cabochon. This variety is known as "star sapphire," of which there are numerous synthetics (often referred to in the trade as "Linde" [pronounced Lin'dee]).

In addition to blue sapphire, we are now beginning to see the appearance of many other color varieties, especially yellow, pink, and purple, and in smaller sizes some beautiful shades of green. These are known as *fancy* sapphires. Compared to the cost of blue sapphire and ruby, these stones usually offer excellent value and beauty. *Padparadscha* sapphire is a very rare variety that appears pinkish orange (you must see *both* pink and orange in the stone to be a true padparadscha), and this variety, depending upon size and quality, can exceed the price of the finest blue sapphire.

Inevitably, one can find evidence of every technique known to improve the perceived quality and value of sapphire—the alteration of color, diffusion treatment to apply color to the surface, synthesis, doublets, and so on. We urge you again to be especially cautious of bargains, deal only with reputable jewelers, and have your stone double-checked by a qualified gemologist-appraiser. When buying any fine, rare sapphire, especially those from Burma or Kashmir, or any stone represented to have *natural color,* have the jeweler or gemologist-appraiser submit the stone to a gem testing laboratory for a report to confirm the facts.

❖ Spinel

Spinel is one of the loveliest of the gems but hasn't yet been given due credit and respect. It is usually compared to sapphire or ruby, rather than being recognized for its own intrinsic beauty and value. There is also a common belief that spinel (and similarly zircon) is synthetic rather than natural, when in fact it is one of nature's most beautiful products (although synthetic spinel is also seen frequently on the market). In fact, a spinel adorns the center of one of the most important crowns among England's Crown Jewels—the Imperial State Crown. It contains a large, red spinel, believed for centuries to be a ruby; in fact, it was known as "the Black Prince's Ruby," and it was only after gemological evaluation of the Crown Jewels that it was discovered to be spinel. Interestingly, red spinel occurs in the same region of Burma as the finest rubies, so it is not surprising that there was a case of mistaken identity!

Spinel commonly occurs in red-orange (flame spinel), light to dark orangy red, light to dark slightly grayish blue, greenish blue, grayish green, and dark to light purple to violet. It also occurs in yellow and in an opaque black variety. The most popular varieties are the red (more orange than the ruby red) and blue (a strong Bromo-Seltzer-bottle blue). When compared to the blue of sapphire or the red of ruby, its color is usually considered less intense, but its brilliance can be greater, and unlike ruby and sapphire, its color is usually *natural.* All in all, spinel is a wonderful gem and makes a wonderful choice for an engagement ring.

Spinel may be confused with or misrepresented as one of many stones—ruby, sapphire, zircon, amethyst, garnet, synthetic ruby/sapphire, or synthetic spinel—as well as glass. The synthetic is often used to make composite stones such as doublets. Spinel is a fairly hard, fairly durable stone, possessing a nice brilliance and still providing good value.

This stone is becoming more and more popular today and may, therefore, become more expensive if current trends continue.

❖ Topaz

True topaz, symbol of love and affection, aid to sweetness of disposition, and birthstone for November, is one of nature's most wonderful and least-known families. The true topaz family offers a variety of color options in lovely, clear, brilliant, and durable stones.

Until recently, true topaz was rarely seen in jewelry stores. Unfortunately, most people know only the citrine quartz mistakenly called topaz. In the past almost any yellow stone was called topaz. True topaz is very beautiful and versatile.

Topaz occurs not only in the transparent yellow, yellow-brown, orangy brown, and pinky brown colors most popularly associated with it, but also in a very light to medium red (now found naturally in fair supply, although many are produced through heat treatment), very light to light blue (also often the result of treatment, although it does occur naturally), very light green, light greenish yellow, violet, and colorless.

Topaz is a hard, brilliant stone with a fine color range, but it is much rarer and much more expensive than the stones commonly sold as topaz. It is also heavier than its imitators.

There are many misleading names to suggest that a stone is topaz when it is not. For example, "Rio topaz," "Madeira topaz," "Spanish topaz," and "Palmeira topaz" are types of citrine (quartz) and should be represented as such.

Blue topaz has become very popular in recent years but is not a stone we recommend for engagement rings. While it does occur naturally, this is very rare and virtually all blue topaz sold in jewelry stores today is treated; unfortunately, there is no practical way yet to determine which have been treated and which are natural. It closely resembles the much more expensive aquamarine.

❖ Tourmaline

Tourmaline is a gem of modern times, but nonetheless has found its way to the list of birthstones, becoming an "alternate birthstone" for October. Perhaps this honor results from tourmaline's versatility and broad color range. Or perhaps from the fact that red-and-green tourmaline, in which the red and green occur side by side in the same stone, is reminiscent of the turning of October leaves.

Whatever the case, tourmaline is one of the most versatile of the gem families. It is available in every color, in every tone, from deep to pastel and even with two or more colors appearing side by side in the same stone. There are bicolored tourmalines (half red and half green, for example) and tricolored (one-third blue, one-third green, and one-third yet another color). The fascinating "watermelon" tourmaline looks just like the inside of a watermelon—red in the center surrounded by a green "rind." Tourmaline can also be found in a cat's-eye type.

It is indeed surprising that most people know of tourmaline simply as an inexpensive "green" stone. Today this is changing as people are becoming more aware of the many lovely varieties available in this fascinating gem. Some of the most popular varieties include:

- Chrome—A particularly rare green variety with a distinctive "emerald" green hue
- Rubellite—Deep pink to red (as in ruby)
- Verdelite—All green varieties, in all shades, except "chrome"
- Paraiba—The most costly variety, rivaling sapphire, occurring in intense shades of "sapphire" blue to violet-blue, and neon intensities of green-to-teal shades

While tourmaline is still a very affordable gem, even in large sizes, the paraiba, chrome, and rubellite varieties are priced (depending on size and quality) anywhere from $500 to $10,000 per carat. So much for the "common and inexpensive" myth!

Tourmaline is a fairly hard, durable, brilliant, and very wearable stone with a wide choice of colors. It makes an excellent choice for rings and offers a variety of colors that makes it distinctive.

❖ Turquoise

A birthstone for December, and ranking highest among all the opaque stones, turquoise—the "Turkish stone"—is highly prized throughout Asia and Africa, not only for its particular hue of blue (a beautiful robin's-egg or sky blue), but more important, for its pro-phylactic and therapeutic qualities. The Arabs consider it a lucky stone and have great confidence in its benevolent action. Used in rings, earrings, necklaces, head ornaments, and amulets, it was be-lieved to protect the wearer from poison, reptile bites, eye diseases, and the evil eye. It was also believed capable of warning of impending death by changing color. Also, the drinking of water in which turquoise has been dipped or washed was believed to cure bladder ailments. Buddhists revere the turquoise because it is associated with a legend in which a turquoise enabled the Buddha to destroy a mon-ster. Even today it is considered a symbol of courage, success, and love. It has also long been associated with American Indian jewelry and art.

Turquoise is an opaque, light to dark blue or blue-green stone. The finest color is an intense blue, with poorer qualities tending toward yellowish green. The famous Persian turquoise, which can be a very intense and pleasing blue, is considered a very rare and valuable gem.

All turquoises are susceptible to aging and may turn greenish or possibly darker with age. Also, care must be taken when wearing, both to avoid contact with soap, grease, or other materials that might discolor it, and to protect it from abuse, since turquoise scratches fairly easily. For this reason we don't recommend turquoise for the engagement ring, but we mention it because it is a birthstone and, as such, might make a nice wedding or anniversary gift for the bride.

Exercise caution when buying turquoise. This is a frequently sim-ulated gem. Very fine glass imitations are produced that are difficult to distinguish from the genuine. Very fine imitations and recon-structed stones (made from turquoise powder bonded in plastic) saturate the marketplace, as does synthetic turquoise. There are techniques to quickly distinguish these simulations so, if in doubt, check it out (and get a complete description on the bill of sale: "genuine, natural turquoise").

❖ Zircon

One of the birthstones for December, zircon was known to the ancients as "hyacinth" and was revered for its many powers. It was especially sought after for men (for whom it was believed to keep evil spirits and bad dreams away, give protection against "fascination" and lightning, strengthen their bodies, fortify their hearts, restore appetite, suppress fat, produce sleep, and banish grief and sadness from the mind); for the bride, it also had a very useful "power"—it was believed capable of assisting a woman during childbirth!

Zircons are very brilliant, transparent stones available in several lovely colors. Unfortunately, like spinel, zircon suffers from a strange misconception that it is a synthetic or man-made stone rather than the lovely natural creation that it is. Perhaps this is because they are frequently, if not usually, treated.

Zircons are regularly treated to alter color, as in the blue and colorless zircons so often seen (many might mistake the colorless zircon for diamond because of its strong brilliance), but zircons also occur naturally in yellow, brown, orange, and red.

Colorless zircons, because of their intense brilliance, are often substituted for diamonds. But care needs to be exercised because zircon is brittle and will chip or abrade easily. For this reason, zircon is recommended for rings only if set with a protective setting, and we recommend against this birthstone for engagement rings. Nonetheless, on her next birthday . . .

❖ Zoisite (Tanzanite)

Zoisite was not considered a gem material until 1967, when a blue to purple-blue transparent variety was found in Tanzania (hence the name *tanzanite*). Tanzanite can possess a rich, sapphire blue color (possibly with some violet red or greenish yellow flashes). This lovely gem, in fine quality, can cost over $1,000 per carat in larger sizes.

But one must be cautious. It is relatively soft and somewhat brittle, so we do not recommend tanzanite for engagement rings unless set in a protective setting. We mention it here because of its great popularity, and because it may be a gemstone you are considering for an engagement ring. If it is truly the "stone of her dreams" just be sure that the stone is set in a mounting that provides adequate protection from accidental knocks or blows.

CHAPTER 20

Pearls

A 3,000-Year-Old Tradition for the Bride

June's birthstone, the pearl, pure and fair to the eye, has been recognized since the earliest times as the emblem of modesty, chastity, and purity. It is also the gem most closely associated throughout history with love and marriage, with traditions more ancient than any other gem. We will explain the pearl in some detail since it is so closely associated to the wedding itself and is the traditional adornment of the bride on the wedding day.

❖ Pearls For the Bride—An Ancient Tradition

> *"And Krishna brought forth pearls from the depths of the sea to give to his daughter on her wedding day."*
> —*The Rigveda*, Ancient Hindu Book, c. 1000 B.C.

As we mentioned earlier, some of the most ancient records relating to the pearl are found in Ceylon and India. Long before the Romans were enjoying pearls, the pearl was held in high esteem in India. Pearls are mentioned often in ancient Hindu writings, in the sacred texts known as the Vedas. These provide some of the earliest mentions of pearls associated with longevity, prosperity, and preservation of life. Here the word *krisana* appears—almost 3,000 years ago—translated as "pearl." Here we also find the story of *Krishna, the preserver* (notice the similarity to the word "krisana"). And here, also, we find perhaps the oldest written mention of pearls in association with weddings. We are told how Krishna *brought forth pearls from the depths of the sea to give to his daughter on her wedding day.* What a beautiful story. What a rare and magnificent gift. And what better illustration of the pearl's great value. The Hindu story is perhaps the earliest mention of pearls and marriage . . . and the start of a centuries-old tradition of pearls as the appropriate adornment of the bride!

The ancient Greeks also believed that pearls should be part of the wedding experience; believing that pearls would help ensure marital bliss and prevent newlywed brides from crying, they were considered "the wedding gem." During the period of the Crusades, we find that pearls were the gift of many a gallant knight returning from the Middle East, bestowed upon his "fair lady" for her wedding day. By the fourteenth and fifteenth centuries, we find pearls at the height of "wedding fashion" with royal weddings in the House of Burgundy taking place in a veritable "sea of pearls." Historical accounts document that virtually everyone from the bride herself to her male guests were adorned in glistening pearls. Botticelli, one of the most famous of the Renaissance painters, equates love itself to the pearl, when in his famous work, "The Birth of Venus," he likens Venus—the goddess of love—to the pearl, bringing her up from the sea, born of the pearl-producing oyster!

The Russian Czarina on her wedding day, in the early 20th century

From Queen Elizabeth I to our modern Queen Elizabeth II, the tradition has continued through the centuries. At the beginning of the twentieth century, pearls were as much a nuptial gem in the United States as diamonds are today; pearls accounted for over 75 percent of jewelry sales in the United States at the turn of the century. Today, the tradition of bestowing pearls upon the bride for her wedding day, often by the father of the bride, or by the groom himself, continues as it has for hundreds of years.

19th-century *natural* pearl and diamond engagement ring

❖ The Pearl Market Today Is a Cultured Pearl Market

Today there are more pearl varieties, in more colors, sizes, and shapes, than ever before. Prices range from a few dollars, to many thousands of dollars for a single pearl. We will limit the discussion here, however, to the classic round white pearls known as "akoya" pearls—the pearl that comes to the minds of most people when we mention the word pearl, although round, white Chinese freshwater pearls can also make an attractive choice at a much lower price. For

The pearl is the "wedding gem" today, as it has been for hundreds of years.

those who wish to know more about pearls, and the many other varieties that might be appropriate as a gift for the bride on her wedding day, or for an important anniversary, we recommend our book *The Pearl Book* (see "Selected Readings" in the appendix).

A fine natural or *Oriental* pearl—the true "natural pearl"—has always been considered a precious gem because of its rarity. This is even truer today than ever before. Virtually all pearls sold today are *cultured*. But fine cultured pearls are also very expensive, and prices seem to continue to rise.

Natural pearls are produced by oysters (not the edible variety) and by mussels in freshwater lakes and rivers. When a foreign substance, such as a tiny sea parasite, accidentally finds its way into the oyster's body, and the oyster can't get rid of it, it becomes an irritant. To soothe the irritation, the oyster produces an iridescent substance called nacre (nay-ker) with which it covers the intruder. This substance builds up over many years, creating the pearl.

Cultured pearls are created by the oyster in essentially the same way. However, in the case of the cultured pearl the "irritant" is *implanted by man* into the tissue of a live oyster. Over time, the oyster secretes a coating of nacre over it (which should be approximately one-half millimeter thick in a good cultured pearl), creating the cultured pearl. The thickness depends in part on the length of time the bead remains in the oyster. Sometimes the cultured pearl is removed from the oyster prematurely, so that the nacre coating is too thin and may begin to wear through in only a few years. In other cases, the cultured pearl is so fine as to require an expert to tell it from a fine, genuine natural pearl.

In terms of quality and value, the same factors are used to determine the quality and value of a cultured pearl as for natural pearls. But a pearl must always be clearly described as cultured or natural (Oriental), and this should be stated in writing on your bill of sale.

As with all gems, quality and value vary. The quality and value of the pearl are determined by:

- **Luster**—the pearl's "glow," or reflective quality. Don't confuse this with a surface shine. Luster is a quality that seems to emanate from within the pearl itself. Some pearls also show a rainbow-like play of color that produces a shimmering effect (this is called "orient" and is seen only in the finest pearls). As you shop, compare the depth and richness of the luster. This is the most important factor in terms of the pearl's beauty.

- *Color*—the most desirable round pearls are white with a rosé overtone, although there are also white pearls with a creamy overtone that are highly desirable. Pearls with a strong yellowish or greenish overtone are less expensive. Keep in mind as you shop, however, that it is important to try pearls on to see what color really looks best with the coloring of your own skin, hair, and eyes. Some women look better in creamier shades, others in whiter shades. You may find you prefer a creamier shade, which may be more affordable.
- *Cleanliness* or surface perfection (skin texture)—freedom from skin blemishes such as blisters, pits, or spots. Perfectly spotless pearls are rare, but the cleaner, the better.
- *Roundness*—while it is extremely rare to find a strand of perfectly round pearls, the closer they come to being perfectly round, the better. Check closely for roundness, and within strands, for careful matching of the pearl shape throughout the strand. Sometimes slightly out-of-round pearls can give the impression of being round when worn and might be a good alternative. But slightly out-of-round pearls sell for less, so be sure the price reflects this.
- *Size*—natural pearls are sold by weight, which is given in *grains* (there are four grains to a carat). Cultured pearls are measured and sold by millimeter size. The larger the pearl, the costlier. There is a dramatic price jump, for example, between 7 1/2 and 8 millimeters, or between 9 1/2 and 10 millimeters. An 8-millimeter pearl is large, a 9-millimeter very large. The price jumps upward rapidly with each millimeter once you pass 8.

A fine pearl necklace, or any strung pearl item, requires very careful matching—of size, roundness, luster, color, and cleanliness. Graduated pearls—a strand containing larger pearls in the center, with the pearls becoming progressively smaller toward the ends—also require careful sizing. Failure to match carefully will detract from both the appearance of the piece and the value.

Pearls should be handled with care. It is best to keep them in a separate pouch and to exercise some caution when wearing. Avoid contact with substances such as vinegar (when making a salad), ammonia, inks, and certain perfumes, since these can spot the pearl's surface. Also, the frequent application of hair spray while wearing pearls will coat them and make them very dull, but this coating can be removed with a soft cloth moistened with clear, acetone-based nail polish remover (which will *not* hurt the pearl in any way).

❖ Is It Real or Simulated?

Simulated or imitation pearls are sold everywhere. Many of the finest imitations have been mistaken for the real thing. One quick test that normally reveals the fake is to run the pearl gently across the edge of your upper (or lower) teeth. The cultured or genuine pearl will have a mildly abrasive or gritty feel, while the imitation will be slippery smooth. (This test won't work with false teeth.) Try the test on pearls you know are cultured or genuine, and then try it on known imitations to get a feel for the difference.

But once again, when in doubt, seek out a qualified gemologist. The cost of being wrong may be too great to risk it.

❖ A Final Word on Pearls

There are innumerable differences in quality—if roundness is good, luster may be poor; if luster is good, roundness may be poor; if color and luster are good, there may be poor surface texture from too many skin blemishes, or matching in a strand may be poor. Shopping around can teach you a tremendous amount about pearls. Keeping in mind the factors that affect quality—size, luster, color, roundness, skin blemishes—go shopping and compare. You'll be surprised by how quickly you will learn to spot differences that affect cost. Now you can decide which factors are important to you, and what you might want to juggle to get the pearls that are right for you.

Cultured pearl strands

PART FIVE

Design and Style:
Getting the Look You Want

CHAPTER 21

Choosing the Shape

Today's bride-to-be has more choices in engagement ring design and style than ever before. But the first step in creating the look you want is selecting the shape of the stone, a shape that's right for you. There are many shapes from which to choose, but it's important to choose the right shape because it will affect the overall design and look of your ring.

Round brilliant

❖ Modern Diamond Shapes

In choosing a design and style that suits your taste, budget, and personality, one of the first steps is to decide on the diamond shape you want. Today, in addition to the classic, round shape, there are many popular "fancy" shapes from which to choose.

Pear shape

As we mentioned earlier, there are many exciting new shapes (see chapter 6), as well as the traditional "fancy" shapes—any shape other than a round, brilliant cut. Some of the new shapes lend themselves to very distinctive designs that would be difficult to create with other shapes; some exhibit unique personalities, not possible in any other shape; and some can even help you stay within your budget (some appear larger, for their weight, than traditional cuts, enabling you to get the *size* you want in a diamond that actually weighs less than you might have thought you needed). One of the most exciting parts of searching for your ring is discovering what is really available today!

Marquise

Oval

Emerald

You should keep in mind, however, that fancy shapes, new and old alike, can vary in their width and length, and in their basic proportioning, and these differences can result in a totally different look and feel on your hand. For example, an emerald-cut diamond that is cut in a very long shape will look

Emerald

Heart shape

very different from one that is more squarish; a broad-shouldered pear shape might look too triangular for the hand, while one with softer, more rounded shoulders might be just what you want. To some extent, the choice of shape is a very personal matter, and there is no standard "ideal" range that is applied to shapes other than round, but you must be careful that the stone is not cut in such a way that its liveliness and brilliance is reduced or adversely affected (see chapter 6).

As you begin to look at diamonds, try on *all* of the shapes; you may discover you like a shape you might not have considered otherwise! Try them in a solitaire style (a single diamond at the center) and in designs that incorporate diamond accents or colored stone and diamond accents. It won't be long before you have a clear idea of the shape that best suits your personal style and taste, the shape that you really like best.

Creative use of *pear-shape* diamonds to accent a colored gemstone creates a soft flow in this classic design.

Cushion-shaped center stone flanked by half-moon cut diamonds

❖ Popular Cuts Frequently Used as Side Stones for Accent

In addition to the fancy shapes described in the preceding section, there are several cuts that are frequently used as side accents. The most popular include straight baguettes, tapered baguettes, and two new shapes—the trilliant and princess. There are also "specialty" cuts that are used to create very distinctive rings. These unusual shapes include half-moon shapes, trapezoids, kite shapes, and bullets, and can be especially lovely accents with colored gemstones or emerald-cut diamonds.

Baguettes have been popular for many years and create a very traditional look. In both straight and tapered shapes, they are understated and serve simply to lead the eye to the important center stone. Today there are also "brilliant-cut" baguettes—both straight and tapered—which some people prefer to use with a "brilliant-cut" center stone; the overall impression across the top of the ring is then more uniformly brilliant.

Prong-set round diamond flanked by shield-shaped rubies and small channel-set round diamonds

The trilliant is a relative newcomer that has quickly become one of the most popular choices to create an elegant and classic look. It is a triangular shape that has been cut with extra facets to create tremendous brilliance and liveliness. The trilliant, because it is cut from a very flat piece of diamond rough, also gives a very large look for its actual weight. It provides an important look to balance a large center stone, within a reasonable budget. They are popular choices to use with diamonds or colored gemstones.

A lovely solitaire ring with trilliant as center stone

The princess cut is also very popular as a choice for side stones, especially for channel-set or bezel-set designs.

Again, the use of side stones to accent a center stone, and the shape of the side stone, is a matter of personal choice. In addition to the shapes mentioned here, almost any of the other popular shapes can be found in small sizes and can be used to create an interesting and distinctive ring.

Emerald flanked by princess cuts

Emerald cut with single tapered baguette on each side

Cushion-cut sapphire flanked by three tapered baguette diamonds that form graceful curving arch across top of finger

Radiant cut flanked with single straight baguette on each side, set perpendicular to ring shank

Emerald-cut emerald flanked by three straight baguettes set in a step-like fashion

Tapered or straight baguettes, used creatively, make elegant choices for diamonds or colored gemstones.

Cushion-cut ruby flanked by diamond trilliants

Use of straight baguettes to complement the center emerald-cut ruby creates a very unusual ring not only because of the design, but also because it is so rare to find ruby in this shape.

Oval center stone flanked by half-moon shaped diamonds

❖ Popular Shapes in Colored Gems

Colored gems can be found in any of the shapes described for diamonds. In addition, they are often seen in the *cushion cut,* a modified oval. Keep in mind that some gems are more easily found in particular shapes than in others. For example, emeralds are most often seen in a rectangular shape (actually called "emerald cut") because this is the shape that tends to present emerald to its best advantage. In addition, the natural crystal shape of emerald lends itself particularly well to a rectangular shape. Rubies and sapphires are often seen in the cushion cut, as pictured below. This is due in part to the shape of rough rubies and sapphires, but also to the fact that this cut seems to reveal the rich, lush color of these stones more fully than other cuts. Thus, it may be very difficult to find a sapphire or ruby in an emerald cut. Once again, your choice is very much a personal matter, but be aware that it may be very difficult, or impossible, to find certain types of gemstones in certain shapes.

Emerald-cut center stone framed by straight baguettes

Art Deco period (1920s) squarish emerald-cut diamond flanked by *trapezoid*-shaped white diamonds, baguettes, and square cuts creates a unique and distinctive ring.

Emerald-cut center stone flanked by princess-cut diamonds and trilliant-cut rubies

CHAPTER 22

Choosing Your Setting

The setting you choose will be determined primarily by personal taste. Nevertheless, it is a good idea to be familiar with a few of the most common settings so that you have a working vocabulary and some idea of what is available.

Bezel setting. With a bezel setting, a rim holds the stone and completely surrounds the gem. Bezels can have straight edges, scalloped edges, or can be molded into any shape to accommodate the stone. The backs can be open or closed. One advantage of the bezel setting is that it can make a stone look larger. The bezel setting can also conceal nicks or chips on the girdle. It can also protect the girdle from becoming chipped or nicked.

Bezel-set center stones with "grosgrain textured" platinum and 18-karat gold

Keep in mind that if you use yellow gold in a bezel setting, the yellow of the bezel surrounding the stone will be reflected into the stone, causing white stones to appear less white. On the other hand, a yellow gold bezel can make a red stone such as ruby look even redder, or an emerald look greener.

A variation on the bezel setting is the collet setting. The collet setting has a similar appearance to the bezel setting but involves the use of gold tubing.

Partial bezel-set solitaire

Prong setting. Prong settings—those that have little "fingers" holding the stone—are perhaps the most common type of setting. They come in an almost infinite variety. There are four-prong, six-prong, and special styles such as fishtail and Tiffany-type. In addition, prongs can be pointed, rounded, flat, or V-shaped. Extra prongs provide added security for the stone and can make a stone look slightly larger. However,

Graceful intertwined prongs hold these diamonds in five-stone bands.

POPULAR SETTINGS

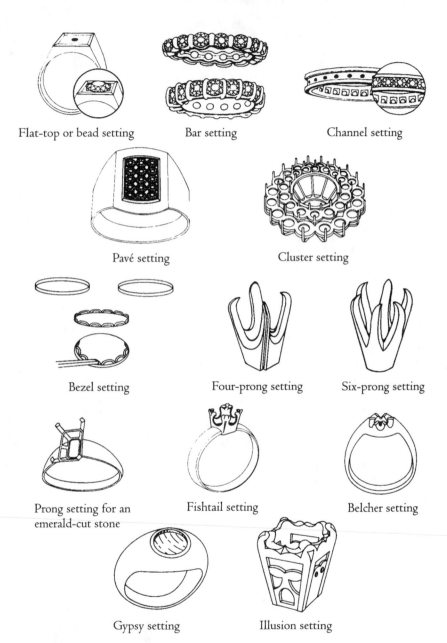

Flat-top or bead setting

Bar setting

Channel setting

Pavé setting

Cluster setting

Bezel setting

Four-prong setting

Six-prong setting

Prong setting for an emerald-cut stone

Fishtail setting

Belcher setting

Gypsy setting

Illusion setting

The drawings above illustrate some of the most popular setting techniques. There can be many variations, such as the shape of the "prong," thickness of "bezel," detailing along bezel, and so on, but this should familiarize you with the basic terminology to help you describe what you like or want to see.

too many prongs hold-
ing too small a stone can
overpower the stone and
make the stone look
smaller, and the mount-
ing look heavy. When
setting a marquise, heart
shape, or pear shape, we

V-shaped prongs protect
point of heart.

Marquise-shaped
diamonds in this
ring show use of
V-shaped prongs
to protect the
points.

recommend that the point or points be held by a V-
shaped prong, which will best protect the point(s). For
emerald-cut stones that have "canted" corners (a corner
with a small diagonal edge rather than forming a 90 degree angle), flat prongs are the preferred choice.

Gypsy setting. In this type of setting, the metal at the
top of the ring (around the stone) is much heavier than
the shank. The stone is set flush into a hole at the top.

Illusion setting. The illusion setting is used to make the
mounted stone appear larger. There are numerous styles
from which to choose.

Channel setting. This setting is used extensively today,
especially for wedding bands. The stones are set into a
channel with no metal separating them. In some cases
the channel can continue completely around the ring,
so that the piece has a continuous row of stones.

Bar setting. This setting, which resembles a channel
setting, combines the contemporary and classic look. It is
used in a circular band, and, rather than using prongs,
each stone is held in the ring by a long thin
bar, shared between two stones.

Pavé setting. This setting is used for numerous small stones set together in a cluster with no metal showing through. The
impression is that the piece is entirely
paved with stones. The setting can be flat
or dome-shaped, and can be worked so

In this grouping,
lower ring shows a
gypsy setting;
upper ring shows
collet setting.

Channel-set
baguettes in a
wedding band

Bar-set bands

Several interesting solitaire designs: prong-set with a scroll motif or twist, and "tension" mounted

A three-stone diamond ring

A three-stone ring with a ruby in the center and an oval diamond on each side, and one with a sapphire at the center and emerald-cut diamonds on each side

that the piece almost appears to be one large single stone. Fine pavé work can be very expensive.

Cluster setting. A cluster setting usually consists of one large stone and several smaller stones as accents. A cluster setting is designed to create a lovely larger piece from several small stones.

❖ A Few Popular Ring Designs

Solitaire. The solitaire is precisely what its name denotes: a single (solitary) stone mounted in a setting. The stone can be any shape (brilliant, emerald, pear, etc.), and the setting can be any style that sets off the stone to its best advantage (prong, illusion, fishtail, etc.).

A solitaire can also have *small* side stones that enhance the important center stone. The most classic solitaire look using side stones normally has a tapered baguette on each side or, for a newer look, the trilliant. This style is equally beautiful whether you use a diamond or colored center stone. Today, we are also seeing diamond center stones with *colored side stones*.

Multi-stone rings. Multi-stone rings usually contain several stones of comparable size, each one being important. This ring style almost always contains an odd number of stones—three, five, or seven—that create the most pleasing aesthetic balance. Some people, however, prefer the center stone slightly larger to achieve a slight tapering in the shape of the ring. Multi-stone rings offer many creative alternatives. One can use diamonds alone, colored stones alone, a mixture of colored stones and diamonds, and/or a mixture of shapes.

Multi-stone rings can create a very important look that will also be more affordable than a single, larger stone. Today's designers and jewelry manufacturers are showing some of the most exciting multi-stone designs ever. A wide variety is available so be sure you take the time to shop around to see what is right for you.

❖ Distinctive Contemporary Settings

There is an increasing number of engagement and wedding ring designs that appeal to the more independent woman who seeks to make a more personal statement. There is also an increasing number of custom jewelry designers catering to the market. The result is an almost limitless choice, ranging from wide, sculpted gold and platinum combinations containing unusual fancy-cut stones, to intricate antique reproductions, as you can see from the variety of styles shown in the color insert section. The choice of metal—yellow gold, white gold, platinum, or mixed-metals—is a personal choice, but there are some differences between the metals that might affect your choice. Refer to chapter 23 for additional information about gold and platinum.

Fine pavé work in diamond and pearl engagement rings, and in a wedding band

❖ Wedding Ring Sets

Many couples prefer wedding ring sets. There are many lovely designs, textures, and shapes from which to choose. Wedding ring sets offer the benefit of an interlocking or perfectly fitting wedding band, often with a matching band for the groom. In addition, sets usually offer distinctive styling at a more affordable price than custom design.

Stylish new wedding ring sets

❖ Settings to Suit Your Lifestyle

It is important to consider your lifestyle when selecting the shape of the stone and the design of your ring. Be realistic about the wear-and-tear your ring must take and realize that while "diamonds are forever," no piece of jewelry is indestructible. Remember, even diamond, the hardest natural substance known, can chip or break if exposed to a sharp accidental blow.

Active outdoor types, for example, might be better off avoiding the marquise or pear shape. The pear shape has a point at one end and the marquise has two points, one at each end. Points are more vulnerable to chipping and breaking,

Designs add protection for active lifestyles

which could result from a sudden or sharp blow to which a very active person might be more vulnerable.

The shank as well as the prongs of a ring worn daily by a very active person will also show the effects of wear; any detailing on your ring will blur over time as the result of gardening, playing on the beach, mountain-climbing, handling ski equipment or bicycles, etc.

The classic four- or six-prong setting served a less active generation well, but may not be as well suited to today's woman. If your daily schedule features a great deal of activity, you would be wise to consider a sturdier engagement ring and wedding band. Remember: sturdy and graceful are not mutually exclusive. Bezel settings do not detract from a gemstone's brilliance, yet they will afford you greater security.

Note: It is important to have a reputable jeweler check mountings and settings periodically, at least once a year. Chlorine attacks soldering links and stress points, so if you swim regularly in a chlorinated pool, take your ring off when you swim and/or have it checked frequently.

In terms of design, rings are usually round, fingers aren't. Top-heavy rings will turn on the finger unless the diameter, or outline, is square or stirrup-shaped to conform to the shape of the finger. Also, remember that rings worn together side by side quickly begin to wear on each other.

In considering which metal is best, remember that color is a personal choice. The higher the gold karatage, the richer the color; but the higher the karatage, the softer the metal. Also, white gold is stronger than yellow. Platinum is expensive, but it is also tougher than gold—rather than abrading easily, platinum tends to "roll over itself" much like warm wax does when you roll it between your fingers. This tends to make a platinum setting more durable than a gold setting, but both metals dent and scratch equally.

❖ Shopping Tips

- *Set a realistic budget* range to eliminate confusion and temptation that can result in disappointment.
- *Shop around and familiarize yourself with current styles* to educate your eye and learn what really appeals to you.

- *Try on different styles*—rings look different on the hand than they do in the window. We know of women who really disliked a ring in the showcase and then loved it on their hand.
- *Decide what is important to you.* Is size important? Do you prefer size to other qualities? Do you feel you need a smaller stone because you have very tiny fingers; or, if you have very long fingers, do you feel you must have a larger stone so that it won't look lost? What shape looks best? If you're considering a colored gem, do you prefer lighter or darker shades of color? Do you prefer yellow gold or white gold/platinum? Will yellow gold or white gold provide the best setting for your stone? What width should the ring be for your finger?
- *Consider the wedding band when you select your engagement ring.* As you select your engagement ring, remember that you will also be wearing a wedding band. Be sure to select a style that will complement the type of wedding band you are considering.

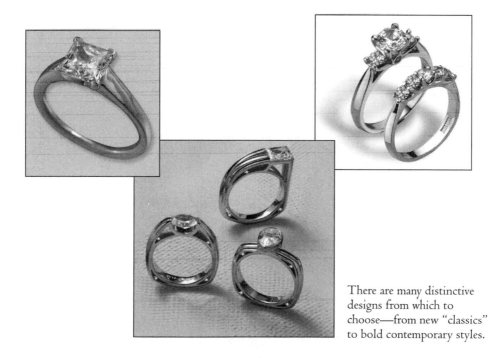

There are many distinctive designs from which to choose—from new "classics" to bold contemporary styles.

CHAPTER 23

Gold or Platinum for Your Rings?

❖ The Gold Ring

Since primitive times, brides and bridegrooms have sealed their wedding vows with a symbolic exchange of rings. As illustrated in folklore and fantasy, once this exchange takes place, the marriage begins.

The history of the gold wedding band is indeed long and illustrious. Before the introduction of coinage, gold rings were circulated as currency. A man would give his bride a gold ring as a sign that he trusted her with his property. Under Roman law, a bridegroom would furnish a ring as a sign of security, a form of collateral to protect the interests of the bride-to-be. Some believe that the idea of using a ring to seal the pact dates back to a time in Iceland when a marriage pledge was made by a man passing his hand through a large iron ring to clasp the hand of his beloved.

During the engagement period in Elizabethan times, three rings were distributed: one to be worn by the groom, one to be worn by the bride, and one to be worn by a witness. At the time of the wedding, all three would be united on the bride's finger!

The pharaohs of Egypt wore their wedding ring on the fourth finger of the left hand because of the *vena amoris,* a vein that they believed ran from that finger directly to the heart. In many cultures, the wedding ring is worn on another finger, but the pharaoh's finger remains the choice of most American brides and grooms.

To the ancients, the circular shape of the ring symbolized eternity. Even today, in some religious ceremonies, the couple is married with rings that have no stones or other "interruptions" that might affect the heavenly circle—the circle of life and happiness that has no beginning and no end.

In modern times, millions of couples exchange gold bands at

their wedding ceremony. The circlet of gold has become the universal symbol of trust and commitment between two loving people. The simple gold wedding band probably uses more of the world's gold than any other single type of jewelry.

❖ What Is Gold?

Gold is one of the world's most precious metals. It combines four basic characteristics that have made it a treasured possession since earliest times: lustrous beauty, easy workability, rarity, and virtual indestructibility. Gold is so soft and malleable that one ounce can be stretched into a wire five miles long, or hammered into a sheet so thin it covers 100 square feet. Gold is so rare that only an estimated 102,000 tons have been taken from the earth during all of recorded history. More steel is poured in one hour than gold has been poured since the beginning of time. Since it does not rust, tarnish, or corrode, gold virtually lasts forever. Coins found in centuries-old sunken galleons are as bright and shiny as the day they were cast.

Through the years, gold has held a preeminent position as the metal most desired for jewelry. In many parts of the world, the finest pieces of jewelry are fashioned in 18- or 22-karat gold. In the United States, 14- or 18-karat gold is often preferred for fine jewelry because it is more durable than higher karat gold.

Although gold is everywhere around us—in the earth's crust, in our seas, rivers, and plants—it is difficult and expensive to extract. Two and a half to three tons of ore must be extracted to yield just one ounce of the precious metal. It is easy to appreciate why gold remains so rare and valuable, and has become such an appropriate symbol commemorating the rarity and value of a good marriage. The leading producers of gold today include Australia, Brazil, Canada, the former USSR, Union of South Africa, and the United States.

❖ What Is a Carat? Or Is It Karat?

In jewelry, the term *carat* (or karat) has a double meaning: *carat* is used as a measurement of weight for gemstones, with one carat weighing one-fifth gram; *carat* is also used in countries around the world to indicate the amount of pure gold in a piece of gold jewelry. In the United States, however, when using the word to indicate gold content rather than gemstone weight, it is spelled with a K—hence "karat"—to avoid confusion. Jewelry should always be marked to indicate how much pure gold it contains.

In the United States a karat mark, abbreviated K or KT, indicates the amount of pure gold present in the metal. The word "karat" (carat) is derived from the word for the fruit of the carob tree: in Italian, *carato;* in Arabic, *qirat;* in Greek, *keration.* The seeds of the fruit were used in ancient times for weighing gems. Also, the pure gold Byzantine coin called the *solidus* weighed 24 "karats." Therefore, a 24-karat mark (24K or 24KT) became the mark used to indicate that something was pure gold.

To understand the concept as applied to gold, imagine that "pure gold" is a pie divided into 24 equal "slices" or parts. Each karat equals one part of the pie. So, 24K would mean that 24 parts (out of a total of 24) are gold. In other words, 24K would be 100 percent gold—or, pure gold. In 18-karat gold jewelry, 18 parts are pure gold and 6 are another metal (or, 18/24 = 3/4 = 75 percent pure gold); in 12-karat, 12 parts are pure gold, 12 parts another metal (12/24 = 1/2 = 50 percent pure gold). And so on.

In some cultures, 24-karat gold jewelry is required for certain jewelry pieces, but it's generally agreed that 24-karat, or pure gold, is too soft for jewelry use. In some parts of the world, 18- or 20-karat is preferred because of its brighter yellow color and because it is considered "purer" and more precious.

In the United States, as we said earlier, many prefer 14- or 18-karat gold because it is more durable than higher karat gold. We caution clients about the risk of high-karat gold (20-, 22-, or 24-karat) for a gem-studded setting because prongs can too easily bend open accidentally, resulting in loss of stones.

Some new alloys—such as *gold 990*—may change the American preference for 14- or 18-karat gold. Gold "990" is an alloy of gold and a very small amount of another element, titanium. The result is almost "pure" gold (990/1000 pure gold), with greatly increased durability. The titanium produces a color that is much less yellow, however, than one expects from such a high-karat gold, more closely resembling the color of straw. In color, it is very similar to 14-karat, which reduces its universal appeal to some extent. Nonetheless, it offers the preciousness

Pure gold ring (24K) with a hammered finish

of a very high-karat, almost pure gold, with added durability.

In some countries, such as Italy, the percentage of pure gold is indicated by a number representing how many parts—out of a total of 1,000 parts—are pure gold. *One thousand* parts would be the equivalent of 24-karat; *seven hundred fifty* means that 750 parts out of 1,000 are pure gold: 750/1000 = 3/4 = 75 percent pure gold. This corresponds to 18K.

The following chart shows how different international gold markings correspond to one another.

Gold Marks		
AMERICAN MARKING (KARATAGE)	PURE GOLD CONTENT	EUROPEAN MARKING (FINENESS IN PERCENT)
24K	100%	1,000–999
22K	91.6%	916
20K	83%	833
19K (used in Portugal)	79.2%	792
18K	75.0%	750
15K (seen in antiques)	62.5%	625
14K	58.3%	585
12K	50.0%	500
10K	41.7%	417
9K	37.5%	375

❖ To Be Called Gold, What Is the Minimum Gold Content?

Many countries have established minimum standards that must be met for items to be legally called "gold." The laws governing the actual content of gold required in a piece of jewelry, however, vary. In the United States, to be called "gold," the item must be at least 10K; in England and Canada, 9K; in Italy and France, 18K.

❖ The Many Colors of Gold

Pure gold is always yellow. But because pure gold is too soft for most jewelry use and must be mixed with other metals (alloys) to increase its hardness, the color can be modified by adding varying amounts of these other metals. Those usually added to gold for jewelry use include copper, zinc, silver, nickel, platinum, and palladium (a metal in the platinum family). Depending upon which alloys are used, a variety of colors can be produced. Another practice is to plate 14K gold jewelry with 18K for an 18K gold *color,* that is, a stronger yellow color. White gold is also frequently plated with rhodium, a rare and more expensive metal from the platinum family, to create a whiter, brighter finish.

Using some combination of one or more of the metals shown below will result in various colors.

How Alloys Affect Color	
Color	Composition
Yellow Gold	Gold, Copper, Silver
White Gold	Gold, Nickel*, Zinc, Silver, Platinum, Palladium
Green Gold	Gold, Silver (much more than in yellow gold), Copper, Zinc
Pink (red) Gold	Gold, Copper (sometimes a small amount of silver is used)

*Note: Some people are allergic to nickel and should not wear white gold containing nickel. For this reason, a white gold alloyed with palladium is being used by some manufacturers. White gold that contains palladium will be more expensive than yellow gold or white gold containing another alloy, but is still less expensive than pure platinum.

Gold Finishes

Gold has excellent working qualities that make it particularly desirable for fine jewelry. As you will see as you shop for your gold wedding bands, gold is available in a wide range of finishes and styles to suit individual tastes.

Popular Finishes and Techniques

Polished gold

Polished gold with milgraining

Florentine finish with milgraining

Appliqué: Soldering a design worked in gold to another piece of gold; soldering one color gold to another.

Chasing: Accent technique, outlining the detail of repoussé.

Diamond cut: Sections of the surface are cut to achieve bright reflections; can create interesting design effects.

Embossing: Ornamentation to create a bas-relief-like impression.

Enameling: Fusing colored glass onto metal surface.

Engraving: Cutting a design into the surface.

Filigree: Gold wire twisted and soldered onto other metal in intricate patterns; also used to describe any intricate openwork.

Florentine: A finish created by texturing the surface with a special tool.

Granulation: Tiny round balls fastened to another metal by a heating process.

Hammering: Forming indentations in metal to create interesting patterns and texture.

High polish: Mirror-like.

Matte: Soft, flat, non-reflective finish.

Milgraining: A detail that resembles a string of tiny beads applied as an ornamental border.

Repoussé: Forming a design by punching or pressing out portions from inside the ring.

Satin: Grained texture of satin cloth; has a softer shine than "high polish."

Gold Look-Alikes

There are several manufacturing methods that result in jewelry that may look like gold, but actually cannot be considered within the quality range of fine or karat gold. Beware of gold look-alikes and remember that the following terms are used for metal products that are *not* gold in the legal sense: gold filled, gold over-lay, double d'or, gold plate, rolled gold plate, plaque d'or lamine, gold electroplating, gold wash or gold flash, and vermeil.

❖ The Platinum Ring

Platinum is even more rare and valuable than gold. The platinum family is composed of six elements: platinum, palladium, iridium, osmium, rhodium, and ruthenium. These six silvery white metals are generally found together in nature, with platinum and palladium the most abundant and ruthenium and iridium the rarest (and most expensive). Platinum is rarer and heavier than other precious metals and is the purest metal—often referred to as the "noblest." Because platinum is so pure, it does not cause allergic reactions. This is greatly appreciated by sensitive people who experience reactions to, or skin discoloration from, jewelry containing base metals. In addition, platinum is much stronger than other precious metals. Because of its many excellent qualities, platinum makes an excellent choice for fine jewelry. Platinum prongs are preferred by many jewelers because they can be maneuvered around a fragile stone with less risk of damaging the stone.

Unlike gold, platinum is not identified by karat marks. In the United States, platinum is marked with the word *platinum*, the abbreviation *PLAT,* or with *Pt950* or *950Plat*. Some platinum jewelry from other countries may be stamped Pt850, but this usually applies only to platinum chain. Some pieces are composed of 90 percent platinum and 10 percent iridium, which once was the most commonly used platinum alloy in the United States. These are stamped Pt900 or 900 PLAT. Some older rings will still have the stamp IRID-PLAT or the stamp "90% platinum 10% iridium" inside.

Platinum is alloyed for strength. Typically, platinum alloys are designed to fulfill a specific function. Platinum/iridium is used for fabrication, platinum/ruthenium is used for machining of wedding rings, and platinum/cobalt is designed to give the finest detailed castings.

In the United States, to be described or marked "platinum," a piece must contain at least 50 percent platinum; anything less cannot be stamped with the word platinum or any mark indicating platinum.

New Platinum Alloys

There are growing numbers of new platinum alloys on the market that are designed for specific functions. Among them are the *hard-cast* and *heat-treatable* alloys. These alloy combinations are proprietary, and they are designed to make the manufacturing of jewelry in platinum easier. Many so-called tension rings are made of such alloys. Pt950 S+1 and S+2 are among the heat-treatable versions. These alloys can be hardened, for extra durability, after the piece has been made. Another new alloy for all around use is called PlatOro, and it contains gold as the alloying metal. Interestingly, platinum can be alloyed with gold, copper, iridium, ruthenium, palladium, tungsten, and cobalt, and there are very minor color differences between these alloys.

Rhodium Plating

Rhodium, another member of the platinum family, is the brightest and most reflective of all the platinum metals. Because of these qualities, it is frequently used to coat silver, gold, and palladium jewelry, and it is used as an electroplate finish. Rhodium is even harder and whiter than platinum, and it is highly resistant to corrosion. Because rhodium is so hard, it does not wear off as quickly as yellow gold plating. As rhodium plating is designed to simulate the look of platinum, fine jewelers do not rhodium plate platinum.

Rhodium plating is especially helpful for people who are allergic to the alloys in 10K or 14K gold. Rhodium plating can eliminate allergic reactions caused by the alloys, and it is also used to change the color of yellow gold to white for those people who prefer a white metal but are allergic to nickel and can't afford platinum.

❖ Yellow Gold, White Gold, or Platinum: Which One?

The first choice you must make is one of color. This selection usually depends on personal preference, skin tone, and the color of other jewelry you may own. If your choice is yellow gold, keep in mind that it is available in several different shades, including a pure yellow, a pinkish yellow, and a greenish yellow.

If your choice is yellow, the only decision you must make is whether you prefer 14K, 18K, or higher karat gold. The least expensive is 14K gold, but it is also the hardest. One noticeable difference is that the yellow is not as bright in 14K gold as in higher karat gold.

The higher the karat, the brighter and more vivid the yellow color becomes. If you prefer a brighter yellow, ask for 14K gold with an 18K *finish*. After several years the finish may wear off, but it can be replated for a minimal charge.

If you prefer a white metal, your choice may be more difficult. Even though white gold and platinum are similar in appearance, they are very different metals. As we mentioned, platinum is much more expensive, so if you're on a limited budget, white gold may be the better choice. In addition to being more affordable, 18K white gold is harder and more resistant to scratches than most platinum alloys. White gold often exhibits a brownish or yellowish cast, which must be covered by rhodium plating. The plating will wear off after a time, but a jeweler can have it replated at a modest cost.

One significant disadvantage of white gold is that it is more brittle than both platinum and yellow gold. So if you decide on white gold, be sure to have your jeweler check the setting—especially the prongs—at least once a year. White gold is also subject to stress corrosion, which does not occur in platinum. There is also the allergy consideration; nickel-alloyed white gold can result in an allergic reaction and is actually prohibited in Europe for this reason.

Platinum is somewhat softer and more malleable than white gold, making it an ideal choice for very intricate settings that require intensive labor. It is much easier to use platinum for pavé work—that is, designs in which the stones are set as closely together as possible. With platinum, the jeweler can also make a safer setting because a larger prong can be used, since platinum conforms so easily to the shape of the stone, reducing the risk of damage. The most important benefit of platinum is that, while it is softer than white gold and can scratch, it is more durable and does not wear down or abrade like gold. Therefore, over time, platinum settings hold up and last longer than gold ones.

Today there are more styles in platinum, and in platinum and gold combinations, than ever before, and the introduction of the new platinum alloys we discussed earlier is also having a positive effect on the increasing availability of platinum designs.

In the final analysis, it is up to you to weigh the advantages and disadvantages of each in terms of your own needs. Whichever precious metal you choose, you can find many beautiful styles and designs. With proper care, whatever choice you make should last a lifetime.

❖ Engraved Messages Add an Intimate, Romantic Touch

Engraving a message on the ring or a hidden message inside the wedding band (or even on the girdle of a stone—see chapter 28) adds a very personal and intimate touch. Secret messages have been engraved in rings for centuries, and today is no different from bygone eras. To some extent, the size and width of the ring limit the message, but a creative couple can always find a way to convey a romantic thought! It may simply be the couple's initials and date of the wedding, a brief sentiment such as "love always", or a few words from a favorite song or poem. The cost is usually nominal and is based on the number of letters in the inscription. Your jeweler can arrange to have rings engraved or refer you to a reliable engraver. Hand engravers usually cost a little more, but they can add flourishes that may not be available by machine.

Personal sentiment
encircling ring

Secret message inscribed
inside this hinged ring

Love, spelled in any
language

CHAPTER 24

Choosing the Wedding Bands

There are virtually hundreds of styles of wedding bands from which to choose, for both the bride and the groom. While the traditional band for both is a simple, round gold ring, today they can be simple or elaborate, wide or thin, gem-studded or not. It is not unusual, even in the groom's ring, to find gemstone accents.

Traditionally, the woman receives two rings—one upon consenting to marriage and the second at the wedding ceremony. Today, this tradition continues to be the most popular choice. However, couples sometimes opt for a more important wedding band that incorporates the gem of choice and eliminates the need for an engagement ring, as such. For example, rather than purchasing an engagement ring with a one-carat diamond followed by a simple wedding band, one might purchase for the same price a diamond wedding band that contains four carats total weight of diamonds encircling the finger.

The diamond wedding band then becomes the single focal point and combines the symbolism of the simple round ring with the symbolism of the diamond or other stone of choice. It can create an important and classic look. Another example might involve the purchase of a single diamond that is then set within a very wide, gold wedding band, again combining the gem traditionally received at an earlier moment within the wedding band itself.

The choice as to whether to have one or two rings is largely personal, but keep in mind that the length of the engagement may affect your decision. If the engagement period is going to be long, rather than waiting for the wedding day the bride-to-be may prefer to have an engagement ring to announce her commitment and, thus, the change in her status and the upcoming event.

❖ Important Considerations Before You Make the Choice

To help you make the right choice for the wedding ring, here are some important factors to consider.

Wedding Band Widths

2 mm

3 mm

4 mm

5 mm

6 mm

8 mm

10 mm

Actual width in millimeters

How does the wedding band look with the engagement ring? If an engagement ring is given, it is very important to consider how the wedding band will look with it on the hand. (We hope that before making the final decision on your engagement ring, you also give some thought to your wedding band.) It's a good idea to try on different styles of wedding bands with the engagement ring to see how they look together. The width of the band can dramatically affect the way it works with the engagement ring. Remember also that certain details such as milgraining (see chapter 23) or a particular type of finish may look great when worn alone, but can detract from the overall appearance when worn together with the engagement ring.

What width looks best? The width of the wedding band is measured in millimeters. The standard ladies' simple gold or platinum band ranges from 2 millimeters to 4 millimeters; the men's ranges from 3 1/2 millimeters to 6 millimeters. Stock sizes can go as wide as 10 millimeters. It is important to try the same style band in different widths because you will be surprised to see how different the effect created by width alone can be. Avoid very wide rings that feel uncomfortable when you try them on. You will not get used to them. While a very wide band may be beautiful from a design standpoint, keep in mind that it may be less comfortable in very hot climates.

Do you prefer a "flat" band or a "half-round" band? A flat band is flatter on the finger, while a half round has a somewhat curved or dome-like shape to it. The decision is purely a matter of personal taste.

Do you prefer "matching" bands? Most wedding ring manufacturers today offer a wide selection of matching ladies' and men's wedding bands.

Do you plan to wear the wedding band without the engagement ring? If you think you may frequently wear your wedding band without your engagement ring, you may prefer a different type of band. For example, some women prefer to wear only their wedding band at the office; some prefer to wear their engagement ring only in social situations. If you think this might be the case with you, you may prefer a larger or more important looking band, one that will stand on its own.

A flat band

For Gem-Studded Bands

Should the stones completely encircle the ring? This is a decision that depends on personal taste, budget, comfort, and fit. Many prefer that the stones continue around the entire finger, while others want the stones set only across the top. The primary benefit in having stones all around is that you never need to worry about the ring twisting on your finger. A significant disadvantage is that some of the stones (those on the underside of the finger) are subjected to strenuous wear, which can result in breakage and loss. The choice is really not an economic one—by juggling the size and quality of the stones and the width of the ring, you can get either look on any budget.

A half-round band

Does the ring fit properly? When selecting a gem-studded style, be sure to try rings that actually fit your finger properly. Otherwise you may find that a ring feels very uncomfortable on your finger, when, in fact, it would be very comfortable if it fit properly. This is particularly true for rings with larger stones held by prongs. Also, for rings with stones going part way around, proper fit is critical to comfort because it affects the contour of the top portion of the ring.

Contemporary gem-studded bands

We will not discuss the many different styles of wedding bands here since the selection is truly limitless. We have provided photographs of a variety of the most popular styles in the color insert section, and we encourage you to use your own imagination.

Classic diamond-studded bands

CHAPTER 25

The Heirloom Ring

Rings passed from one generation to another carry with them the history and tradition of a family, and add a romantic element—and emotional value—difficult to match with a "new" ring. In addition to the true "heirloom," which has been passed down through the family, young couples today enjoy the unique and distinctive character and workmanship found in antique rings and rings from earlier by-gone days. Antique as well as *antique reproduction* rings have also become very popular and offer a distinctive look with a nostalgic element. Some of the most popular periods include the Art Nouveau period (1895–1915) with its graceful, curving lines, floral motifs, and other images from nature; the Edwardian period (1901–1914) with its lacy character and romantic themes such as garlands of flowers; and the Art Deco period (1920–1930) with its clean, geometric feeling and use of interesting shapes such as trapezoids, triangles, and half-moons, often combined with tiny colored gemstone accents. Simple pieces from the 1950s and 1960s are also gaining in popularity.

If you are thinking of giving an heirloom or estate piece as an engagement or wedding ring, or are considering taking stones out of an heirloom piece, you must remember that the stones may not be what they appear to be, especially if purchased from a source other a than reputable jewelry firm, or they may have been chipped or damaged in some way that might pose a problem if you are remounting them.

The first step is to have the piece appraised by a qualified gemologist-appraiser. The appraisal will verify that the ring is what you believe it to be, will

New rings with an authentic vintage look

fully describe its quality, and identify whether or not there are any problems; that is, if the stone is chipped or cracked in such a way that it may be vulnerable to breakage. With full knowledge of the stone, you can take any necessary precautions when wearing or re-setting it. For example, if a diamond has been chipped from wear over the years and the chip has resulted in a small fracture that penetrates the stone, you have to consider what kind of setting is best when resetting it. Can a prong conceal and protect the stone? Possibly a bezel setting will be most advantageous.

Today, there are many styles of rings that can accommodate almost any stone, but keep in mind one point when updating or resetting an heirloom: Some require custom-made settings that are more expensive than already-made settings, especially if the shape of the stone is unusual.

It is much easier and less expensive to find a desirable setting if you are using a round stone. A stone other than a round one may require custom setting or a skilled jeweler who can customize part of another setting to suit the shape of your stone.

In cases where you love the ring, but it requires some minor repair such as re-tipping a prong, or it needs only to be re-sized, be sure to take extra precaution with antique settings. Chances are the setting has been repaired over the years and may well have been improperly fixed. This is frequently the case with platinum pieces. Often platinum settings have been restored or repaired with white gold solder, which is actually a different color from the original piece.

It is a good idea to closely examine any antique platinum piece for minute cracks that may have formed around open work or bridgework. A jeweler may have inadvertently damaged the platinum in the process of doing a minor repair (a jeweler unaccustomed to working with platinum may immerse the piece in sulfuric acid after soldering—this breaks down the molecular structure of the metal, causing it to begin to crack and deteriorate). A platinum piece that has begun to crack as a result of sulfuric acid *cannot be restored* and is *unstable*. Be sure to check for signs of deterioration in the prong areas and in other thin places. (*Note:* Should this be the case with an heirloom ring that has been in the family for many years, a skilled jeweler may be able to remake the ring, retaining the original appearance and workmanship.)

❖ Tips on Updating an Heirloom or Older Piece

When to Redesign

- *When you don't like the style of the ring,* whether it looks outdated or is simply not your taste.
- *When the setting is in need of repair,* but the techniques involved are too expensive to make it worthwhile. Take, for example, a ring with extensive damage to the enameling, or a ring with delicate granulation or extensive filigree.
- *When the overall piece is too small for your taste.* A new setting using a bold gold or platinum design can add size and importance to a smaller stone.
- *When you wish to use just the stone(s)* from another piece of jewelry, such as a pendant or brooch.

❖ How to Create Something New from Something Old

Getting Started

The first step in creating a new look out of an antique or old piece is to know exactly what you have and what condition it is in. Have the piece examined and evaluated by a qualified gemologist-appraiser. The examination should include:

1. *Verification of what the stone is.* Is it what you believe it is or something else? Is it genuine, synthetic, or imitation? Just because it has been in the family is no guarantee of its true identity. For your protection and the jeweler's, check it out first. For more information about enhancement techniques used in antique and estate jewelry, *Gem Identification Made Easy, 2nd Edition* (GemStone Press, Woodstock, Vt., 1998) describes them in a chapter devoted to this subject.

2. *Full description of the stone.* (The Four C's, discussed in chapters 6–9 and 16.)

3. *Notation of condition and any problem areas,* including any scratches, chips, cracks, etc. It is helpful if these are indicated on a sketch, showing their positions on (or in) the stone. If there is anything else that the jeweler should know about your stone before beginning work on your ring, have the appraiser make a notation. For example, some stones can't take high

temperatures and any jewelry technique using intense heat could damage the stone.

Be sure to give the jeweler who will be making the ring a copy of this information so proper precautions can be taken.

Selecting the Jeweler

- *Be sure to select a fine jeweler* who has experience working with stones as well as metal. A jeweler who creates beautiful gold or silver jewelry is not necessarily skilled at making jewelry that uses stones. Also, if you are using a stone other than a diamond for your ring, the jeweler should be experienced in colored gems as well—they are more difficult to work with than diamonds. *Ask for recommendations* from friends or acquaintances who have had pieces remade.
- *Ask your appraiser for recommendations.* If you don't know anyone who can offer a recommendation, ask your appraiser; they are often aware of good jewelers in the community and familiar with their work.
- *Meet with the jeweler and look at his work.* Jewelry design is like art . . . what appeals to someone else may not appeal to you; what is considered "great" by someone else may not be to your own personal liking. Try to find someone whose work excites you.

Working with the Jeweler to Design the Ring

When you find someone whose work you like, give him or her as much information as you can about what you like and what you're looking for. Look through magazines and catalogues and clip pictures of rings you admire, even if there are little details you would want to change. Give these to the jeweler and discuss the details you like or don't like. Do your best to help the jeweler clearly understand what you want.

Have the jeweler provide sketches, if possible, showing both *top and side views.* Some jewelers won't do this, but will be happy to make a wax model. Always request a model so that you can have a clearer view of what the finished piece will look like. This way alterations can be made before the ring is cast and stones are set. Do keep in mind, however, that the wax models have a heavier, clunkier look than the finished piece. A little imagination is required to get a real sense of the ring. Even so, important details can be refined and altered at this stage more easily than after the ring is completed.

Remember: Jewelers are not mind readers. You may have an idea in mind that you think you can describe in words. Most people can't. It is difficult to communicate with words alone an image that only you can see. All too often the big day arrives, you go to get your ring, and your heart sinks upon seeing it. This is why it is so important to take the extra time to work with sketches and models—to help ensure that your heart will soar when you see the ring you will treasure forever!

Vintage Styles Old & New. A nostalgic feeling is evoked with designs from bygone eras. Today many styles for engagement and wedding rings are being reproduced, often from original molds dating back to earlier eras.

PART SIX

Important Advice Before You Buy

CHAPTER 26

What to Ask When Buying the Stone

Asking the right questions is the key to knowing what you're getting when it comes to buying gemstones. It is also the only way you can be sure what you are comparing when considering gems from different jewelers. Be sure the jeweler can answer your questions or can get the answers for you. Then, be sure the jeweler is willing to put the answers *in writing* on your bill of sale. Finally, verify the facts—double-check that the stone is as represented—by having your stone examined by a qualified gemologist-appraiser (see chapter 28). In this way you'll be able to make an informed choice about quality and value, you'll have no doubt about what you are getting, and you'll begin to develop a solid relationship with the jeweler from whom you make the purchase, based on confidence and trust. And, in the event the stone is not as represented, you'll know in time—and have the information you need—to get your money back.

❖ Questions to Ask When Buying a Diamond

You should always have very specific information before purchasing a fine diamond weighing one carat or more. For smaller stones, the information may not be so readily available, since most jewelers don't take the time to grade them precisely. An experienced jeweler, however, should be able to provide information regarding quality for stones from a half-carat and up, or offer to find it for you. Indeed, some laboratories are now providing grading reports for diamonds as small as a half-carat or smaller.

Also keep in mind that since it is not possible to grade mounted diamonds accurately, we recommend that fine diamonds weighing one carat or more be purchased unmounted, or removed from the setting and then remounted. In jewelry containing numerous small diamonds, the stones are graded before they are set and the information may be on the sales tag. If not, it is extremely difficult to know for sure what the true quality is, and much can be concealed by a setting. We recommend buying such pieces only from a knowledgeable jeweler with a good reputation.

Here are the basic questions to ask and information that needs to be included on the bill of sale for a diamond or diamond ring:

1. *What is the exact carat weight?* Be sure the stone's weight is given, not its spread (see chapter 9).
2. *What is its color grade?* And what grading system was used (see chapter 7)?
3. *What is its clarity (flaw) grade?* Again, ask what system was used (see chapter 8).
4. *What shape is it?* Round, pear, marquise (see chapter 6)?
5. *Is it well cut for its shape?* How would the "make" be graded: ideal, excellent, good (see chapter 6)?
6. *What are the exact millimeter dimensions of the stone?*
7. *Is this stone accompanied by a diamond grading report or certificate?* Ask for the full report (see chapter 11).

Be sure to find out what system was used to grade the stone. If GIA terms are used, ask if GIA standards and methods have been applied to grading the stone.

Be sure to get the *exact* millimeter dimensions of the stone; the dimensions can be approximated if the stone is mounted. For a round stone, be sure you are given two dimensions for the stone's diameter; since most are not round, you need the highest and lowest. For fancy shapes, get the dimensions of the length and width. Always get the dimension from the table to the culet as well, that is, the depth of the stone.

Be especially careful if the diamond is being taken out on consignment, on a jeweler's memorandum or sales slip, or on a contingency sale. Having the measurements in writing helps protect you from being accused of switching should you have to return the stone for any reason.

Always ask if the stone has a certificate or diamond grading report, and, if so, make sure it accompanies the stone; if you are taking the stone on approval, ask for a copy of the report. If there is no report or certificate, find out who determined the color and flaw grades; make sure the seller puts that information on the bill of sale, and insist that the sale be contingent upon the stone's actually having the grades represented.

❖ Additional Questions to Help You Make Your Selection

Is it large enough? This is a valid question and you should be honest with yourself about it. If you think the diamond is too small, you won't feel good about wearing it. Remember that other factors such as clarity and color can be juggled several grades with little visible difference, and this might enable you to get a larger diamond. And remember that the color and type of setting can also help you achieve a larger look.

Does this stone have a good make? Does this stone have good proportions? How do its proportions compare to the "ideal"? Remember, much variance can exist and a stone can still be a beautiful, desirable gem even if it does not conform to "ideal" standards. Nonetheless, you won't want a stone with poor proportions, so if you have any question about the stone's brilliance and liveliness—if it looks lifeless or dull in spots—you should ask specifically about the proportioning of the cut. In addition, you should ask if there are any cutting faults that might make the stone more vulnerable to chipping or breaking as, for example, an extremely thin girdle would.

Has this stone been clarity-enhanced? Be sure to ask whether or not the diamond has been laser treated or fracture-filled (see chapter 8). If it is accompanied by a GIA report, the report will indicate lasering, if present. However, GIA won't issue a report on a fracture-filled stone and some jewelers don't know how to detect them. If there is no GIA report, be sure to ask explicitly, and get a statement in writing that the diamond is or is not clarity-enhanced, whichever the case may be. Getting this fact in writing may save you a big headache should you learn later that the stone is enhanced.

Does this stone show any fluorescence? If a diamond fluoresces *blue* when viewed in daylight or under daylight-type fluorescent light, it will appear *whiter* than it really is. This can be a desirable quality so long as the stone has not been graded or classified incorrectly. A diamond may also fluoresce yellow, which means that in certain light its color could appear worse than it actually is. If the stone has a diamond grading report, any fluorescence will be indicated there. If there is no report, and if the jeweler can't tell you whether or not the stone exhibits any fluorescence, the stone's color grade may be incorrect.

❖ Special Tips When Buying a Diamond

Ask the jeweler to clean the stone

Don't hesitate to ask to have the stone cleaned before you examine it. Cleaning will remove dirt, grease, or indelible purple ink. Cleaning is best done by steaming or in an ultrasonic cleaner. Cleaning also helps to ensure that you'll see the full beauty of the stone; diamonds can become very dirty just from customers handling them and, as a result, look less brilliant and sparkling than they really are.

View the stone against a dead-white background

When looking at unmounted stones, look at them only against a *dead-white background* such as white blotter paper or a white business card, or on a grading trough. Examine the stone against the white background, through the side, not down through the table (see chapter 7). Tilt the stone toward a good light source; a daylight fluorescent lamp is best. If the stone shows any yellow body tint when viewed through the girdle, if it is not as colorless as an ice cube, then the diamond is not "white" or "colorless."

Get the facts on a bill of sale

Ask that all the facts concerning the stone be put on the bill of sale. These include the carat weight, the color and flaw grades, the cut, and the dimensions. Also, be sure you obtain the report on any "certificated" stone, as diamonds accompanied by laboratory reports are sometimes called.

Verify facts with a gemologist

If a stone is one carat or larger and not accompanied by a respected laboratory report, make the sale contingent on verification of the facts by a qualified gemologist, gem testing lab, or the GIA. While the GIA will not estimate dollar value, it will verify color, flaw grade, make, fluorescence, weight, and other physical characteristics.

Weigh the facts

Decide what is important to you and then weigh the facts. Most people think color and "make" are the most important considerations when buying a diamond, but if you want a larger stone, you may have to come down several grades in color, or choose a slightly spread stone, or select one of the new shapes that look much larger than traditional cuts. The most important thing is to know what you're getting and get what you pay for.

❖ What to Ask When Buying a Colored Gemstone

As with diamonds, it's very important to ask the right questions to help you understand the differences in gems you may be considering. Asking the following questions should help you gain a greater understanding of the differences, determine what's right for you, and have greater confidence in your decision.

1. *Is it a genuine, natural stone, or a synthetic?* Synthetic stones are genuine, but not natural (see chapter 17).

2. *Is the color natural?* Most colored gemstones are routinely color-enhanced (see chapters 16 and 17). See information on specific gems (chapters 19 and 20) to determine whether or not this is an important question for you to ask.

   Be especially cautious when buying any blue sapphire; make sure you ask whether or not the stone has been checked for diffusion treatment. Today, with diffused sapphire being found mixed in parcels of natural sapphires and unknowingly set into jewelry, it's possible that one may be sold inadvertently (see chapter 17).

3. *Is the clarity acceptable, or do too many inclusions detract from the beauty of the stone?* Are there any flaws, inclusions, or natural characteristics in the stone that might make it more vulnerable to breakage with normal wear? This is a particularly important question when considering a colored stone (see chapter 16).

   While visible inclusions are more common in colored gems than in diamonds, and their existence has much less impact on value than they have on diamond value, value is nonetheless reduced if the inclusions or blemishes affect the stone's durability or are so numerous that they mar its beauty.

Be especially careful to ask whether or not any inclusion breaks the stone's surface, since this may weaken the stone, particularly if the imperfection is in a position normally exposed to wear, like the top of the stone or around the girdle. This would reduce the stone's value significantly. On the other hand, if the flaw is in a less vulnerable spot, where it can be protected by the setting, it may be of minimal risk and have little effect on value.

A large number of inclusions will usually detract noticeably from the beauty, especially in terms of liveliness, and will also generally weaken the stone and make it more susceptible to any blow or knock. We recommend that you avoid such stones as the choice for an engagement ring, since this is a ring one hopes to wear for many years to come, for a lifetime.

4. *Do you like the color?* How close is the color to its pure spectral shade? Is it too light? Too dark? How does the color look in different types of light? Learn to look at color critically. Become familiar with the rarest and most valuable color of the gem of your choice. But after you do this, decide what you really like for yourself. You may prefer a color that might be less rare, and therefore more affordable. Be sure the color pleases you—don't buy what you think you *should* buy unless you really like it.

5. *Is the color permanent?* This question should be asked in light of new treatments (such as diffusion) and also because color in some stones is prone to fading. Amethyst is an example; some fade, but it is impossible to know which ones will fade and which ones won't, and how long the process might take. This phenomenon has never affected the popularity of amethyst, but we feel you should be aware of it.

6. *Does the stone need a protective setting?* The setting may be of special importance when considering stones like tanzanite, opal, and emerald. They require a setting that will offer some protection—for example, one in which the main stone is surrounded by diamonds. A design in which the stone is unusually exposed, such as in a high setting or one with open, unprotected sides, would be undesirable.

7. *Does the stone have a pleasing shape? Does it have a nice "person-ality"?* This will be determined by the cutting. Many colored gems are cut in fancy shapes, often by custom cutters. Fine cutting can enrich the color and personality, and increase the cost. However, with colored gems, brilliance and sparkle are less important than the color itself. The most critical considerations must focus on color, first and foremost. Sometimes a cutter must sacrifice brilliance in order to obtain the finest possible color. But if the color isn't rich enough or captivating enough to compensate for less brilliance, ask if the jeweler has something that is cut better and exhibits a little more sparkle. Keep in mind, however, that the more brilliant stone may not have the precise color you like, and that when buying a colored gem, *color* is the most crucial factor. Unless you find the stone's personality unappealing, don't sacrifice a beautiful color for a stone with a less appealing color just because it may sparkle more. Compare, and decide based upon what you like, and what you can afford.

When considering a pastel-colored gem, remember that if it is cut too shallow (flat), it can lose its appeal quickly (but only temporarily) with a slight build up of greasy dirt on the back; the color will fade and its liveliness will practically disappear. This can be immediately remedied by a good cleaning.

❖ Special Tips to Remember When Buying a Colored Stone

- *When looking at unmounted stones, view them through the side as well as from the top.* Also, turn them upside down on a flat, white surface so they are resting on the table facet and you can look straight down through the stone from the back. Look for evenness of color versus color zoning—shades of lighter or darker tones creating streaks or planes of differing color.
- *Remember that color is the most important consideration.* If the color is fine, the presence of flaws or inclusions doesn't detract from the stone's value as significantly as with diamonds. If the overall color or beauty is not seriously affected, the presence of flaws should not deter a purchase. But, conversely, flawless

stones may bring a disproportionately higher price-per-carat due to their rarity, and larger sizes will also command higher prices. In pastel-colored gems, or stones with less fine color, clarity may be more important.

- *Check the stone's color in several different types of light.* View the stone under spotlight, sunlight, fluorescent, or lamplight before making any decision. Many stones change color—some just slightly, others dramatically—depending upon the light in which they are viewed. Be sure that the stone is a pleasing color in the type of light in which you expect to wear it most. An engagement ring will be worn all the time, in all lights, so color "trueness" is especially important.
- *Remember to give special attention to wearability.* Since the engagement ring will be worn most of the time, this is especially important in terms of the stone you select and the design of the setting.

❖ Get the Facts on the Bill of Sale

If a colored stone is over one carat and exceptionally fine and expensive, make the sale contingent on verification of the facts by a qualified gemologist-appraiser or gem testing lab, such as GIA or American Gemological Laboratories (AGL).

Always make sure that any item you purchase is clearly described in the bill of sale exactly as represented to you by the salesperson or jeweler. For diamonds, be sure each of the Four C's is described in writing. For colored gems, essential information also includes the following:

- The identity of the stone or stones and whether or not they are genuine or synthetic, and not in any way a composite (doublet, triplet).
- A statement that the color is natural, if it has been so represented; or, in the case of sapphire or ruby, a statement that the stone either is surface diffused or *not* surface diffused.
- A statement describing the overall color (hue, tone, intensity).
- A statement describing the overall flaw picture and whether or not it has been clarity-enhanced (especially for emerald). This is not always necessary with colored stones. In the case of a

flawless or nearly flawless stone it is wise to note the excellent clarity. In addition, note any unusual flaw that might prove useful for identification.

- A statement describing the cut or make. This is not always necessary but may be useful if the stone is especially well cut, or has an unusual or fancy cut.
- The carat weight of the main stone or stones, plus total weight if there is a combination of main and smaller stones.
- If the stone is to be taken on approval, make sure that the *exact* dimensions of the stone are included, as well as any other identifying characteristics. The terms and period of approval should also be clearly stated.

Other Information that Should Be Included for Jewelry

- If the piece is being represented as having been made by a famous designer or house (Van Cleef & Arpels, Tiffany, J. E. Caldwell, Cartier, etc.), and the price reflects this, the name of the designer or jewelry firm should be stated on the bill of sale.
- If the piece is represented as antique (technically, an antique must be at least one hundred years old) or as a "period" piece from a popular, collectible period like Art Deco, Art Nouveau, Edwardian (especially if made by a premier artisan of the period), this information should be stated on the bill of sale along with the approximate age or date of manufacture and a statement describing "condition."
- If made by hand, or custom-designed, this should be indicated on the bill of sale.

CHAPTER 27

Deciding Where to Make the Purchase—Retailer or E-retailer

❖ Finding a Reputable Jeweler

It would be very difficult to give any hard-and-fast rules on this matter since there are so many exceptions. Size and years in business are not always absolute indicators of reliability. Some one-person jewelry firms are highly respected; others are not. Some well-established firms that have been in business for many years have built their trade on the highest standards of integrity and knowledge; others should have been put out of business years ago.

One point worth stressing is that for the average consumer, price alone will not be a reliable indicator of a jeweler's integrity or knowledge. Aside from the basic differences in quality that affect price, and which usually will not be readily discernible to the consumer, there are cost differences resulting from differences in jewelry manufacturing processes. There are many jewelry manufacturers selling mass-produced lines of good-quality jewelry to jewelers all across the country. Mass-produced items, many of which show beautiful, classic designs (often very similar to those from the most prestigious firms), are usually cheaper than items having a more limited production. Then there are designers who create unique pieces or limited quantities of their designs, which are available in only a few select establishments. A premium is always charged for handmade or one-of-a-kind pieces, since the initial cost of production is being paid by one individual rather than being shared by many, as in mass-produced pieces.

Furthermore, jewelers do not all use the same retail markup. Markup depends upon operating costs and credit risks, among other things.

The best way to select wisely is by shopping around. Go to several fine jewelry firms in your geographic area and compare items and the prices being asked for them to get a sense of what is fair in your market area. *But as you do, remember to ask the right questions to be sure you're comparing stones of comparable quality, and pay attention to design and manufacturing details.* Also, as part of this process, it may be helpful to consider these questions:

- *How long has the firm been in business?* A quick check with the Better Business Bureau may reveal whether or not there are serious consumer complaints.
- *What are the gemological credentials of the jeweler, manager, or owner?* Is there a gemologist on staff? Does the store have its own laboratory?
- *How would you describe the store window?* One of jewelry nicely displayed? Or incredible bargains and come-on advertising to lure you in?
- *How would you describe the overall atmosphere?* Professional, helpful, tasteful? Or hustling, pushy, intimidating?
- *What is their policy regarding returns?* Full refund or only store credit? How many days? What basis for return?
- *Will they allow a piece to be taken "on memo"?* It won't hurt to ask. Some jewelers will. However, unless you know the jeweler personally, this is not often permitted today because too many jewelers have suffered from stolen, damaged, or switched merchandise.
- *To what extent will they guarantee their merchandise to be as represented?* Be careful here. Make sure you've asked the right questions and get the right information on the bill of sale, or you may find yourself stuck because of a technicality. And if you're making the purchase on a contingency basis, put the terms of the contingency on the bill of sale. If they can't or won't provide the necessary information, we recommend you go to another jeweler.

Never allow yourself to be intimidated into "trusting" anyone. Beware of the person who says "Just trust me" or who tries to intimidate you with statements such as "Don't you trust me?" A trustworthy jeweler will have no problem giving you the information you request—in writing.

- *What is their repair or replacement policy?* Be sure they give you a receipt that provides a full description. Be sure to find out if their insurance covers any damage to your piece while being repaired, redesigned, or sized.

Again, in general, you will be in a stronger position to differentiate between a knowledgeable, reputable jeweler and one who isn't if you've shopped around first. Unless you are an expert, visit several firms, ask questions, examine merchandise carefully, and then you be the judge.

If You Want to File a Complaint

If any jeweler has misrepresented what they sold you, please contact the Jewelers Vigilance Committee (JVC), 25 West 45th Street, Suite 400, New York, New York 10036, (212) 997-2002. They can provide invaluable assistance to you, investigate your complaint, and take action against firms believed to be guilty of fraudulent activity in the jewelry industry.

❖ Buying on the Internet

"E-commerce" is the current buzzword, and gem and jewelry websites are springing up almost daily. You can find unmounted diamonds and gemstones, along with numerous engagement and wedding ring styles. The Internet opens doors to more choices than ever imagined, often at prices that are comparable, or lower, than what is typically found in traditional jewelry stores. Buying on the Internet can be fun, and there are an increasing number of reliable e-retailers such as BlueNile.com, which have been in business long enough to have a good track record and a reputation for reliability.

Bluenile.com is a well-known company that offers a wide range of ring styles.

But e-commerce is not for everyone, and the risk of buying something that is not properly represented is higher when you buy on-line; it is essential to buy only from a source with an established reputation, and from one you can actually find should it be necessary (carefully check their contact information). Before flying off into cyberspace, take time to consider some of the pros and cons.

For many, the major attraction of shopping on-line is convenience and the "money-back guarantee" with no questions asked. It is fast, easy, and private, enabling you to make decisions without feeling pressured or intimidated by salespeople. For those who live in remote areas far from fine jewelry stores, and for those with too little time to visit numerous jewelry stores in the quest for that "perfect" ring, it provides an opportunity to see what is available and what's new and exciting. The Internet can enable you to learn more about everything from gemstones to the latest award-winning designers. Many online vendors also provide educational sites to help you understand more about what you are buying.

It is easy to see the allure of Internet shopping, but in all-too-many cases it is not all that it appears to be. The first disadvantage is the inability to see and compare the stones firsthand and to determine how well made the ring is or how it might compare to alternatives. It is impossible to accurately judge beauty and desirability from a static photo, and, as we've pointed out, you can't see and appreciate the unique "personality" of any gemstone from an on-line image. On the other hand, we realize that many couples—perhaps most—are not as passionate about the "personality" of a particular stone as we are. Whether shopping on-line or at a jewelry store, your main concern may simply be that it sparkles and looks like a diamond! In such cases, the benefits of buying on-line may outweigh this "negative." As long as the site offers a money-back guarantee (and it is a reliable site with an established reputation), you can always return it should you be disappointed. Just be sure to ask about the vendor's return policy and read the fine print. Find out how quickly merchandise must be returned and whether you will receive a refund; be leery of vendors who will only give a credit toward future purchases. And keep in mind that unless you've done your homework in checking out the source, you may not be able to find them to get your money back!

Another serious problem is the absence of any screening mechanism to help you determine the reliability of information provided on many online sites. Sales information pertaining to gems or jewelry being sold is often incomplete and inaccurate.

It is also difficult to find reliable information about the competence

or trustworthiness of many online vendors, and written representations or statements regarding return policies may be meaningless
unless you can work out a way to verify facts before making payment
to the vendor. Carefully check information given on the site with regard to how you can contact them: Is there a physical address? A
phone number with local area code as well as an 800 number? Do
they provide the names of corporate management, etc.? Have you
checked with the Better Business Bureau to see whether or not any
complaints have been filed?

In general, everything we have warned about in previous chapters
applies when purchasing from an online vendor. As we have stressed
repeatedly, many of the factors affecting quality and value cannot be
accurately judged without gemological training, experience, and
proper equipment. Yet often there is no information about the on-
line vendors and whether or not they have experience and are knowledgeable. This is usually because they lack the requisite knowledge
and skill, which means their representations may be unreliable.

We cannot emphasize too strongly the importance of taking
every precaution to protect yourself and ensure you are getting what
you think you are getting, at an appropriate price. Remember that
many Internet companies and individual vendors are unknown en-
tities, without reliable track records or well-established reputations.
This means that problems might be more difficult, or impossible, to
resolve satisfactorily, regardless of "guarantees" made before purchase.
You must also remember that it may be difficult, or impossible, to
find the seller "off-line," and you cannot rely on vendor ratings because they can be easily rigged by the unscrupulous.

Appraisals and Laboratory Reports Provide a False Sense of Security

Appraisals and gem-testing laboratory reports issued by reliable
laboratories, such as GIA, AGS, or EGL, are being used increasingly
by online sellers to increase confidence among prospective buyers
and can provide an accurate description of quality. But this is not
always the case. Unfortunately, unreliable reports issued by unknown labs and, in some cases, by fictitious labs, are also being used
increasingly by the unscrupulous. We are seeing an increase in
bogus appraisals and fraudulent lab reports that have duped

unsuspecting buyers into purchasing something that has been mis-represented. We have also seen diamonds accompanied by reports from highly respected labs, where the quality of the stone does not match the description on the report. *Be sure to get independent verification of any documentation provided by the seller* (see chapter 13), before payment if possible.

Remember also that you cannot properly judge a gem based on a lab report or appraisal alone. We've seen many diamonds with "great reports" that were not beautiful (and should sell for less than one might surmise based on the report alone), and others with "questionable" reports that were exceptionally beautiful (and should cost more than the report would indicate). In other words, you really must see the stone along with the report; this is just one more good reason to buy only from a known firm that will refund your money if you are not satisfied.

Other problems that are surfacing on the web include the following:

- **Failure to comply with Federal Trade Commission (FTC) guidelines.** The FTC has found extensive failure to comply with FTC guidelines. Most notably, descriptions provided by sellers often omit critical information pertaining to quality factors, exact weight, and treatments used on diamonds, colored gemstones, and pearls.
- **Prices are often higher than fair retail.** Don't assume you will pay a lower price, and beware of fictitious "comparative retail" prices that lead you to believe you are getting a bargain. Prices are often no lower than those at a local jewelry store, and many e-retailers sell jewelry at prices significantly higher than what you would pay for comparable quality from knowledgeable, independent jewelers. Before buying on-line, check prices from a variety of sources, including your local jeweler.
- **"Wholesale" claims may be misleading.** "Wholesale" online offerings present even greater risks to consumers than buying in any wholesale jewelry district (see chapter 13), because you do not see the actual gem or jewelry firsthand and have no guarantee you are buying from a bona fide wholesaler. Many people buying "wholesale" through online sources are not getting the bargains they believe they are getting and many mistakes would have been avoided had

the buyer seen the jewelry first or had an opportunity to compare it to alternatives.

In some cases, arrangements can be made to allow you to view the piece before the vendor receives payment, using a local bank or gemological laboratory, for example, as an intermediary. We recommend this be done wherever possible.

- *Here today, gone tomorrow.* In numerous reported cases, buyers have never received the merchandise for which they paid, or received merchandise that was not as represented. Often there is no recourse because vendors cannot be located once the transaction is complete.

Form of Payment May Provide Protection

There are several payment options that might provide some protection. Credit cards offer the most consumer protection, usually including the right to seek a credit through the credit card issuer if the product isn't delivered. If the seller won't agree, other options include setting up an escrow arrangement (for which there is usually a nominal fee) or using a reliable third party for verification, such as a well-known gem-testing laboratory, before an exchange of products or money.

To sum up, if you are buying an engagement or wedding ring on-line—from e-retailers, auction sites, or individuals—the rewards may be great, but the risks are much higher than buying from traditional sources. For additional information on how to reduce the risk in buying on-line, or to file a complaint, write to the Federal Trade Commission, Consumer Response Center, 600 Pennsylvania Avenue, NW, Washington, DC 20580, or see their website: www.ftc.gov.

❖ Buying at Auction—Rewards and Rip-offs

Fine auction houses are just beginning to attract the attention of couples seeking beautiful engagement and wedding rings and pearls and other gifts for the wedding day, and online auction sites are also attempting to lure the about-to-be-engaged couple. The attraction is partly price, but also the elaborate workmanship found in many rings from bygone eras, details that cannot be duplicated today. The auction venue also provides an important source for those seeking fine, rare natural gemstones.

But the risks involved in buying at auction, especially online sites, are much higher than anywhere else. It can be a rewarding experience, but keep in mind that even at the best firms there is an element of risk. One must be very knowledgeable, or work with an expert consultant, to recognize opportunities and spot pitfalls. Over the years we've seen many pieces acquired from reputable auction firms that contained synthetic stones, fracture-filled diamonds, and diffusion-treated sapphires.

The advice one needs to compete in the auction arena is a book in itself. So, if this venue is of interest to you, we strongly recommend that you first read *Jewelry & Gems at Auction: The Definitive Guide to Buying & Selling at the Auction House & on Internet Auction Sites.*

❖ To Sum Up

We hope you are now better informed about engagement and wedding rings and how to buy them. Use the information we provide here, but remember, it takes years of formal training and experience to become a true expert. For important purchases, always verify the facts with a qualified gemologist-appraiser. The worksheet in the appendix will help you ask the right questions and keep a record of important information you are given.

PART SEVEN

Important Advice After You Buy

CHAPTER 28

Choosing the Appraiser and Insurer

❖ Why Is It Important to Get an Appraisal?

Whether you have bought a diamond or a colored gemstone ring, getting a professional appraisal and keeping it updated is critical. An appraisal is necessary for four reasons: to verify the facts about the jewelry you have purchased (especially important with the abundance of new synthetic materials and treatments); to obtain adequate insurance to protect against theft, loss, or damage; to establish adequate information to legally claim a ring recovered by the police; and, if your rings are lost or stolen, to provide sufficient information to make sure that they are replaced with rings that actually are of "comparable quality," if that is what your insurance policy provides.

The need for appraisal services has increased greatly because of the high incidence of theft and sharp increases in the prices of diamonds and colored gems. It has become a necessity to have any fine gem properly appraised given the potential for serious financial loss at today's prices, if the gem is not accurately represented.

It is also important, given recent price increases, to update value estimations from old appraisals; this is especially true if you have received a family heirloom, to be sure you have adequate insurance coverage in the event of loss or theft.

❖ How to Find a Reliable Appraiser

The appraisal business has been booming over the past few years and many jewelry firms have begun to provide the service themselves.

We must point out, however, that there are essentially no officially established guidelines for going into the gem appraising business. Anyone can represent himself as an "appraiser." While many highly qualified professionals are in the business, others lack the expertise to offer these services. So it is essential to select an appraiser with care and diligence. Further, if the purpose of the appraisal is to verify the identity or genuineness of a gem, as well as its value, we recommend that you deal with someone who is in the business of gem identification and appraisal and not primarily in the business of selling gems.

To help you find a reliable gemologist-appraiser in your own area, here is a list of organizations that award highly respected designations to qualifing members (a list of internationally respected gem-testing laboratories is provided in the appendix):

The American Society of Appraisers
P.O. Box 17265
Washington, DC 20041
(703) 478-2228
• Ask for a current listing of *Master Gemologist Appraisers*.

The American Gem Society
8881 W. Sahara Ave.
Las Vegas, NV 89117
(702) 255-6500
• Ask for a list of *Certified Gemologist Appraisers* or
  Independent Certified Gemologist Appraisers.

The Accredited Gemologists Association
888 Brannan St., Ste. 1175
San Francisco, CA 94103
(415) 252-9340
• Ask for a list of *Certified Gem Laboratories* or
  Certified Master Gemologists.

The National Association of Jewelry Appraisers
PO Box 6558
Annapolis, MD 21401-0558
(410) 897-0889
• Ask for a list of *Certified Master Appraisers* or
  Certified Senior Members.

In addition, when selecting a gemologist-appraiser, keep the following suggestions in mind:

Obtain the names of several appraisers and then compare their credentials. To be a qualified gemologist-appraiser requires extensive formal training and experience. You can conduct a preliminary check by telephoning the appraisers and inquiring about their gemological credentials.

Look for specific credentials. The Gemmological Institute of America and the Gemmological Association of Great Britain provide internationally recognized diplomas. GIA's highest award is G.G. (Graduate Gemologist), and the Gemmological Association of Great Britain awards the F.G.A.—Fellow of the Gemmological Association (F.G.A.A. in Australia; F.C.G.A. in Canada). Some hold this honor "With Distinction." In Germany, the D.G.G. is awarded; in Asia, the A.G. Make sure the appraiser you select has one of these gemological diplomas. In addition, when seeking an *appraiser,* look for the title "Certified Gemologist Appraiser" (C.G.A.), which is awarded by the American Gem Society, or "Master Gemologist Appraiser" (M.G.A.), which is awarded by the American Society of Appraisers. Some fine gemologists and appraisers lack these titles because they do not belong to the organizations awarding them, but these titles currently represent the highest awards presented in the gemological appraisal field. Anyone holding these titles should have fine gemological credentials and adhere to high standards of professional conduct.

Check the appraiser's length of experience. In addition to formal training, to be a reliable gemologist-appraiser requires extensive experience in the handling of gems, use of the equipment necessary for accurate identification and evaluation, and activity in the marketplace. The appraiser should have at least several years of experience in a well-equipped laboratory. If the gem being appraised is a colored gem, the complexities are much greater and require more extensive experience. In order to qualify for C.G.A. or M.G.A. titles, the appraiser must have at least several years of experience.

Ask where the appraisal will be conducted. An appraisal should normally be done in the presence of the customer, if possible. This is important to ensure that the same stone is returned to you and to protect the appraiser against charges of "switching." Recently we appraised an old platinum engagement ring that had over twenty years' filth compacted under its high, filigree-type box mounting that was typical of the early 1920s. After cleaning, which was difficult, the diamond showed a definite brown tint that was easily seen by the client, who had not noticed it when the ring was dirty. She had just inherited the ring from her deceased mother-in-law, who had told her it had a blue-white color. If she had not been present when the ring was being cleaned and appraised, it might have resulted in a lawsuit, for she would certainly have suspected a switch. This particular situation does not present itself often, but appraisers and customers alike need to be diligent and watchful.

It normally takes about a half hour per item to get all of the specifications, but it can take much longer in some cases.

❖ Appraisal Fees

This is a touchy and complex subject. As with any professional service, there should be a suitable charge. Fees should be conspicuously posted or offered readily on request so that the customer knows beforehand what to expect to pay for this service. Fees are essentially based on the expertise of appraisers and the time required of them, as well as the secretarial work required to put the appraisal in written form, since all appraisals should be done in writing. While it used to be standard practice to base appraisal fees on a percentage of the appraised value, this practice is no longer acceptable. Today, all recognized appraisal associations in the United States recommend that fees be based on a flat hourly rate, or on a per-carat charge for diamonds.

There is usually a minimum appraisal fee, regardless of value.

The hourly rate charged by a professional, experienced gemologist-appraiser can range from $50 to $150, depending on the complexity of the work to be performed and the degree of expertise required.

Find out beforehand what the hourly rate is and what the minimum fee will be.

For certification or special gemological consulting that requires special expertise, rates can easily be $125 to $150 per hour. Extra services, such as photography, radiography, Gemprint, or spectroscopic examination of fancy-color diamonds, will require additional fees.

Be wary of appraisal services offering appraisals at very low rates and of appraisers who continue to base their fee on a percentage of the "appraised valuation." The Internal Revenue Service, for example, will not accept appraisals performed by appraisers who charge a "percentage-based" fee.

Some appraisers can photograph the ring, which we suggest. On the photo, the appraiser should note the approximate magnification and the date, along with your name as the owner. This provides a means of identifying your ring should it be stolen or lost and subsequently recovered by police. The photo can also be useful with the U.S. Customs Service should you take your honeymoon outside the United States and find yourself having to prove that the ring was not purchased abroad.

❖ Protecting Your Diamond with Gemprint™

Gemprint is a unique service offered by many jewelers and appraisers. While not totally foolproof (recutting the diamond may affect Gemprint's reliability), it is playing an increasingly important role in the recovery and return of lost and stolen diamonds, and we strongly recommend it where available.

Gemprint offers a fast and practical way to identify a diamond, even one already mounted, by capturing the image of the pattern of reflections created when the diamond is hit by a low-level laser beam. Depending upon the Gemprint system being used by the jeweler or appraiser, the image can be captured and stored on computer with digital imaging, or a photograph of the image may be taken. Each diamond produces a unique pattern, which is documented by this service. As with human fingerprints, no two Gemprints are ever alike.

The process takes only a few minutes. The jeweler or appraiser will provide you with a certificate of registration that includes either a photograph or scanned image of the stone, along with other pertinent information about it. The information about your diamond is kept in the jeweler's or appraiser's file and is also transferred to Gemprint's international database, whereby interested law enforcement agencies can verify ownership of a diamond when recovered.

If your stone is ever lost or stolen, you or your insurer sends a notice-of-loss form to Gemprint, which will then notify appropriate law enforcement agencies. Police can then verify with the registry the identification of recovered diamonds, many of which are thereby returned to their rightful owners. As another safeguard, Gemprint also checks each new registration against its lost-and-stolen file before confirming and storing the registration. Gemprint can also be useful in checking a diamond that has been left for repair, cleaning, or resetting, to assure you that your stone has been returned.

Whether purchasing a diamond, or repairing, re-sizing, or remounting an heirloom, getting a Gemprint is another way to secure your investment. Increasingly, jewelers are offering Gemprint at no additional charge to customers making a diamond purchase. Whatever the case, the cost is nominal ($35 to $50) and may actually save you money in the long run since some insurance companies give 10 percent off the annual premium you pay if the diamond you are insuring has a Gemprint.

Gemprint is available in about 650 locations in the United States. For the location nearest you, contact Gemprint at 1-888-GEMPRINT.

❖ Laser Inscriptions Add Protection As Well As Romance

Several gem testing laboratories now offer laser inscription services whereby an inscription is lasered onto the girdle edge of the diamond. While not easily discernable without magnification, inscriptions can provide the number of your diamond grading report or a secret message. In addition to the romantic touch, laser inscriptions offer another means of identification in cases where lost or stolen diamonds are recovered. Check directly with the lab to learn whether or not this service is offered (see appendix).

❖ Choosing an Insurer

Once you have a complete appraisal, the next step is to obtain adequate insurance. Most people do not realize that insurers differ widely in their coverage and reimbursement or replacement procedures. Many companies will not reimburse the "full value" provided in the policy, but instead exercise a "replacement" option by which they offer a *cash sum less than the amount for which the jewelry is insured,* or offer to replace it for you. Therefore, it is important to ask very specific questions to determine the precise coverage offered. We recommend asking insurance companies at least the following:

- *How do you satisfy claims?* Do you reimburse the insured amount in cash? If not, how is the amount of the cash settlement determined? Or do you replace the jewelry?
- *What involvement do I have in the replacement of an item?* What assurance do I have that the replacement will be of comparable quality and value to the original?
- *What is your coverage on articles that cannot be replaced?*
- *Exactly what risks does my policy cover?* All risks? Mysterious disappearance? In all geographic areas? At all times?
- *Are there any exemptions or exclusions?* What if the loss involves negligence?
- *What are the deductibles, if any?*
- *What documentation do you expect me to provide?*

To help with insurance claims, keep a "photo inventory" of your ring and other pieces of jewelry. Take a photo and store it in a safe place (a bank safe deposit box). In case of theft or fire, a photo will be useful in helping you describe your ring, and also in remembering other pieces that are missing, and in identifying them, if recovered. A photo is also useful for insurance documentation.

CHAPTER 29

Caring for Your Engagement and Wedding Rings

You will most likely wear your engagement and wedding rings more than any other piece of jewelry, so it is important to know how to care for and protect them. The following tips should help you in properly caring for your rings.

- *Try not to touch the stones in your rings* when putting them on or taking them off. Instead, take rings on and off by grasping the shank or metal portion that encircles the finger. Slipping rings on and off by grasping the metal shank rather than the stone will prevent a greasy buildup on the stone's surface, which greatly reduces the brilliance and sparkle of a stone.

- *To keep rings sparkling, get into the habit of "huffing" them.* This is a little trick we use to remove the dirt and oily film on the stone's surface (which occurs from incorrectly putting rings on and taking them off, or from occasionally "fingering" them—which most of us do without even realizing). Each time the stones are touched, a layer of oily film is applied to the top and the stone's beauty is diminished. To restore its sparkle, just "huff" it. Simply hold the ring close to your mouth, "huff" on it with your breath—you'll see the stone fog up—and wipe it off with a soft, lint-free cloth, such as a handkerchief, scarf, or coat/blouse sleeve. You'll be amazed at how much better your rings can look simply by removing even the lightest oil film from the surface!

- *Don't take off rings and lay them on the side of the sink* unless you're sure the drain is closed. Also, never remove your rings to wash your hands when away from home (all too many have been forgotten . . . and lost).

- *Don't wear your ring while doing any type of rough work,* such as house cleaning or gardening, or sports like mountain climbing. Even diamonds can be chipped or broken by a hard blow in certain directions.
- Avoid contact with chlorine, the principal ingredient in many bleaches, household cleaners, and swimming pool disinfectants. Chlorine can cause pitting and discoloration to the mounting of your ring and to your gold or platinum wedding band.
- *Don't carelessly toss jewelry in a case.* Diamonds can scratch other gemstones very easily, and can also scratch each other. To prevent scratching, diamond jewelry should be placed in a case with dividers or separate compartments, or each piece placed in a soft pouch or individually wrapped in tissues or a soft cloth.
- *Have a reliable jeweler check your ring every eighteen months* to make sure the setting is secure, especially the prongs. If you ever feel (or hear) the stone moving in the setting, it's a warning that the prongs or bezel need tightening. Failure to repair this may result in loss or damage to the stone.

❖ How to Clean Your Jewelry

Keeping your ring clean is essential if you want it to sparkle to its fullest. Film from lotions, powders, and your own skin oils will dull stones and reduce their brilliance. As we repeatedly point out, you will be amazed at how much a slight film can affect the brilliance—and color—of your gems.

It's easy to keep it clean. To clean your rings, wash with warm, sudsy water. This is perhaps the simplest and easiest way to clean any kind of jewelry. Prepare a small bowl of hot, sudsy water, using any kind of mild liquid detergent. Soak your ring for a few minutes and then brush gently with an eyebrow brush or soft toothbrush, keeping the piece submerged in the sudsy water. Rinse thoroughly under running water; make sure the drain is closed (some prefer to place jewelry in a wire strainer before placing under the running water) and pat dry with a soft lint-free cloth or paper towel.

To clean your diamonds only, make a solution of hot water and ammonia (half water/half ammonia) and soak your diamond in this solution for about fifteen minutes. Lift it out and tap it gently from the sides and back and then brush it gently with a soft toothbrush. This technique is especially effective for diamond rings with a heavy build up of oily dirt. It may take several "soaks" if the ring hasn't been cleaned in a long time. Rinse and dry with a soft cloth or paper towel.

To clean your wedding band or any other gold jewelry without gemstones, rubbing with a soft chamois cloth will restore much of the luster. Tarnish can be removed with a solution of soap and water, to which a few drops of ammonia have been added. Using a soft toothbrush, brush the rings with this solution, rinse with warm water, and dry with a soft cloth. Grease can be removed by dipping in plain rubbing alcohol.

While more convenient, commercial jewelry cleaners are not necessarily more effective than the methods suggested above. *Never let colored gemstone jewelry soak in commercial cleaners for more than a few minutes.* Leaving stones such as emerald or amethyst in some commercial cleaners for any length of time can cause etching of the surface, which reduces the stone's luster.

We do not recommend ultrasonic cleaning for most gems and think it should be restricted to the cleaning of diamonds and gold jewelry only. Washing with hot, sudsy water is simple, effective, and safe for all jewelry.

❖ Store Jewelry Carefully

- It is important to store your rings carefully, in a dry place. Avoid extremes of temperature and humidity.
- Keep gemstone jewelry, pearls, gold, and silver pieces separated from each other to prevent scratching. Keep fine jewelry in soft pouches or wrapped in a soft cloth (or, except for pearls, in a plastic Ziploc-type bag) to help protect it.
- Don't overcrowd your jewelry box. This can result in misplacing or losing pieces that might fall unnoticed from the case. Forcing jewelry into the box can cause damage, such as bending a fragile piece, or chipping a fragile stone.

PART EIGHT

Appendices

A Selected List of Laboratories
That Provide Internationally Recognized
Reports of Genuineness and Quality

American Gemological Laboratories
  (AGL)
580 Fifth Avenue, Suite 706
New York, NY 10036

American Gem Trade Association
  Gemological Testing Center (AGTA)
18 East 48th St., Suite 1002
New York, NY 10017

Asian Institute of Gemological
  Sciences (AIGS)
919/1 Jewelry Trade Center, 33rd Floor,
  North Tower
Silom Road, Bangrak,
Bangkok 0500
Thailand

CISGEM-External Service for
  Precious Stones
Via Ansperto, 5
20123 Milano
Italy

European Gemological
  Laboratory (EGL)
6 West 48th St.
New York, NY 10036

Gemmological Association and Gem
  Testing Laboratory of Great Britain
27 Greville St.
London EC1N 8SU
England

Gemological Association of All Japan
Katsumi Bldg., 5F, 5-25-8
Ueno, Taito-ku
Tokyo 110
Japan

Gem Certification and Appraisal Lab
580 Fifth Avenue, Suite 1205
New York, NY 10036

Gemological Institute of America
  Gem Trade Laboratory (GIA/GTL)
580 Fifth Avenue
New York, NY 10036

Gemological Institute of America
  Gem Trade Laboratory (GIA/GTL)
5345 Armada Dr.
Carlsbad, CA 92008

German Gemmological Laboratory
and Foundation for Gemstone Research
  (DSEF)
Prof.-Schlossmacher-Str. 1
D-55743 Idar-Oberstein
Germany

Gübelin Gemmological Lab
Maihofstrasse 102
CH-6006 Lucerne 9
Switzerland

Hoge Raad voor Diamant (HRD)
Hoveniersstraat, 22
B-2018 Antwerp
Belgium

International Gemmological Institute
579 Fifth Avenue
New York, NY 10017

Professional Gem Sciences (PGS)
5 South Wabash, Suite 1905
Chicago, IL 60603

Swiss Gemmological Institute
SSEF—Schweizerische Stiftung für
  Edelstein-Forschung
Falknerstrasse 9
CH-4001 Basel
Switzerland

International Ring Size Equivalents

American	English	French/Japanese	Metric
½	A	–	37.8252
¾	A½	–	38.4237
1	B	–	39.0222
1¼	B½	–	39.6207
1½	C	–	40.2192
1¾	C½	–	40.8177
2	D	1	41.4162
2¼	D½	2	42.0147
2½	E	–	42.6132
2¾	E½	3	43.2117
3	F	4	43.8102
3¼	F½	–	44.4087
3¼	G	5	45.0072
3½	G½	–	45.6057
3¾	H	6	46.2042
4	H½	–	46.8027
4¼	I	7	47.4012
4½	I½	8	47.9997
4¾	J	–	48.5982
5	J½	9	49.1967
5¼	K	10	49.7952
5½	K½	–	50.3937
5¾	L	11	50.9922
6	L½	–	51.5907
6¼	M	12	52.1892
6½	M½	13	52.7877
6¾	N	–	53.4660
7	N½	14	54.1044
7	O	15	54.7428
7¼	O½	–	55.3812
7½	P	16	56.0196
7¾	P½	–	56.6580
8	Q	17	57.2964
8¼	Q½	18	57.9348
8½	R	–	58.5732
8¾	R½	19	59.2116
9	S	20	59.8500
9¼	S½	–	60.4884
9½	T	21	61.1268
9¾	T½	22	61.7652
10	U	–	62.4026
10¼	U½	23	63.0420
10½	V	24	63.6804
10¾	V½	–	64.3188
11	W	25	64.8774
11¼	W½	–	65.4759
11½	X	26	66.0744
11¾	X½	–	66.6729
12	Y	–	67.2714
12¼	Y½	–	67.8699
12½	Z	–	68.4684

A Worksheet to Help You Select Your Rings

Ring sizes: Bride's_____ Groom's_____
Wedding band width: Bride's_____millimeters
                              Groom's_____ millimeters

Jewelry Store: _____

Address: _____

Phone Number: _____ Store representative's name: _____

Price of ring: $ _____

Description of ring: _____

_____

Setting (circle appropriate descriptions)

Metal: 14k   18k   22k   yellow gold
                 white gold   platinum   platinum iridium
Custom-made: yes   no
Is this a designer ring? yes   no
If yes, name of designer: _____
Identity of main stone: _____ Weight: _____ Shape: _____
Dimensions (millimeters):   X   X

Additional Information (including answers to questions in chapter 11):

For Diamonds

Is the stone accompanied by a diamond grading report?*

If so: Issued by: _____ Date: _____
Color grade (circle one): D E F G H I J K L M N O P Q R S T U V W X Y Z
Clarity (Flaw) grade (circle one): FL IF VVS$_1$ VVS$_2$ VS$_1$ VS$_2$ SI$_1$ SI$_2$ I$_1$ I$_2$ I$_3$

For Colored Gems

Is the stone accompanied by a colored gemstone report?*

If so: Issued by: _____ Date: _____
Color grading date:_____ Hue/tone/saturation: _____
Clarity grade (circle one):   FL VVS   LI VS   LI SI   MI I   HI

Please make additional copies of this worksheet to take with you as you shop for your rings.

*Ask for a copy of the report to take with you (see chapters 11 and 16).

Selected Readings

Arem, Joel E. *Color Encyclopedia of Gemstones.* New York: Van Nostrand Reinhold, 1987. Excellent color photography makes this book interesting for anyone. An invaluable reference for the gemologist.

Bruton, E. *Diamonds. 2nd Edition.* Radnor, Pa.: Chilton, 1978. An excellent, well-illustrated book, good for both amateur and professional gemologist.

Desautels, Paul E. *The Jade Kingdom.* New York: Van Nostrand Reinhold, 1986. Important resource on world occurrences, history, uses, and identification.

Hofer, Stephen C. *Collecting and Classifying Colored Diamonds.* New York: Ashland Press, 1998. The book is a treasure of information on one of the world's rarest and most valuable gems: natural-color diamonds.

Kunz, G.F. *The Curious Lore of Precious Stones.* Reprinted, with *The Magic of Jewels and Charms.* New York: Dover Publications.

———. *Rings for the Finger.* Unabridged republication of 1917 edition. New York: Dover Publications, 1973. Fascinating for young and old, for the historical romantic.

Levi, Karen, ed. *The Power of Love: Six Centuries of Diamond Betrothal Rings.* London: The Diamond Information Centre, 1988. Wonderful photographs and fascinating historical anecdotes tracing diamond betrothal rings from the middle ages to the present.

Matlins, Antoinette Leonard & A. C. Bonanno. *Gem Identification Made Easy: A Hands-On Guide to More Confident Buying & Selling. 2nd Edition.* Woodstock, Vt.: GemStone Press, 1997. A nontechnical book that makes gem identification possible for anyone—even without a science background. A "must" for beginners, and the experienced may pick up a few tips, too. Practical, easy to understand.

———. *Jewelry & Gems: The Buying Guide. 5th Edition.* Woodstock, Vt.: GemStone Press, 2001. How to buy diamonds, pearls, colored gemstones, gold, and jewelry. Invaluable for both the novice and the connoisseur.

Matlins, Antoinette. *Colored Gemstones: The Antoinette Matlins Buying Guide— How to Select, Buy, Care for & Enjoy Sapphires, Emeralds, Rubies and Other Colored Gems with Confidence and Knowledge.* Woodstock, Vt.: GemStone

Press, 2001. Covers every aspect of gemstones in detail, from their symbolic attributes to current frauds.

———. *Diamonds: The Antoinette Matlins Buying Guide—How to Select, Buy, Care for & Enjoy Diamonds with Confidence and Knowledge.* Woodstock, Vt.: GemStone Press, 2001. Covers every aspect of diamonds, from how to read a diamond grading report to singing diamonds.

———. *Jewelry & Gems at Auction: The Definitive Guide to Buying and Selling at the Auction House & on Internet Auction Sites.* Woodstock, Vt.: GemStone Press, 2002. Covers all the unique risks and opportunities of the auction arena. Includes information on everything from period pieces to new diamond ring styles.

———. *The Pearl Book: The Definitive Buying Guide—How to Select, Buy, Care for & Enjoy Pearls. 3rd Edition.* Woodstock, Vt.: GemStone Press, 2002. How to select, buy, care for and enjoy pearls. Covers every aspect of pearls, from lore and history to complete buying advice. An indispensable guide.

Miller, Anna M. *Cameos Old & New.* 3rd ed. Woodstock, Vt.: GemStone Press, 2002. A valuable resource for cameo lovers. Beautifully illustrated.

Pagel-Theisen, V. *Diamond Grading ABC.* New York: Rubin & Son, 1990. Highly recommended for anyone in diamond sales.

Schumann, W. *Gemstones of the World.* Translated by E. Stern. New York: Sterling Publishing Co., 1977. This book has superior color plates of all of the gem families and their different varieties and for this reason would be valuable to anyone interested in gems.

Sofianides, Anna S., and George E. Harlow. *Gems & Crystals.* New York: Simon & Schuster, 1991. Features 150 stunning full color photos of 400 different gems and crystals from the collection of the American Museum of Natural History.

Zucker, Benjamin. *Gems and Jewels: A Connoisseur's Guide.* New York: Thames and Hudson, Inc., 1984. Lavishly illustrated book on principal gems and "great" gemstones of the world, with fascinating historical facts, mythological tidbits, and examples of jeweler's art from widely differing cultures.

Text and Color Insert Credits

Page v: Diamond Information Centre.

Page 1: Mary Evans Picture Library, London, and Diamond Information Centre.

Page 4: Benjamin Zucker, Precious Stones Company, New York.

Page 7: Diamond Information Centre.

Page 8: Top to bottom: Kunsthistoriches Museum, Vienna, Austria, and Diamond Information Centre; Diamond Information Centre; Christie's; Benjamin Zucker, Precious Stones Company.

Page 9: All photos courtesy of Benjamin Zucker, Precious Stones Company.

Page 10: Top: Benjamin Zucker, Precious Stones Company. Center: Christie's.

Page 11: Top: Benjamin Zucker, Precious Stones Company. Bottom: private collection, courtesy of Diamond Information Centre.

Page 12: Copy made by Julie Crossland, courtesy of Diamond Information Centre.

Page 14: Diamond Information Centre.

Page 15: Chatham Created Gemstones.

Page 27: Gabrielle® diamond, courtesy of Suberi Brothers Inc.

Page 32: Mappin & Webb and Diamond Information Centre.

Pages 39 and 41: EightStar Diamond Company (photo/Richard von Sternberg).

Pages 45–46: Radiant and princess from Eugene Biro Corp.; Crisscut® from Christopher Designs (photo/Christony Inc.); Quadrillion™ from Ambar Diamonds; trilliant from MEFCO Inc. (photo/Sky Hall); Noble Cut™ from Doron Isaak; Gabrielle® from Suberi Brothers (photo/Peter Hurst); Spirit Sun® and Context® from Freiesleben; Lucida™ from Tiffany and Company (photo/Monica Stevenson); modern cushion-cut ring from Jonathan Birnbach for J. B. International; Royal Asscher® from Royal Asscher Diamond Company Ltd. (photo/Donald Barry Woodrow).

Page 48: Old Asscher from Jonathan Birnbach for J. B. International; old cushion from Antiquorum Auctioneers. Trapezoids and half-moons from Doron Isaak.

Page 70: Courtesy of Suberi Brothers.

Page 85: Left: Antiquorum Auctioneers. Right: Designed by Brian Sholdt of Sholdt Design.

Page 129: Top: Circle Round the Moon. Bottom: Benjamin Zucker, Precious Stones Company.

Page 131: Benjamin Zucker, Precious Stones Company.

Page 138: Richard Kimball.

Page 141: James Breski & Co.

Page 153: Courtesy of Jack Abraham, President of Precious Gem Resources.

Page 196: Top: Kunz and Stevenson, *The Book of the Pearl*, 1908. Middle: private collection of Antoinette Matlins (photo/T. Ardai); Bottom: Cultured Pearl Information Center.

Page 199: T. Ardai.

Page 201: Alex Primak.

Page 203: Diamond Information Centre.

Page 204: Top: Antiquorum Auctioneers. Middle: J. B. International (photo/Peter Hurst). Bottom: exclusive design by Carvin French, commissioned by Antoinette Matlins (photo/T. Ardai, with permission of David and Agnes Sarns).

Page 205: Top: Benjamin Zucker, Precious Stones Company. Middle: Richard Kimball (photo/Stephan Ramsey). Bottom, left to right: Fullcut Diamond; private collection (photo/T. Ardai); Fullcut Diamond; James Breski & Co.

Page 206: Left, top to bottom: Benjamin Zucker, Precious Stones Company; Antiquorum Auctioneers; James Breski & Co. Bottom, left to right: J. Kleinhaus & Sons (photo/Benjamin Zucker); Antiquorum Auctioneers; James Breski & Co.

Page 207: Top to bottom: Kwiat Couture by Robin Garin; George Sawyer Design; Lazare Kaplan, Inc.

Page 209: Top left: Suberi Brothers. Right margin, top to bottom: Kwiat; Circle Round the Moon; JFA Designs; J. B. International (photo/Peter Hurst). Bottom left: Kwiat.

Page 210: Top to bottom: Suberi Brothers; Lazare Kaplan, Inc.; Kretchmer Designs (photo/Robert Weldon). Bottom two: J. B. International (photo/Peter Hurst).

Page 211: Top to bottom: Barnett Robinson; Cornelius Hollander; designed by Brian Sholdt of Sholdt Design (left); Chris Correia (right); Richard Kimball.

Page 213: Left to right: designed by Brian Sholdt of Sholdt Design; Scott Keating Design (photo/Dave O. Marlow); Scott Kay Platinum.

Page 218: Christian Bauer.

Page 224: Left to right: Memoire Paris; Taköhl Treasure Ring® by Tammy Kohl; Susan Michel.

Page 227: Top to bottom: James Breski; Kwiat.

Page 229: Mark Silverstein.

Page 233: Richard Landi.

Color Insert Exhibits

Page 2: Clockwise from top left: Diamond Information Centre; Benjamin Zucker, Precious Stones Company; Christie's; Diamond Information Centre; Christie's; Diamond Information Centre.

Page 3: Clockwise from top left: Bali ring, ring set with uncut diamond crystals, table-cut and gimmel ring all courtesy of Benjamin Zucker, Precious Stones Company. Rose-cut diamond ring, courtesy of Diamond Information Centre. 16th-century ring, courtesy of Precious Stones Company.

Page 4: Clockwise from top left: James Breski; Jeffrey Howard; James Breski; Circle Round the Moon; Benjamin Zucker, Precious Stones Company; Antiquorum Auctioneers; Precious Stones Company.

Page 5: Clockwise from top left: private collection of Antoinette Matlins (photo/Tibor Ardai); Benjamin Zucker, Precious Stones Company; Antiquorum Auctioneers; designed by Brian Sholdt of Sholdt Design; Richard Landi; Tacori;

Mark Silverstein.

Page 6: Clockwise from top left: Chris Correia; James Breski; Tacori; designed by Carvin French and Antoinette Matlins (photo/T. Ardai courtesy of a private collector); James Breski; Precious Stones Company; natural color sapphire ring, courtesy of a private collection (photo/T. Ardai); two rings by Fullcut.

Page 7: Solitaire variations, left to right: Diamond Information Centre; two rings by Lazare Kaplan International. Selection of diamond engagement rings and wedding bands courtesy of Alex Primak. Multistone rings, clockwise from top left: J. B. International (photo/Peter Hurst); Suberi Brothers; Fullcut; Lazare Kaplan; J. B. International (photo/Peter Hurst); designed by Carvin French and Antoinette Matlins (photo/T. Ardai, with permission of David and Agnes Sarns).

Pages 8–11: Photos courtesy of designers featured. William Richey rings photographed by Robert Diamante. Steven Kretchmer rings © 1990 S. Kretchmer, US Patent Nos. 5,084,108 and 5,188,679 (photo/Robert Weldon). Scott Keating rings photographed by Dave O. Marlow. Jean-François Albert's designs courtesy of JFA Design. Leopoldo Poli's designs courtesy of La Nouvelle Bague. Lisa Chris and Richard Mason's designs courtesy of Barnett Robinson. Robin Garin's designs courtesy of Kwiat Couture by Robin Garin. Martin Gruber's designs courtesy of Nova by Gruber. Whitney Boin rings by T. Flashner Photography.

Page 12: Three traditional flat bands courtesy of GCL, Jewelry Design, Inc., a division of Precimet Corp (photo/David Kaplan). All other wedding bands from Christian Bauer.

Page 13: Clockwise from top left: Alex Primak; Kwiat; James Breski; J. B. International (photo/Peter Hurst); courtesy of Carelle©.

Page 14–15: Photos courtesy of designers shown. Jean-François Albert's rings courtesy of JFA Design.

Page 16: Diamonds cut in classic shapes, courtesy of MEFCO Inc. (photo/Sky Hall). Trapezoid and half-moon diamonds, courtesy of Doron Isaak. Context®, courtesy of Freiesleben. Crisscut®, courtesy of Christopher Designs (photo/Christony Inc.). Lucida™, courtesy of Tiffany and Company (photo/Monica Stevenson). Royal Asscher®, courtesy of Royal Asscher Diamond Company Ltd. (photo/Donald Barry Woodrow). Lily Cut®, courtesy of Lili Diamonds (designed by Siman-Tov Bros.). Quadrillion™ diamond and diamond ring, courtesy of Ambar diamonds. Spirit Sun®, courtesy of Freiesleben. EightStar®, courtesy of EightStar Diamond Company (photo/Richard von Sternberg).

Index